Ron Hazelton's HouseCalls

Ron Hazelton's
HOUSECALLS

WITH RICK PETERS

America's Most Requested
Home Improvement Projects

TIME
LIFE
BOOKS

Alexandria, Virginia

Time-Life Books is a division of Time Life Inc.

TIME LIFE INC.
President and CEO: George Artandi

TIME-LIFE CUSTOM PUBLISHING
Vice President and Publisher: Terry Newell
Vice President of Sales and Marketing: Neil Levin
Director of Acquisitions and Editorial Resources: Jennifer Pearce
Director of Creative Services: Laura Ciccone McNeill
Director of Special Markets: Liz Ziehl
Project Manager: Jennie Halfant

BUTTERICK MEDIA
President and Publisher: Art Joinnides
Managing Editor: Caroline Politi
Project Director: Rick Peters
Design and Page Layout: Sandy Freeman
Photographer: Christopher J. Vendetta
Cover Design: WorkHorse Creative
Associate Editors: Tony O'Malley, Roger Yepsen
Illustrator: Mario Camacho
Editorial Coordinator: Traci Bosco
Copyeditor: Barbara McIntosh Webb
Indexer: Nan Badgett

First printing. Printed in U.S.A.
TIME-LIFE is a trademark of Time Warner Inc., and affiliated companies.

Library of Congress Cataloging-in-Publication Data
Hazelton, Ron.
    Ron Hazelton's HouseCalls ; America's most requested home improvement projects /
Ron Hazelton, with Rick Peters.
        p.   cm.
    Includes index.
    ISBN 0–7370–0016–3 (hardcover)
    1. Dwellings—Maintenance and repair—Amateurs' manuals.   2. Dwellings—
Remodeling—Amateurs' manuals.   I. Peters, Rick.   II. Title.
TH4817.3.H4   1999
643'.7—dc21   99–30132

Books produced by Time-Life Custom Publishing are available at a special bulk discount for promotional and premium use. Custom adaptations can also be created to meet your specific marketing goals. Call 1-800-323-5255.

Acknowledgments

I'd like to thank the kind folks at Time Life and Butterick Media for all their help with this book—in particular, at Time Life, Jennifer Pearce and Jennie Halfant; and at Butterick Media, Art Joinnides, Caroline Politi, and the production staff: Rick Peters, Sandy Freeman, Chris Vendetta, Tony O'Malley, Roger Yepsen, Barbara Webb, and Mario Camacho.

I am grateful to three special people who provided valuable advice, counsel, and constant encouragement during the development and production of this book: Susan Drummond, director and developer for *Ron Hazelton Productions*; Jeanette Boudreau, my attorney; and Lynn Drasin, my wife and partner in both business and life.

I also worked closely with a number of contractors on some of the projects. Their vast experience and willingness to share knowledge is much appreciated:

Mark Amey, General Contractor—Lenhartsville, Pa.
Tom Budinetz, Aesthetic Renovations—Allentown, Pa.
Keith Kauffman, Kauffman Electric—Allentown, Pa.
Dave Moser, Wallpapering and Painting—Zionsville, Pa.
Tony Noel—Macungie, Pa.
William Uhl, General Contractor—Zionsville, Pa.
Carl Urffer, Carl F. Urffer & Son Floor Covering Co.—Emmaus, Pa.

Finally, I want to thank the families who opened their homes and allowed us to take step-by-step photographs of the jobs in progress (one family even prepared a lasagna lunch for us!). Without your gracious invitations into your homes, this book would not have been possible.

Contents

Acknowledgments **5**
Introduction. **8**

KITCHENS

Installing a Vented
Range Hood **12**
Adding a Kitchen Island **18**
Upgrading a Sink **22**
Relaminating a Countertop. . . . **28**
Upgrading a Faucet **36**

Refacing Kitchen Cabinets **40**
Painting Kitchen Cabinets. **46**
Sink Cabinet Storage
Upgrades **50**
Tiling a Backsplash **54**

BATHROOMS

Replacing a Vanity. **60**
Installing a Pedestal Sink. **66**
Upgrading a Medicine
Cabinet. **70**
Replacing Bathroom Lights **74**
Upgrading a Toilet **78**

Installing a Whirlpool Tub **84**
Installing a Bathroom
Exhaust Fan **90**
Installing Shower Doors **94**
Installing Bathroom
Tileboard **100**

WALLS

Stenciling Walls **106**
Painting Walls **110**
Stripping Wallpaper. **114**
Hanging Wallpaper **118**
Adding a Wallpaper Border . . . **124**
Installing Wainscoting **128**
Installing Chair Rail. **134**
Installing Wall Paneling **138**
Refinishing Trim **146**

Building a Fireplace
Surround **150**
Making a Built-In
Window Seat **156**
Installing Bifold Doors **160**
A Faux Wall Finish. **164**
Finishing Off
a Basement Wall **168**
Installing Simple Shelves. **172**

FLOORS

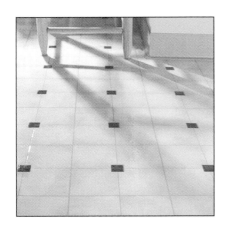

Resilient Sheet Flooring...... **178**

Installing a "Floating"
Laminate Floor............ **186**

Installing Floor Tiles **192**

Refinishing a Wood Floor **198**

Installing Ceramic Tile **202**

Installing Wood
Strip Flooring............. **208**

Installing
Wall-to-Wall Carpeting **214**

CEILINGS

Wallpapering a Ceiling **222**

Installing Crown Molding.... **226**

Installing
a Suspended Ceiling **234**

Soundproofing
a Ceiling................. **240**

Installing Acoustical
Ceiling Tile............... **244**

Adding Track Lighting....... **250**

Installing a Thin-Line
Skylight **254**

Hanging a Ceiling Fan....... **260**

EXTERIORS

Installing a Replacement
Entry Door............... **266**

Making a Window Box **272**

Installing a Window
Greenhouse **276**

Painting Exterior Walls **280**

Painting Exterior Trim....... **286**

Adding Shutters........... **290**

Adding Low-Voltage
Lighting **294**

Installing a Security Light **298**

Installing a Storm Door...... **302**

Adding a Stone Path **306**

A Simple
Brick-and-Sand Patio **310**

Sources.................. **316**

Index **317**

Introduction

In the course of producing *The House Doctor* and *Ron Hazelton's HouseCalls,* I've learned that there's a surprise waiting in every home improvement project—some good surprises, some bad. Whether it's finding a pristine hardwood floor under hideous carpeting or discovering an unexpected gas line in a wall, there's always something. But that's part of the fun—and the way it is in the real world of home improvement. That's why I've made it a point to use actual homes for my show. There's nothing like the real thing, something you won't find in the all-too-perfect world of a studio.

When Time-Life approached me to do this book, I insisted that we use real homes, homes full of surprises, because that's the kind of home that real people have—that you have. To that end, all of the projects in this book were done in actual homes. For example, the kitchen shown on the opposite page *(inset)* really needed help: drab, drab, drab—and no storage or workspace. With a modest investment of time (about three weekends) and money (less than $1,500), we did a complete makeover *(see the opposite page).*

Because we used real homes, every project offered something unexpected. For example, when we went to upgrade the kitchen sink, we found that the cutout for the old stainless steel sink was too big for the new cast-iron sink. The solution: decrease the opening with furring strips. But what if the opening had been too small? No problem. There's a tip on how to accurately increase the opening with a paper template. Real solutions for real problems. That's what this book is all about.

The other thing I insisted on was that the projects in this book had to be projects that homeowners wanted to do. Picking the most requested projects was easy—I simply went to the database I've created over the many years of *The House Doctor* and *Ron Hazelton's HouseCalls* and picked the top most requested projects. Then I screened the list for only those projects that could be completed in a weekend or less. Let's face it: We're all short on time these days. Sure, we want our home to look good and be comfortable. But not at the expense of eating up all our precious free time.

To make it easy for you to select and find projects, I've divided this book into six sections: kitchens, bathrooms, walls, floors, ceilings, and exteriors. You'll find a mini table of contents at the start of each section, detailing the projects. To help you plan, I've included a box at the start of each project that describes the level of difficulty, time requirement, and cost estimate for the typical do-it-yourselfer to complete the job. Every project features detailed step-by-step photography, along with sidebars on "Tool Know-How," "Choosing Materials," and "Pro Tips" to help you successfully complete any project.

Just as with any how-to job that you tackle, I strongly recommend that you read through the entire procedure before starting work. This will ensure that you've got all the materials on hand you'll need—and there will be fewer surprises. Also, it's imperative that you check with your local building inspector before starting any work that will alter your home's electrical or plumbing system. Working on either of these systems requires knowledge of (and compliance with) your local codes. Although there are "standards" for these codes, they vary widely from state to state and from town to town.

I hope that with the help of this book, you enjoy improving your home as much as I've enjoyed helping folks improve their homes over the years.

Ron Hazelton
September 1999

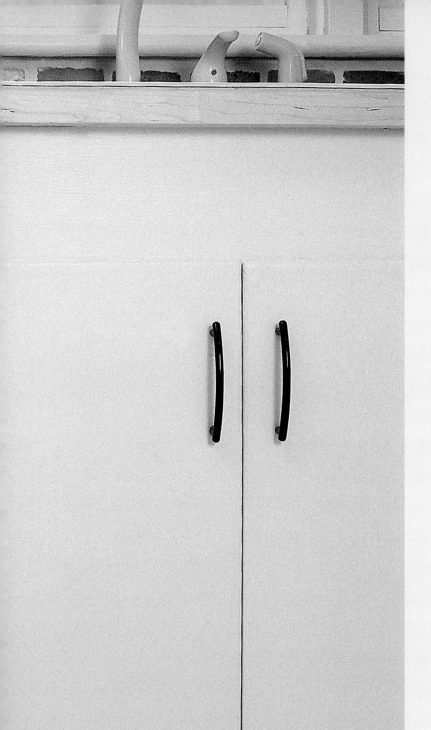

PROJECTS

Installing
a Vented Range Hood 12

Adding
a Kitchen Island 18

Upgrading a Sink 22

Relaminating
a Countertop 28

Upgrading a Faucet 36

Refacing
Kitchen Cabinets 40

Painting
Kitchen Cabinets 46

Sink Cabinet
Storage Upgrades 50

Tiling a Backsplash 54

KITCHENS

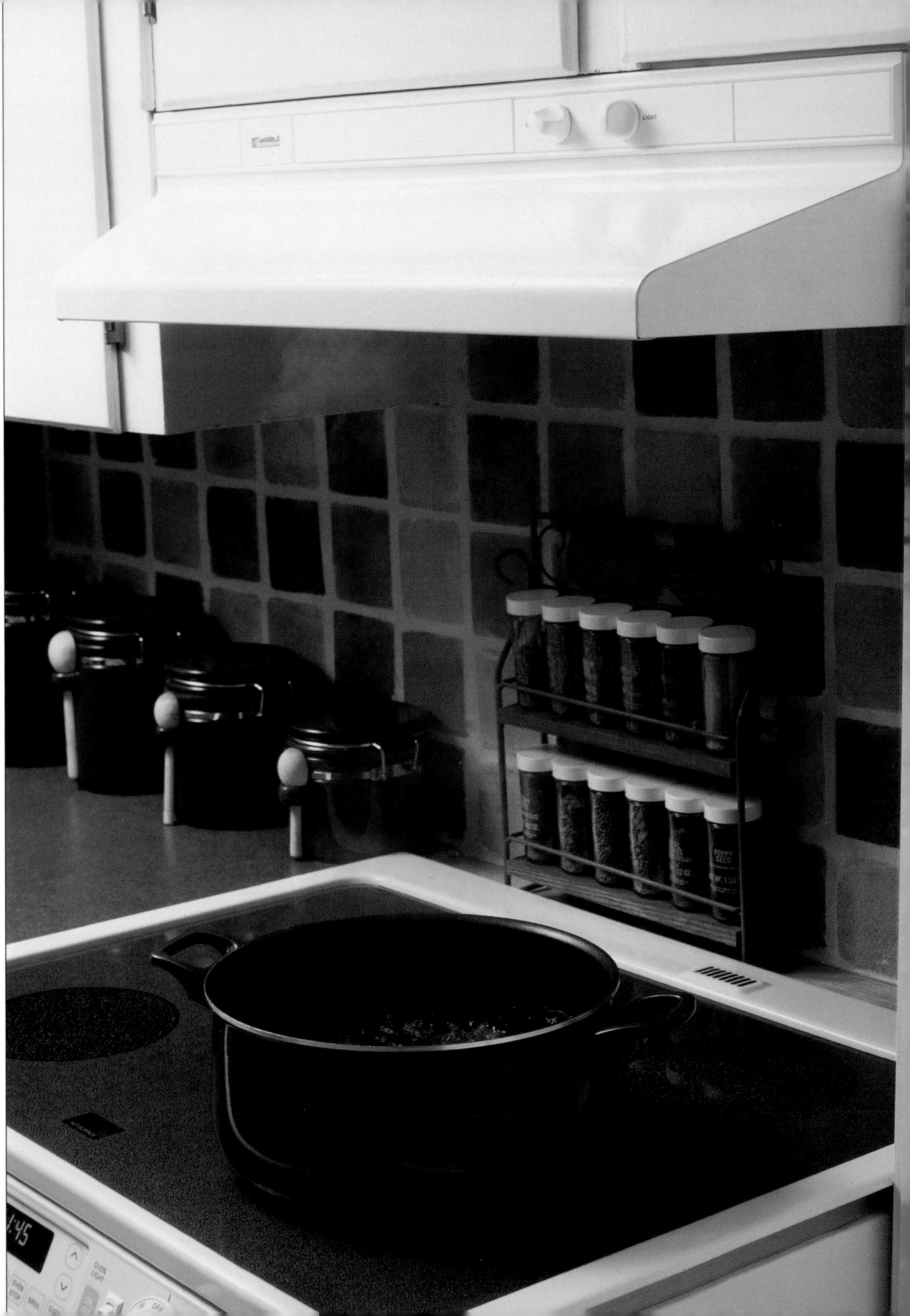
LIGHT
POPPY SEED
OVEN LIGHT
BROIL

Installing a Vented Range Hood

Banish grease and steam from your kitchen.

There's nothing homier than the aromas of good cooking— pancakes and bacon, pasta with a rich tomato sauce, burgers with onions. Still, you can have too much of a good thing. Although a ventless range hood does some filtering, it basically blows hot air right back at you. A better alternative is to whisk grease and vapor out of the house with a vented model.

If the range happens to be along an exterior wall, the job isn't that involved. Otherwise, you'll need to run ducting between the hood and a vent. In a single-story home, ducting can be run straight up through a roof vent. More common is horizontal ducting, through cabinets, soffits, or even in the space between ceiling joists. The ducting used for range hoods is either rectangular or round; I prefer round (typically 5" or 6" in diameter) because it's easier to work with. Check your owner's manual for suggested duct sizing, or consult a heating contractor.

Determine the type of range hood you'll need. They either mount below a wall cabinet or are placed between two wall cabinets (some have decorative vent hoods to conceal the ducting above). Or, as I often point out to homeowners who have ventless models in place, it could be that you don't even need a new range hood: The manufacturer may stock parts for a conversion to exterior venting, as was the case with the installation shown here.

Tools

Tape measure
Stud finder
Phillips-head and flat-head screwdrivers
Electric drill and twist bits
Saber saw or keyhole saw
Tin snips
Cold chisel, hammer, safety glasses, and leather gloves (for masonry walls)
Caulking gun

Materials

Duct tape
Silicone caulk
Vented hood or conversion kit
Ducting (can be found at most home centers, or can be custom-ordered from a heating supply store)
Exterior vent cap

Preparation

Plan the ducting: The shorter the run and the fewer the elbows, the better the range hood's performance and the easier the installation.

If necessary, check whether ducting can be run through the soffits above the cabinets or between ceiling joists.

Empty any cabinets that will be affected; remove doors and shelves that aren't fixed; relocate the stove; protect adjacent countertops with drop cloths.

Determine the power source, and bring the electrical cable to the site (if there's not one already there).

LEVEL OF DIFFICULTY
Challenging

TIME REQUIREMENT
1 day with a helper on hand

COST ESTIMATE
$100 to $250, depending on the length of the ducting

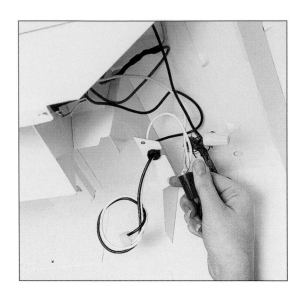

1 DISCONNECT WIRING

If your range doesn't have an existing hood, skip to Step 3.

- If there is an existing range hood (like the ventless one shown here), turn off power to the circuit at the service panel.
- Remove the filters and the bottom cover panel.
- Twist off the wire nuts and disconnect the wires.

2 REMOVE EXISTING RANGE HOOD

- Take out the blower, if possible, to make the hood lighter.
- While a helper supports the hood, back out the screws holding it in place.
- Remove the hood and set it aside.

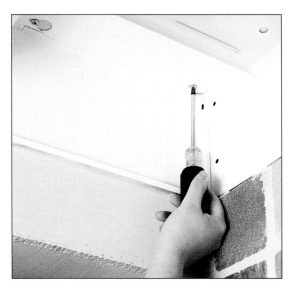

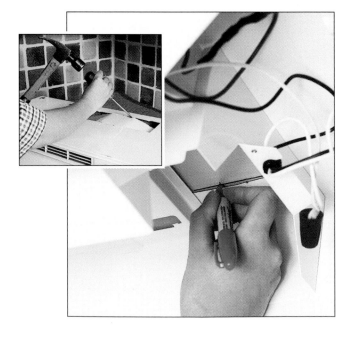

3 MARK OPENING FOR DUCT

- Remove the appropriate electrical knock-out for running cable through the top or back of the hood.
- Remove duct knockouts in the top of the hood for vertical venting, or in the back for horizontal venting *(inset)*, as is the case here.
- With a helper holding the range hood in place, trace the outline of the duct knockout(s) onto the underside of the cabinet bottom.

4 CUT DUCT OPENING

Make an opening in the cabinet bottom for the damper assembly that connects the hood to the ducting.

- Drill one or more ⅜"-diameter starter holes inside the outline you traced *(inset)*. For round openings, drill one hole; if the opening is rectangular, drill holes at each corner.
- Center the damper assembly over the holes in the top side of the cabinet bottom, and trace a cut line 1/16" to 1/8" outside the assembly for clearance.
- Use a saber saw or keyhole saw to cut the opening.

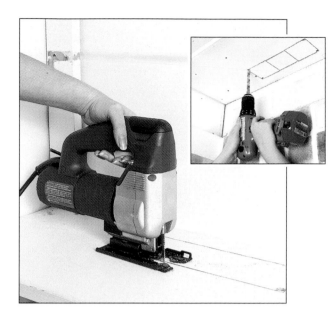

5 ATTACH DAMPER ASSEMBLY

A damper helps prevent backdrafts of out-side air from entering the house.

- Attach the damper assembly with the provided sheet metal screws.
- Make sure the damper pivots freely.
- If you're using a tapering transition piece to switch to a round duct, test-fit the piece now. To keep it from restricting damper movement, add an extension cut from a short length of duct, as done in this project.

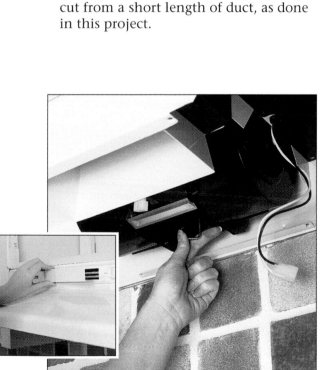

6 INSTALL HOOD

- With a helper holding the hood in place, mark the screw locations.
- Remove the hood, and drill pilot holes for the screws.
- With the helper again holding the hood in place, drive the screws.
- Clip on the plastic cover to close off the front exhaust *(inset)*.
- Make sure the power is off, and recon-nect the wires.
- Reinstall the blower unit, the bottom cover plate, and any other parts as indi-cated by the manufacturer.

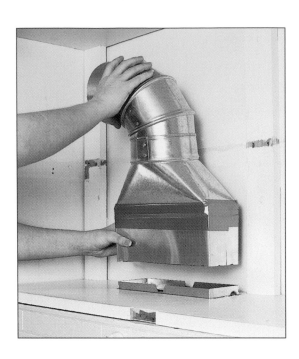

7 INSTALL VERTICAL DUCTING

Vent directly through the exterior wall behind the hood, or run ducting to reach another wall.

- For long runs of ducting, use a transition piece to switch from rectangular to round ducting, as it's easier to work with.
- Use a 90-degree elbow to begin the horizontal run.
- Temporarily attach the transition and elbow to the damper assembly, as shown. (Caution: Edges of ducting are sharp.)

8 CUT HOLES IN CABINET

Plan on a pitch of ½" per 5 horizontal feet of duct toward the exterior wall so that condesation will flow out of the kitchen.

- Measure the duct's height at the end of the elbow, and transfer the mark to the first partition. (You can position this hole toward the back of the cabinet to preserve space.)
- Hold a section of duct in place so the top is flush with the mark you just made, and trace its outline on the partition.
- Drill ⅜"-diameter starter holes at one or more points, and make the cutout with a saber saw or keyhole saw.

TOOL
KNOW-HOW

Saber Saws

Not all power saws scream like a banshee and chew their way through wood. The saber saw is quiet, lightweight, and mild-mannered. Its thin reciprocating blade cuts a narrow kerf and is easy to steer around curves. And for making curved cutouts in a piece of wood, it has no equal. No tool is without its limitations, of course. For making straight cuts in heavy stock, a circular saw can't be beat. But a saber saw will make a reasonably straight cut if you guide it with a fence—either the shoe that comes with most models, or a straightedge that you clamp or tack on to the workpiece.

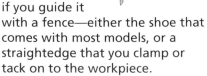

9 INSTALL HORIZONTAL DUCTING

- Run ducting toward the exterior wall, sealing joints with duct tape as you go.
- For frame walls, locate studs with a stud finder.
- Transfer the location of the ducting to the inside of the exterior wall, and trace the outline of a section of duct; for a frame wall, move the hole location as necessary to avoid studs.
- Drill a pilot hole through the center of this outline to determine where the vent hole should be made on the outside of the house; use a wood bit for a frame wall, or a masonry bit for a wall of block, brick, or stone.

10 CUT HOLE IN EXTERIOR

- For a frame wall, make a hole for the duct by working from both inside and outside the house with a saber saw or a heavy-duty reciprocating saw.
- For a masonry wall, wear safety glasses and leather gloves and use a cold chisel and hammer to slowly knock out an opening for the ducting.

11 INSTALL VENT CAP

- Hold the vent cap in position and mark the wall with the locations of the holes for screws or nails.
- Drill pilot holes for screws, nails, or plastic anchors.
- Apply a bead of exterior silicone caulk around the inside of the cap flange, and press the cap into place. Fill any gaps with more caulk.
- Attach the cap to aluminum or vinyl siding with screws; attach it to masonry with masonry screws.
- Restore power and test the range hood to make sure that air flows out the vent.

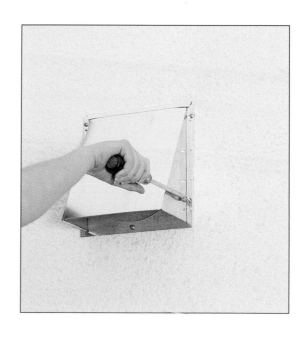

Adding a Kitchen Island

An island provides an informal eating spot, as well as added counter space, without obstructing the work flow of the kitchen.

Some of the most desperate requests for help that I get have to do with a shortage of space in a kitchen. Space for storage, space for seating, and especially a shortage of work space. What most folks do is try to shoehorn in a small table and a couple of chairs. This doesn't help with storage, but it does provide seating (although it often disrupts the work flow), and the table can serve as a temporary food preparation area.

A more elegant solution to these problems is a kitchen island with an overhanging top. The overhanging top serves as a table and allows you to stow chairs (or stools) out of the way when not in use. This creates a streamlined unit that actually enhances work flow by providing a centrally located food prep area. An island can be as small as 24 by 36 inches, but if you want to seat two comfortably, you'll need an area roughly 36 by 36 inches. You can find cabinets this wide, but you may want to consider screwing together two narrower cabinets. The nice thing about using multiple cabinets is you can mix and match cabinets to meet specific storage needs: all drawers, a drawer with a shelf, etc.

Regardless of the configuration, the backs of the cabinets (and perhaps the ends) will need to be covered with finished panels. Most cabinet manufacturers supply these, or you can cut matching plywood panels yourself.

Tools

Electric or cordless drill
Twist bits
Circular saw
3' level
Phillips-head and flat-head screwdrivers
Tape measure
C-clamps
Utility knife

Materials

2 or more base cabinets
Finished end and back panels (purchase with cabinets, or buy plywood that matches cabinets and cut it to fit)
Preformed countertop (available in many standard sizes, or can be custom-ordered)
Vinyl cove base or wood trim
Cove base adhesive or 1¼" finish nails
1⅝" and 2½" drywall screws
Wood shims
Cleats (2 by 4 scraps, 8" to 10" long)
1" brads
Wood putty

Preparation

When determining the size of the island, be sure to leave enough room on all sides for appliance doors and human traffic.

LEVEL OF DIFFICULTY
Moderate

TIME REQUIREMENT
1 to 3 days

COST ESTIMATE
Based on a 3-cabinet island, $200 to $300 for paint-grade cabinets, including plywood for end and back panels; $400 to $600 for finished oak cabinets with raised-panel doors, back, and end panels

1 ASSEMBLE THE CABINETS

Position the cabinets side-by-side and clamp two together at a time, making sure the front edges are flush.

- Drill ⅛" holes through one side and partway into the other, along the top, bottom, and front edge of the cabinet.
- Drive drywall screws into the holes to hold the cabinets together.
- Cut and fit the back and end panels as needed and attach them with glue and small brads.
- Fill brad holes with wood putty to match the cabinet.

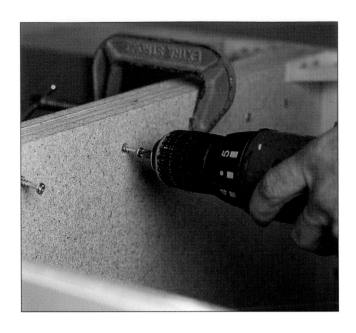

2 LOCATE CLEATS

The island attaches to the floor via a set of cleats (scraps of 2 by 4) screwed directly to the floor.

- Position the assembled island where you want it on the floor.
- Check for necessary clearances—near appliance doors, in walkways, and between the overhang and the nearest wall where the stools will go.
- Mark the perimeter of the island base on the floor.

3 SCREW CLEATS TO FLOOR

First check the bottom of the cabinets to determine where the cleats should go. Take into account the thickness of the cabinet walls when locating the cleats.

- Offset the cleats from the lines you marked on the floor so they will align with the inside edges of the cabinet base.
- Screw the cleats to the floor with 2½" drywall screws.

4 SCREW ISLAND TO CLEATS

- Lift the island onto the cleats.
- Level the island by sliding wood shims under the edges of the base wherever necessary.
- Screw the island base to the cleats with $1\frac{5}{8}$" drywall screws set in countersunk holes. (These screws will be covered later with trim.)

5 INSTALL COUNTERTOP

Many cabinets are supplied with corner brackets that can be used for attaching the countertop. If your cabinets lack these, cut blocks from a piece of 1 by 2 and screw them to the inside corners of the two end cabinets.

- Drill through the corner blocks up into the countertop. Use a depth stop on the drill bit.
- Screw the countertop to the blocks with drywall screws.

6 APPLY COVE BASE OR TRIM

Depending on the look you're after, you can use vinyl cove base or wood trim to cover the screws that attach the island to the cleats.

- For vinyl cove base, apply cove base adhesive to the back of the vinyl and press it firmly against the cabinet base. Work the vinyl around outside corners by pressing it firmly against the corner of the cabinet. If necessary, score the back of the vinyl lightly with a utility knife to help it bend.
- For wood trim, measure and miter the pieces to fit, and nail them to the base of the cabinet.

Upgrading a Sink

Don't remodel

everything

but the

kitchen sink!

Most plumbing jobs get little praise because no one ever sees all the hard work. A kitchen sink is different. Unless you keep it full of dirty dishes, its shiny face will be in full view for anyone to admire. I find that home-owners are delighted with a new sink, out of all proportion to cost and time involved in the job. Whether it's a sturdy stainless steel model or a snazzy enameled number, this humble utility can do as much for your kitchen as the fanciest chef's gadget.

Replacing a sink is straightforward unless you'll be resizing the cutout for the new sink. To minimize the work involved, check the dimensions of the new model against those in your countertop. Note that "rimless" sinks are installed in cutouts larger than their dimensions, allowing space for the mounting rim. "Self-rimming" sinks use a smaller cutout and have a lip that rests on the counter.

Tools

Adjustable wrench
Slip-joint pliers
Phillips-head and flat-head
   screwdrivers
Putty knife
Claw hammer
Saber saw or hand saw
Caulking gun
Ruler or straightedge

Materials

New sink
New strainer (optional)
New faucet (optional)
Plumber's putty
1¼" finish nails
Strips of wood (for reducing
   an opening)
150-grit sandpaper (if you're
   enlarging an opening)
5-minute epoxy
Acetone or lacquer thinner
Silicone caulk
Kraft paper
Denatured alcohol or caulk-
   removing product
Teflon tape

Preparation

If you need to resize the sink opening, have some kraft paper on hand to make a template (*see page 25*).

LEVEL OF DIFFICULTY
  Moderate

TIME REQUIREMENT
  ½ day, with helper

COST ESTIMATE
  $140 to $175 (sink only)

KITCHENS

1 DISCONNECT WASTE AND WATER LINES

- Turn off the shutoff valves for both supply lines. Then turn on the faucet to drain water from the lines.
- From under the cabinet, loosen the coupling nuts for the waste line and remove the trap—it will be full of water, so have a bucket and towel handy.
- Undo the connecting nut attaching each supply pipe to its shutoff valve.
- If your sink is fitted with a garbage disposal, first turn off the power to it. Then loosen the locking ring and temporarily set the disposal in the bottom of the cabinet.

2 REMOVE SINK AND FAUCET

- From under the cabinet, unscrew the clips around the sink's perimeter that hold it in place.
- Use a putty knife to help pry around the edge of the sink.
- If the sink is cast-iron, lift it out with the aid of a helper.

3 REDUCE OPENING IF NEEDED

- If the opening is too large to adequately support the new sink, build up the front, back, and sides of the opening with strips of wood roughly as wide as the counter is thick.
- Attach the strips with 5-minute epoxy and finish nails.

4 ENLARGE OPENING IF NEEDED

- For openings that are too small for the new sink, use a paper template *(see below)* to lay out a larger opening.
- Cut the opening with a saber saw or hand saw.
- Soften the rough-cut edges with 150-grit sandpaper wrapped around a scrap of wood.

5 APPLY SEALANT

- Clean the countertop around the cutout with acetone or lacquer thinner.
- When this area has dried, apply a bead of silicone caulk or plumber's putty around the perimeter of the countertop where the lip will rest on it.

Ron's
PRO TIPS

Using a Paper Template

Cutting a hole in a countertop is not a job you want to botch, and the sink manufacturer may include a paper template to help in making the cutout. To use a template, cut around the outline with scissors, then tape the template in place on the countertop. Trace around its perimeter, remove it, and make the cut with a saber saw. To make your own template for a self-rimming sink, place it upside down on a sheet of sturdy paper, such as kraft paper, and trace its outline. Slide out the paper and draw a second, parallel line sufficiently inside the first so that the cutout will be the right size to support the sink; consult the manufacturer's directions. Cut along this inner line with scissors, and proceed as above.

6 INSTALL FAUCET

- If you're planing on reusing your old faucet, apply a fresh bedding of plumber's putty around its base.
- For a new faucet, use the gaskets provided by the manufacturer.
- Put the faucet (and related components, such as a sprayer or soap dispenser) in place and tighten any mounting nuts.
- Hand-tighten the coupling nuts under the sink, then finish with an adjustable wrench.

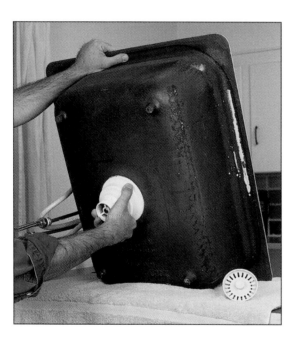

7 INSTALL STRAINER

If you're replacing the strainer, there may be a gasket to ensure a good seal, or you may be instructed to apply a bead of silicone caulk or plumber's putty.

- To assemble a standard strainer, have a helper hold it in place in the sink while you tighten the locknut.
- Or, to assemble a self-tightening strainer, align the notches of the retainer with the corresponding ridges on the base of the strainer, then tighten the thumbscrews.

8 SET SINK IN POSITION

- Put the sink in place. By temporarily placing strips of wood below the corners of a heavy cast-iron sink, you can help prevent pinching fingers as you lower it.
- Promptly clean up any excess caulk with a cloth or sponge dampened with denatured alcohol or a caulk-removing product.
- Tighten the clips under the counter if the new sink uses them.

9 RECONNECT SUPPLY LINES

- Wrap Teflon tape around the threads of both supply pipes. Consider replacing the old lines with flexible tubing *(see Choosing Materials, below)*.
- Attach the supply lines to their respective shutoff valves with the connecting nuts, tightening the nuts with an adjustable wrench.

10 RECONNECT WASTE LINE

- Attach the tail piece to the waste line
- To make the connection easier, you can use a tail piece with a flexible mid-section.
- Turn on the shutoff valves to restore the water supply.
- Check for leaks. If you discover any, tighten the offending slip or connecting nuts to eliminate them.

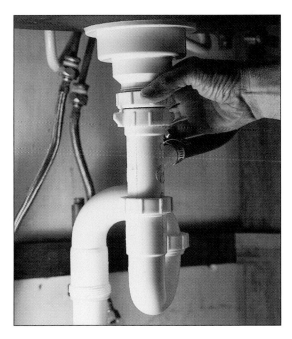

CHOOSING
Materials

Flexible Tubing

Plumbing jobs demand a bit of flexibility, from the person laboring under a sink as well as from the pipes themselves. Fortunately, you can replace unyielding supply and waste lines with flexible replacements that adapt themselves to the available space. Their convenient twist-on ends bring this sort of task within the abilities of homeowners who'd hesitate at the thought of cutting and joining copper pipes.

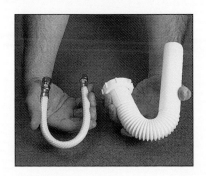

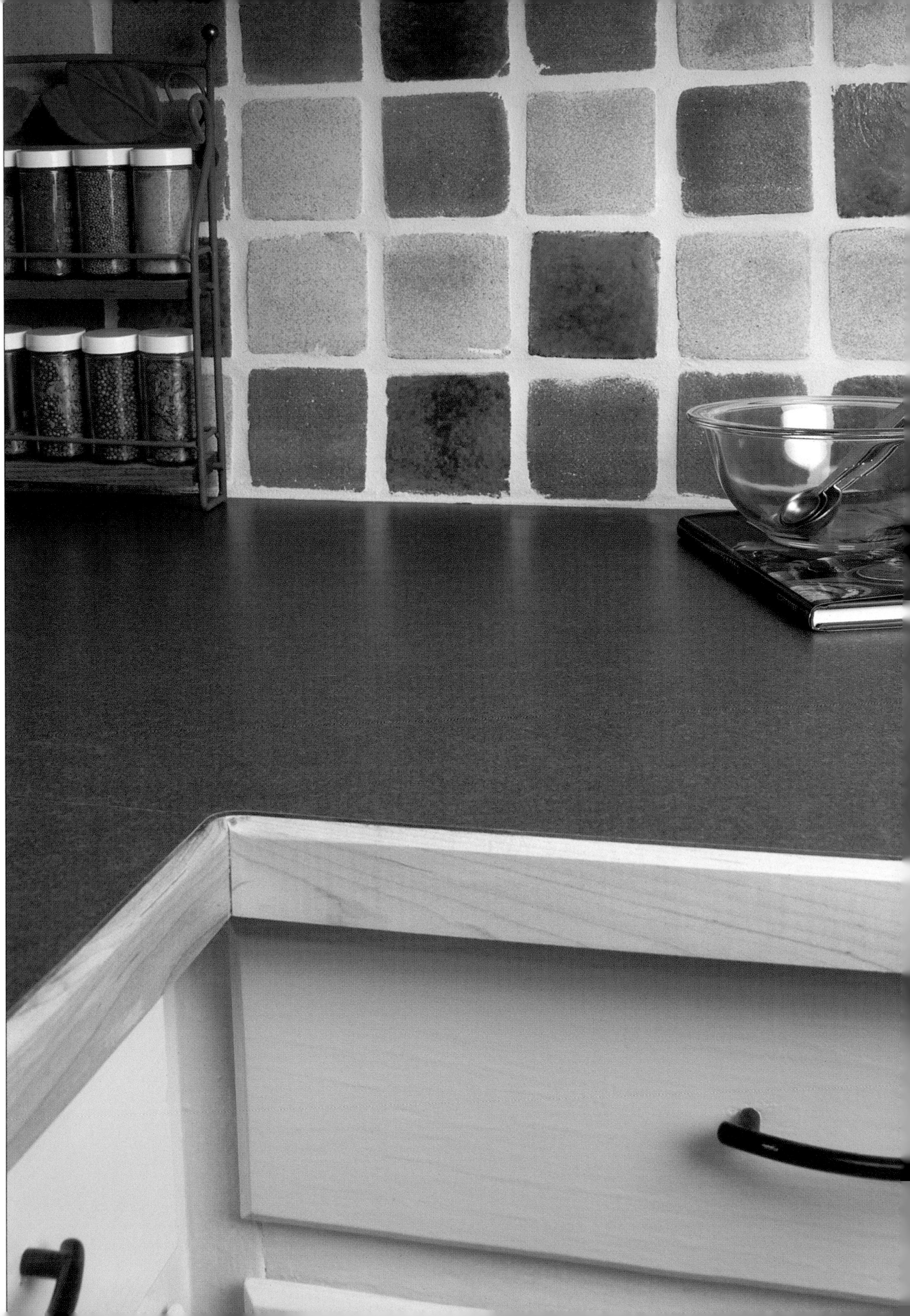

Relaminating a Countertop

You don't have to tear out an old or damaged countertop to replace it; just relaminate it instead.

Changing your kitchen countertop is a low-cost way to give the room a modest face-lift. But why relaminate a countertop when you can replace the whole thing with a ready-made countertop picked up at the home center? I've encountered several scenarios that make relaminating easier than replacing.

First, if your kitchen cabinets are more than 30 years old, it's likely that they are not the standard depth (24") that ready-made countertops are made for. If the cabinets are deeper, there won't be enough overhang on the counter; if they are narrower, there will be too much overhang. Second, removing a countertop usually requires a lot of prying and pulling, and you may damage the countertop, the cabinets, or the surrounding walls in the process. Third, if the countertop is made of several pieces fastened together from underneath (typical of L- and U-shaped countertops) or has specially shaped curves, replacing the counter is likely to be more complicated and just plain more work than relaminating it.

A question that may pop into your head about this is, Can I get a reliable bond laminating right over the old laminate? The experts say you can—as long as you follow the recommended steps outlined here.

Tools

Sanding block
Utility knife and straightedge
Mallet or laminate roller
Claw hammer
Laminate trimmer with a flush-trimming bit
Belt sander (optional)
Fine mill file
C-clamps
Paint roller and tray

Materials

60-grit sandpaper
Acetone
Plastic laminate
Wood edge and backsplash (optional)
Finish nails
Contact cement
Several lengths of dowel
Silicone caulk
Construction adhesive
5-minute epoxy

Preparation

Make sure your original laminate is bonded securely to the countertop. If it's not, don't relaminate directly on top of it—you won't get a good bond. Instead, nail on a layer of ¼" plywood, set and fill the nail holes, and fill the seams with leveling compound.

Safety

Contact cements may be highly flammable (check the label). Turn off any pilot lights and provide adequate ventilation.

LEVEL OF DIFFICULTY
Challenging

TIME REQUIREMENT
2 to 3 days

COST ESTIMATE
$100 to $300, depending on the quality and amount of laminate

1 REMOVE THE SINK AND BACKSPLASH

While relaminating your countertop, it's a good time to consider upgrading your sink. Either way, you'll have to remove it.

- Close the faucet shutoff valves and disconnect the supply and waste lines, and dishwasher hookup if there is one.

- Unscrew the clips that hold the sink to the underside of the countertop, and lift out the sink.

- Carefully pry the backsplash away from the wall, using a scrap block of wood to protect the wall.

Ron's
PRO TIPS

Sealing the Sink Cutout

Most countertops are made using a core of ¾"-thick particleboard which although flat and stable, is porous and can swell up if it gets wet. This can cause the area of the countertop around the sink to bubble up, or the glue bond between the laminate and countertop to fail. Check your countertop—it may already show signs of this. If it has started to swell, flatten any raised areas with a block wrapped with sandpaper. To prevent water from seeping in in the future, apply a waterproof finish to the edge to seal it and prevent future water damage. Use an oil-based paint or primer, polyurethane, or marine varnish. Apply two or more generous coats, and allow it to dry completely.

2 SAND THE OLD LAMINATE

The glue used on countertops is called contact cement. You spread it on both parts, let it dry to the touch, then lay the parts together. While perfectly smooth surfaces will bond, slightly rough surfaces bond even better.

- Abrade the surface of the old laminate with 60-grit or rougher sandpaper wrapped around a sanding block.

- While you're at it, examine the surface for minor loose areas, especially along the edges. Reglue by forcing a wedge under the edge and squeezing some five-minute epoxy into the crevice. Then clamp the area until the epoxy cures.

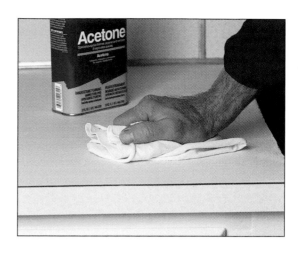

3 CLEAN THE COUNTERTOP

You'll want to remove the sanding dust without leaving any oily residue; so don't use paint thinner, as it's petroleum-based. Instead, use acetone or lacquer thinner. They dry quickly but are highly flammable and give off strong fumes; so open a window or door to let the fumes dissipate.

- Remove the sanding dust and clean the old laminate with acetone or lacquer thinner and a soft rag.

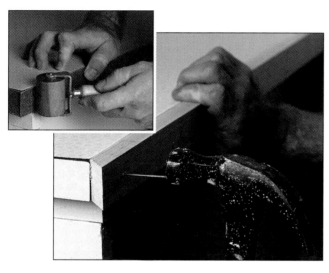

4 APPLY NEW EDGING

There are two basic edge treatments to consider using when relaminating—a wood edge or a laminate edge. In either case, the edge material is applied first, then covered with the top laminate.

- For a wood edge, cut the wood strips to length, mitering inside and outside corners. Then, nail or screw the wood edge to the edge of the countertop; drill pilot holes first. Fill screw holes with wood plugs and nail holes with wood putty.

- With a laminate edge (*inset*), cut strips of laminate ⅛" wider than the existing edge and ½" or so longer. Apply glue to both the laminate and the counter edges. When the glue is dry to the touch, apply the strip to the edge so it extends slightly at top and bottom as well as at the ends. Press the edge strips on with a roller.

TOOL
KNOW-HOW

Laminate Rollers

On a small relaminating job, you can get by using the low-tech approach to bonding the laminate—a block of wood and a mallet (*see Step 10 on page 34*). But if you're planning to work with plastic laminate on other remodeling projects, get the tool the pros use—a laminate roller. The standard tool is a 3"-wide J-roller, a hard rubber wheel mounted on a J-shaped metal frame with cushioned grips. There are also wider rollers for bigger jobs.

A laminate roller allows you to apply pressure more consistently over the laminate surface. That means the bond will be more uniform and reliable. A roller is especially useful for applying laminate edges, where it's harder to get pressure with a block and mallet.

To use a J-roller, simply lean on it with your upper body weight while rolling it back and forth over the laminate.

KITCHENS

5 SAND THE EDGING FLUSH

Before applying the top laminate, sand the edging flush with the existing laminate.

- If you have access to a belt sander, it will make quick work of sanding the edge flush; make sure to wear a dust mask and be carefull not to round-over any edges.
- Alternatively, use a file on a laminate edge and a sanding block with 60- or 80-grit sandpaper on a wood edge.

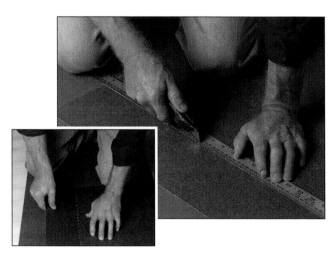

6 ROUGH-CUT THE LAMINATE

Cutting plastic laminate is similar to scoring and snapping a piece of glass, only with plastic laminate you snap toward the score line, not away from it.

- Measure and mark the piece. It should be at least ¼" wider than the counter, and ½" or more longer.
- Set the laminate on the floor, protected with a scrap of wood. Hold a straightedge tightly against the mark and run a utility knife against the straightedge. Make two or three passes, increasing the pressure each time until you've cut through about half the thickness.
- To break the laminate, press down on the larger portion with your knee, and pull up on the smaller piece (*inset*). If you need to trim less than an inch, break it off with a pair of pliers or tile nippers.

Laminate Trimmers

A laminate trimmer is just a small router, but its size and weight make it perfect for laminate work. With a flush-trimming bit, it will trim overhanging laminate flush with an adjacent surface. A standard router will work, but its size is awkward and will limit how close you can trim to a wall.

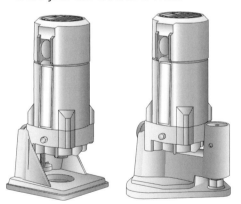

With its small base, the typical laminate trimmer will work to within about an inch of a wall on a countertop (*left*). The rest you'll have to trim by hand. Better still, consider a laminate trimmer with an offset base (*right*). On this tool the bit is offset to the very edge of the base, so you can trim right up to a wall.

KITCHENS

7 MAKE A SEAM

If you must join pieces of laminate together, avoid locating a seam near the sink, where water can weaken the glue bond.

- Mark the edges that will form the seam. Find two pieces of wood or plywood that are as long as the seam; the factory edge on plywood works well.

- Position the plywood under the laminate so ¹⁄₁₆" of laminate extends past the edge. Set the second piece of plywood on the laminate ¹⁄₈" back from the edge. Trim the laminate with a flush-trim bit, with the bearing riding against the lower piece of plywood *(inset)*.

- Repeat the process on the second piece of laminate that forms the seam.

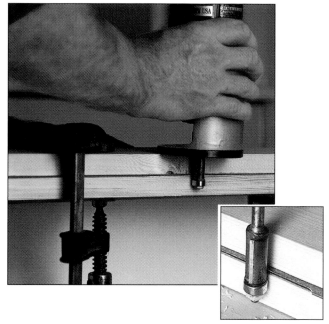

Scribing to a Wall

Ron's PRO TIPS

If your laminate butts up against a wall that isn't concealed by a backsplash, or if your wall isn't straight, you'll need to scribe the laminate to fit neatly against the wall.

If the wall deviates from a straight line by more than ¹⁄₈" or so, use a short scrap block to transfer the contour of the wall onto the laminate. The thickness of the block should be greater than the largest gap between the wall and the laminate. Slide the block with a marking pen held firmly against it along the wall. The block will follow the wall's shape, and the marker will record it.

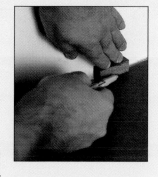

Don't try to cut plastic laminate along an irregular line. Instead cut a straight line that follows the irregular line as closely as possible; then file or sand the laminate to shape.

8 APPLY CONTACT CEMENT

Contact cement is either water- or solvent-based. Although solvent-based contact cements are flammable, they provide a better bond when adhering laminate to laminate.

- Lay the laminate upside down on the counter. Apply the adhesive to the laminate with a low- or medium-nap roller. You want a consistent layer of glue without any globs or heavy ridges. Be sure to cover all the laminate evenly right out to the edges.

- Move the laminate to a spot where it can dry, glue face up, undisturbed.

- Now spread contact cement on the countertop. Allow the adhesive to dry to the touch—typically 10 to 15 minutes.

9 POSITION LAMINATE ON COUNTER

- To prevent the contact cement from bonding prematurely, lay several dowels or thin sticks across the countertop, and then set the laminate on the dowels.
- Position the laminate so the overhang is even along the edges and the ends.
- Remove dowels one at a time, working from one end, pressing the laminate down as you go. When gluing pieces that join together at a seam, apply one piece first, then carefully position the second piece and butt the seam together before pressing down the second piece.

10 APPLY EVEN PRESSURE

Contact cement needs only a little bit of "momentary pressure" to get a good bond.

- You can use a low-tech approach by laying a piece of 2 by 4 on the laminate and pounding it, moderately hard, systematically around the entire area. Or use a rubber laminate "J-roller" made specifically for this job (*see page 31*).
- **Caution:** Don't roll or pound over the sink opening—you may cause a crack that extends onto the good part of the countertop. Apply some masking tape over the sink area to indicate a "no-pressure zone."

11 FLUSH-TRIM THE EDGE

You can trim small amounts of laminate with a file, but it's slow going and tedious. I prefer a laminate trimmer (*see page 32*) with a flush-trimming bit.

- Set the bit height so ¼" of the cutter overlaps the laminate and the bearing rides along the edge of the counter.
- Trim the laminate flush to the edge, keeping the base flat on the countertop.
- Where the counter meets a wall, you'll be left with a section that the router can't reach. Trim these end sections with a file (or use an offset laminate trimmer).

12 ROUT A PROFILE ON THE EDGE

With the top laminate trimmed flush to the edge, you're just about finished. But the edge is sharp to the touch and fragile. It needs to be softened a bit.

- For a wood edge, rout a profile with a router or laminate trimmer and a profiling bit. A chamfering bit is a good choice: It cuts a clean bevel across the wood and the laminate.

- On a laminate edge, rout a much smaller bevel—it can't be more than $1/16$" or else you'll rout through the laminate itself. Another option would be to file a small bevel with a mill file. Work your way carefully along the entire edge.

13 MAKE THE SINK CUTOUT

You can cut the sink opening out with a saber saw or a laminate trimmer; a laminate trimmer works best and will leave the edge crisp and clean, requiring no sanding.

- Drill a $1/2$" or larger hole through the laminate a few inches out from the edge of the sink opening.

- With a flush-trim bit positioned in the hole, turn on the laminate trimmer and cut out the sink opening.

14 INSTALL A BACKSPLASH

You can make or buy a backsplash that matches the laminate counter, or one that matches the wood edge if you've used one.

- Cut the backsplash to length.

- If you apply a backsplash at the ends, miter the inside corners of both the back piece and the end pieces.

- Check that the backsplash fits correctly, then glue it to the wall with construction adhesive.

- Apply a bead of silicone caulk between the backsplash and the counter, and between the backsplash and the wall.

- Replace the sink (*see page 22*).

KOHLER

Upgrading a Faucet

If your hardworking faucet is looking and acting tired, replacing it will be a satisfying afternoon's project.

You use your kitchen faucet dozens of times a day, so it should function well—no drips!—and look good, too. Faucets aren't just chrome-plated these days; you might be surprised at the range of models carried by the larger home centers. A wide variety of colors and finishes are available, from satin or brushed brass to high-gloss red or green.

New features such as extended spouts and pullout sprayers take the drudgery out of many kitchen tasks: Extended spouts make washing both dishes and food easier, as well as filling pitchers and other tall containers. Some spouts are even designed to be lifted out to function as a sprayer as well.

I'm often surprised to find that many homeowners don't consider upgrading a faucet unless they're replacing the sink. Nonsense. You can replace a faucet anytime you're looking for a fresh look in the kitchen. All it takes is an afternoon.

Tools

Phillips-head and flat-head screwdrivers
Adjustable wrench
Basin wrench
Putty knife

Materials

New faucet
Plumber's putty, if required
½" Teflon tape
Flexible supply lines

Preparation

A faucet requires holes in the sink for its mounting hardware and water-supply lines. Go under the sink with a flashlight and note both the number of holes and their spacing; use this information when shopping for a new faucet. To avoid buying a fixture that won't fit, you can remove the old faucet and bring it with you to the store.

LEVEL OF DIFFICULTY
Easy

TIME REQUIREMENT
½ day

COST ESTIMATE
$50 to $150

KITCHENS

1 DISCONNECT WATER SUPPLY

You'll get a geyser if you remove the old faucet without first turning off the supply lines running to it, both hot and cold.

- The shutoffs should be under the sink; if not, you'll have to trace the pipes to the basement or utility space and turn off the water there.
- Then open the faucets to drain the lines.
- Undo the connecting nut attaching each supply pipe to its shutoff valve.

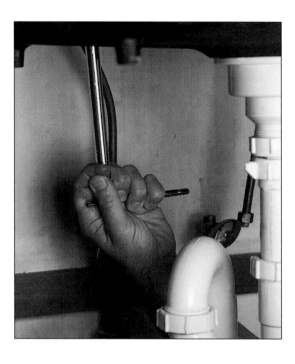

2 DISCONNECT MOUNTING NUTS

- Remove the nuts that hold the faucet in place; they are on the underside of the sink, just below the fixture.
- A basin wrench, with its long extension, makes this job less awkward; see "Tool Know-How" on the opposite page.
- If the mounting nuts won't budge, or if you don't have a basin wrench, you may have to remove the sink to gain access to the nuts. Disconnect the waste line, loosen the mounting clips, and lift out the sink.

3 REMOVE OLD FAUCET

- Carefully lift out the old faucet.
- Then clean the sink where the new faucet will go. Scrape off any old plumber's putty with a putty knife, taking care not to scratch the surface.
- Remove any residue by wiping down the faucet area with acetone.

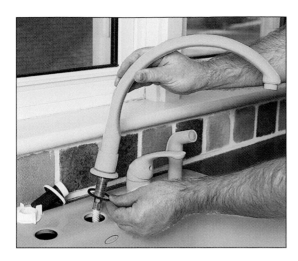

4 INSTALL NEW FAUCET

- To create a seal between the faucet and sink, position the gasket provided over the faucet opening. If there is no gasket, check the installation instructions to see if you should apply plumber's putty.

- Put the faucet in position and tighten the nuts to hold the faucet in place.

- If there is a spray hose, attach it to the connector on the body of the faucet.

- Reconnect the water supply using flexible supply lines (*see page 27*).

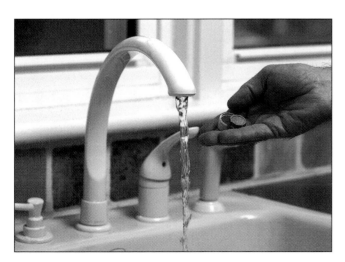

5 FLUSH FAUCET

- Unscrew the collar and run the water to flush out any debris that may have been in the faucet.

- Rinse out the collar's strainer, then put the collar back in place.

TOOL
KNOW-HOW

Basin Wrench

When you work on plumbing, you soon find yourself wishing your arm had two elbows, or even three. That's especially true of under-the-sink jobs, because everything is tucked out of sight and is almost always inaccessible.

A basin wrench (*above*) is a specialty tool that gives you that extra elbow. It has a long extension arm that allows you to loosen or tighten faucet fittings with your hand in the clear space as shown below.

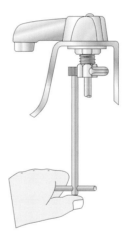

Another helpful feature is that the serrated jaws are self-adjusting, and they close to fit around the nut as pressure is applied. You can find basin wrenches at virtually any hardware store or in the plumbing section at most home and building centers.

KITCHENS

Refacing Kitchen Cabinets

Instead of replacing tired, old kitchen cabinets, reface them for a fresh look.

What's the biggest, heaviest thing in your house? Unless you have a very unusual hobby, the answer probably is the kitchen cabinets. When they become dingy and outmoded, it's a lot easier—and cheaper—to simply redo the surfaces you see, allowing the structural parts to stay. Flip through the yellow pages, and you'll find local companies that specialize in doing just that. But you can do the job yourself, without advanced woodworking skills or special tools. Only the doors of cabinets and drawers are replaced, leaving you to cover the cabinet's "face frame" with veneer—thin sheets of real wood that come with peel-and-stick or iron-on adhesive.

You can order refacing kits through home centers, complete with doors, drawer fronts, veneer, plywood cabinet ends, and hardware. You'll have a choice of woods (most commonly oak, ash, maple, and birch) and finishes (prefinished, ready to finish, paint grade, and laminated). And you should be able to find a style that complements your kitchen, including doors with beveled or leaded glass.

Tools

Phillips-head and flat-head screwdrivers
Putty knife and utility knife
Sanding block
Electric drill and twist bits
Tape measure and straightedge
Iron (for iron-on veneer)
Laminate roller (can be rented)
2" varnish brush

Materials

Replacement cabinet doors and drawer fronts
Veneer sheets
Wood edge banding (optional)
¼" plywood for cabinet ends (optional)
Construction adhesive
1" brads
1¼" wood screws
100-grit sandpaper
Satin or gloss varnish
New hardware (optional)
Wood putty

Preparation

Measure the inside openings for doors and drawer fronts, and order replacements. You'll also need veneer for the face frames, and either veneer or plywood for the cabinet ends.

Decide on whether to buy new hardware.

Apply finish to drawers and doors before installation to reduce the kitchen's downtime.

LEVEL OF DIFFICULTY
Moderate

TIME REQUIREMENT
2 to 3 days

COST ESTIMATE
For average oak door, $30 unfinished or $44 finished; for average oak drawer front, $23 unfinished or $29 finished. Add $55 for a 2' by 8' roll of oak veneer.

KITCHENS

1 REMOVE OLD DOORS AND DRAWERS

- Unscrew door hinges from cabinets, and remove drawer fronts.
- If you will be reusing the hinges and handles, remove them and save the screws.
- Putty large dents, as well as hinge holes that would show.
- Paint the cabinet interiors if you wish.

2 SAND FACE FRAMES

Since most cabinets typically have a glossy surface (whether painted or finished clear), the veneer will adhere better after some prep work.

- Wash all of the surfaces to be veneered with warm, soapy water or a mild solution of TSP (trisodium phosphate).
- Rinse well and let dry.
- Sand with 100-grit paper wrapped around a sanding block. Safety Note: If your cabinets were built prior to 1978, they may have been decoarted with lead paint. See page 287 before sanding.

CHOOSING
Materials

Veneers and Plywood

Cabinet refacing wouldn't be a very attractive option if it weren't for paper-thin sheets of real wood—veneer. The stuff is good looking, flexible, easy to cut, and affordable. And no one but a cabinetmaker or experienced wood-worker is likely to notice that the beauty of your refaced cabinets is only skin deep. Veneer comes in sheets, for covering larger surfaces, and rolls of 1"-wide banding for running along edges.

3 CUT VENEER TO ROUGH SIZE

- Measure for the pieces of veneer, adding ½" extra to each dimension to ensure full coverage.
- If you want to cover the inside edges of door openings, cut strips from rolls of edge-banding veneer.
- Working on a flat surface, cut the veneer with a sharp utility knife and a metal straightedge.

4 ATTACH VENEER

- For veneer backed with heat-sensitive glue, attach using a household iron on the setting for cotton, then roll immediately with a laminate roller *(inset)*.
- For self-adhesive veneer with a peel-off backing, begin at one corner, peeling only enough paper to get started, then continue peeling as you smooth the veneer into place.
- For the face frames, apply vertical pieces first, and trim as shown in the next step.
- Next, apply horizontal pieces so that they overlap the vertical pieces; cut through the overlap with a utility knife, using a metal straightedge as a guide.

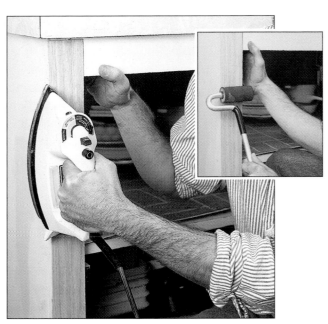

5 TRIM VENEER EDGES

- Carefully trim away excess veneer with a utility knife.
- On edges that protrude just slightly, use 100-grit sandpaper wrapped around a sanding block.

6 SAW OFF DRAWER LIPS

• If your drawers have "integral fronts" (that is, fronts that can't be detached from the drawer), saw the lips off them so that the new fronts will be flush with the face frame when the drawers are closed.

7 ATTACH NEW DRAWER FRONTS

• To center each drawer front, drive two 1¼" wood screws from inside the drawer box until the tips protrude about ⅛".

• Position the drawer box in the cabinet so that it is flush with the face frame. (Have a helper hold the drawer in position.)

• Center the new drawer front over its opening and press it into place so that the screw tips leave marks on its back.

• Remove the front and drawer box, and drill holes slightly larger then the diameter of the screws through the box. Then press the front in place as guided by the screw tips and their marks, and drive in the screws to secure the front.

Ron's
PRO
TIPS

Hardware-Mounting Template

Here's a time saver used by production shops to locate pilot holes for hardware. Templates aren't much use if you've got only a couple of holes to drill. But since you're looking at an entire kitchen's worth of hardware, you might give this simple template a try. It's just a piece of wood with holes in it to guide drilling the pilot holes in each door or drawer front. The cleats on the back allow you to hold the template in exactly the same place for every door or drawer front. I made the one shown here from workshop scraps, gluing and clamp-

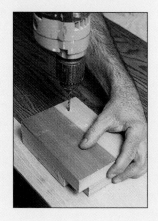

ing the cleats in place. To use the template, place it with the cleats snug up against adjacent sides of a door or drawer front, and drill through the holes.

KITCHENS

8 ATTACH DOOR HARDWARE

- If you're replacing the old hardware with new hardware, first drill pilot holes for hinges and handles on the doors and drawer fronts.
- To speed up the placement of locating holes, use a template as described in Ron's Pro Tips on the opposite page.
- Screw the hinges to the doors. (A little parafin applied to the threads of the screws makes it easier to drive them in.)

9 MOUNT DOORS

- Position each door so that it overlaps evenly all around, then mark the face frame for the hinges.
- Drill pilot holes and then drive screws through the hinges.
- If the hinges allow for making adjustments, fine-tune the fit of the doors.

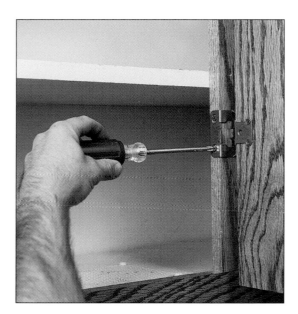

10 ADD SIDE PANELS

You can use veneer to cover the ends of cabinets, but I prefer panels of matching ¼" plywood for base cabinets that will be subjected to daily wear and tear.

- Measure and cut the plywood to fit the end of the cabinet.
- Attach the side panels to the cabinet with construction adhesive and 1" brads.
- Set the heads of the brads and fill with matching putty.

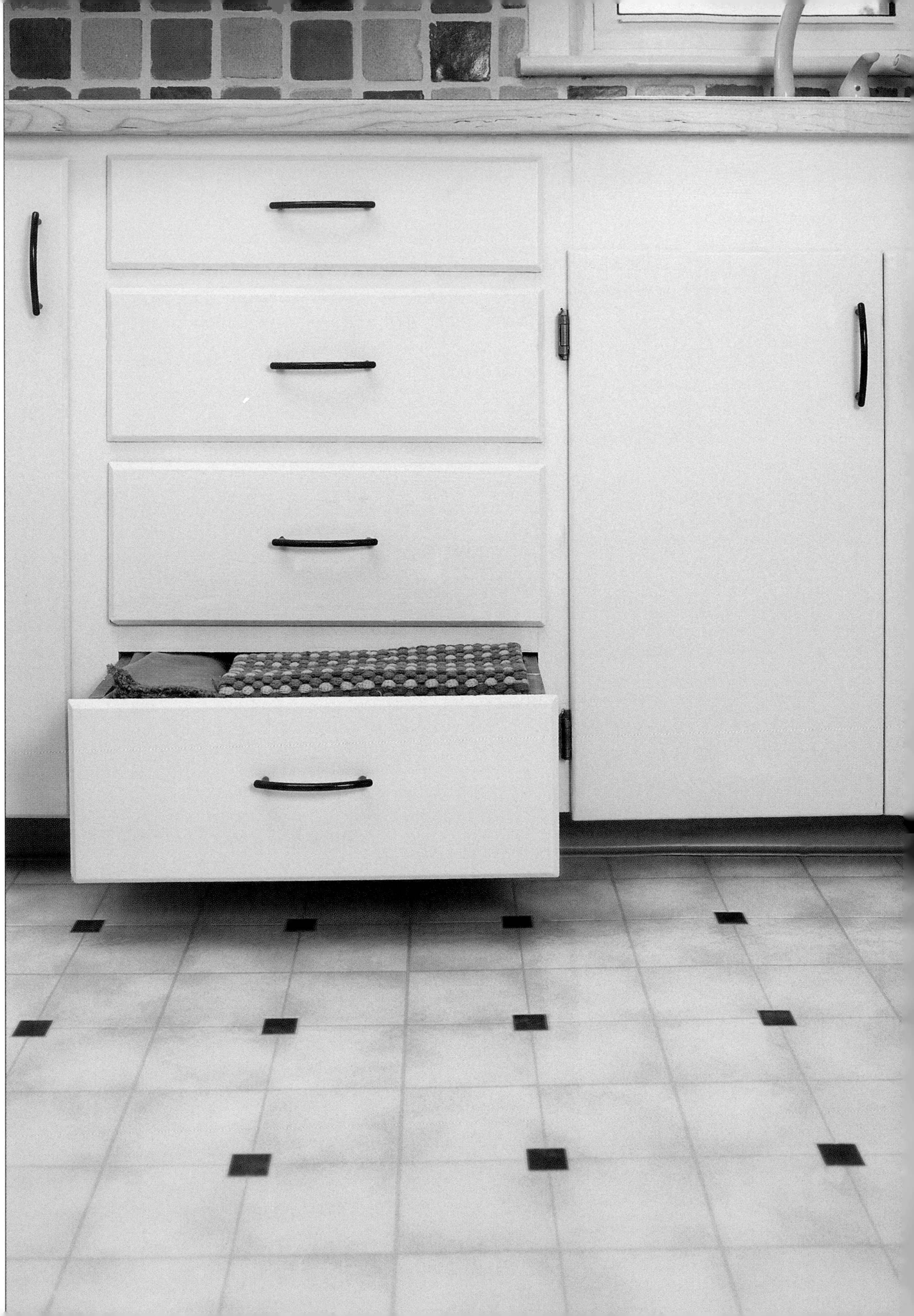

Painting Kitchen Cabinets

Painting cabinets will give a kitchen a quick and inexpensive face-lift.

Every kitchen is built around the cabinetry. When considering kitchen remodeling, replacing the cabinets is by far the most substantial part of the job. And the cost of new cabinets is usually greater than all the other costs combined. That's why I often suggest to homeowners painting the cabinets as an economical alternative.

Any kitchen cabinets can be painted—whether the doors are flush panels or frame-and-panel construction. (Note: Pre-1978 cabinets may have been decorated with lead paint, see the Safety note on page 287 before beginning work.) Choose any color in the rainbow, and the cost will be the same: very little. Paint the walls and ceiling at the same time, perhaps add a new floor, and painted cabinets can be the centerpiece of a substantial—but reasonably priced—kitchen makeover.

Since this is such an inexpensive project, invest in a high-quality paint. I prefer a latex enamel with a satin finish. It will hide future scratches and dings and will clean up easily. If your cabinets have a natural, clear finish (as opposed to paint), apply a coat of primer before the topcoat.

Tools

Phillips-head and flat-head screwdrivers
Putty knife
Sanding block
2" paintbrush
Paint roller with tray
Sponge

Materials

120-grit sandpaper
Masking tape
Spackling compound
Trisodium phosphate (TSP)
Paint
Drop cloth or newspaper
Felt or rubber bumpers
New hardware (optional)

Preparation

Set up a place where you can paint as many of the parts as possible without needing to move them around. In a small kitchen, the countertop may be the best place—just cover it well with newspaper. Or set up sawhorses in the garage or basement and paint there.

Before you start, make a rough plan drawing of the kitchen and give each cabinet a number; then label the doors and drawers according to the plan. Drawers can be labeled on the bottom; doors, behind one of the hinge plates. This will ensure that you'll get all the parts back in their proper place.

LEVEL OF DIFFICULTY
 Easy

TIME REQUIREMENT
 1 to 3 days, depending on the size of the kitchen

COST ESTIMATE
 $30 to $100

KITCHENS

1 REMOVE DOORS, DRAWERS, AND HARDWARE

Painting kitchen cabinets involves only the exposed parts—doors, drawer fronts, and the cabinet face frames. The first step is to remove the hardware from the doors and drawers.

- Remove all the handles and pulls.
- Unscrew the doors from their hinges, then remove the hinges.
- If the drawer fronts are detachable, take them off the drawer boxes. Some drawers have integral fronts; on these you'll have to pull out the entire drawer box.

2 CLEAN THE SURFACES

Paint adheres well only to clean surfaces. Kitchen cabinets pick up a lot of dirt over time, especially greasy dirt. So you'll need to clean them well before sanding. Don't try to sand the dirt off the wood—it will gum up the sandpaper and create a mess.

- Scrub the doors, drawer fronts, and face frames with soap and water and a sponge or abrasive pad such as Scotch-Brite. Use a mixture of water and trisodium phosphate (TSP) to really clean the wood.
- Then wipe the surfaces dry.

3 FILL IMPERFECTIONS

- Check the surfaces to be painted for dents, gouges, and scratches, and apply spackling compound with a putty knife.
- Let the spackling dry thoroughly.
- If you'll be using new hardware that mounts differently, fill any unwanted holes.

KITCHENS

4 SAND THE SURFACES

Wood takes paint best when it is lightly abraded.

- Wrap some 120-grit sandpaper around a sanding block or a scrap of wood.
- Sand all the flat wood parts consistently. Make sure all the edges are slightly rounded over.
- On raised-panel doors, use a small piece of sandpaper and mold it in your fingers to the shape of the panel edge. Then sand each edge of the panel.

5 PAINT DOORS, DRAWERS, AND FACE FRAMES

- Paint the back faces of the doors and drawer fronts first, then the front faces.
- Paint the face frames using a small roller (or a 2" brush). Paint the doors with a detail or standard-sized roller. Use a brush to paint the edges of the doors, drawer fronts, and face frames.

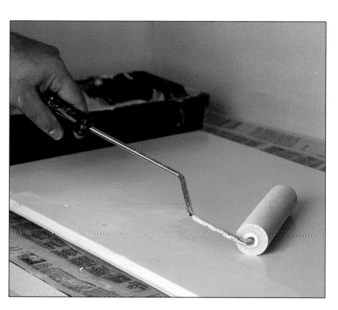

6 ATTACH HARDWARE

Allow the paint to dry thoroughly before putting everything back together.

- Screw the hinges to the doors, then to the face frames.
- Reattach the handles and pulls; or replace them with new hardware for a fresh look. (Drill holes for the new hardware as necessary.)
- Apply rubber or felt bumpers on the backs of the doors and drawer fronts to prevent the paint from sticking.

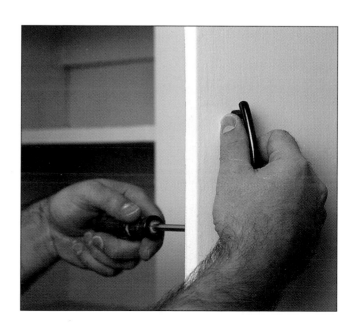

Sink Cabinet Storage Upgrades

Create more storage space under your kitchen sink with these easy-to-install add-ons.

If I had to choose one area in a kitchen that could really use help with storage, I'd pick the sink; there is so much to store there—cleaning supplies, dish racks, towels, buckets, etc.—and so little usable space. There isn't any room for drawers at the top because of the sink. And the plumbing gets in the way of using the bottom area of the cabinet. Although many people store their cleaning products under the sink along the front edge where they're easy to reach, it still leaves a lot of wasted space in the back.

Here are two simple ideas I often recommend for quick improvements. First, you can add flip-out trays behind the false drawer fronts. These are great for storing sponges, dish cloths, steel wool pads, and other small items. Down below, you can install slide-out wire baskets that extend all the way out of the cabinet to give you complete and easy access to everything stored there. These are especially easy to install because the slide mechanism is a single unit, not two separate tracks that have to be carefully aligned.

Tools

Electric drill
Phillips-head and flat-head
  screwdrivers

Materials

Flip-out trays and hinges
Slide-out wire basket

Preparation

Before buying the hardware for the flip-out trays, check to see how the false drawer fronts are mounted on your cabinet. Make sure you can remove them without removing the sink (unless you're willing to do that as well).

Also check the usable depth of the cabinet at the bottom, because the plumbing lines reduce the amount of usable space for a slide-out basket.

LEVEL OF DIFFICULTY
Easy

TIME REQUIREMENT
½ day

COST ESTIMATE
$50 to $75

Flip-out trays

1 SCREW HINGES TO FALSE DRAWER FRONTS

The hinges that allow the false fronts to pivot out rest on the bottom face frame and get screwed to the vertical face frame.

- Detach the false fronts by unscrewing the tabs inside the cabinet that hold them in place.
- Follow the positioning instructions provided to drill the mounting holes; then screw the hinges to the false fronts.

2 DRILL TRAY MOUNTING HOLES

- Center the tray on the inside face of the false drawer front so it will clear the face frame when the assembly is closed.
- Drill the holes for mounting the tray, but don't attach it now.

3 ATTACH HINGES TO FACE FRAME

The hinges are self-closing, and you need to hold them in the open position to mount them to the face frame.

- Mark the mounting holes and drill pilot holes in the vertical face frame.
- Mount the hinges with their screws.
- Once the drawer front is hinged, attach the tray and tighten the screws that hold it.
- Check for smooth operation, and adjust hinge placement as needed.

Slide-out wire basket

1 MOUNT SLIDE MECHANISM

To start, fit the wire basket into its slide mechanism. Position the assembly where you want it in the cabinet. Make sure it fits all the way into the cabinet when in the closed position.

- Mark the slide mechanism mounting holes on the bottom of the cabinet.

- Remove the basket, if necessary, and screw the slide mechanism to the cabinet bottom.

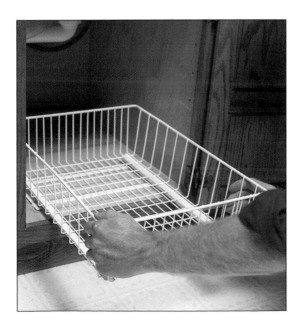

Cordless Drills and Drivers

Cordless drills (*below right*), which double as power screwdrivers, make drilling holes and driving screws a lot easier these days. They're typically lighter than corded drills, and they go anywhere— no power cords to get in the way and no need for an outlet nearby.

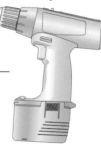

There is a huge selection of styles, power ratings, and options. Power ranges go from 7.2 volts all the way up to 18 volts. Most cordless drills have at least two speeds, while some have two variable speed ranges. Better models have a clutch, which lets you drive screws without stripping the heads. And many models come with a second battery so you can keep on working when one battery runs out of juice.

A cordless screwdriver (*left*) is an inexpensive option, especially if all you plan to use it for is light-duty jobs like hanging curtains. But these models drive screws only— they don't have a chuck for drilling holes.

2 INSTALL WIRE BASKET

- Slide the wire basket into its slide mechanism and test that it slides smoothly all the way out and back in.

- If the action is not smooth, apply light oil to lubricate the slide.

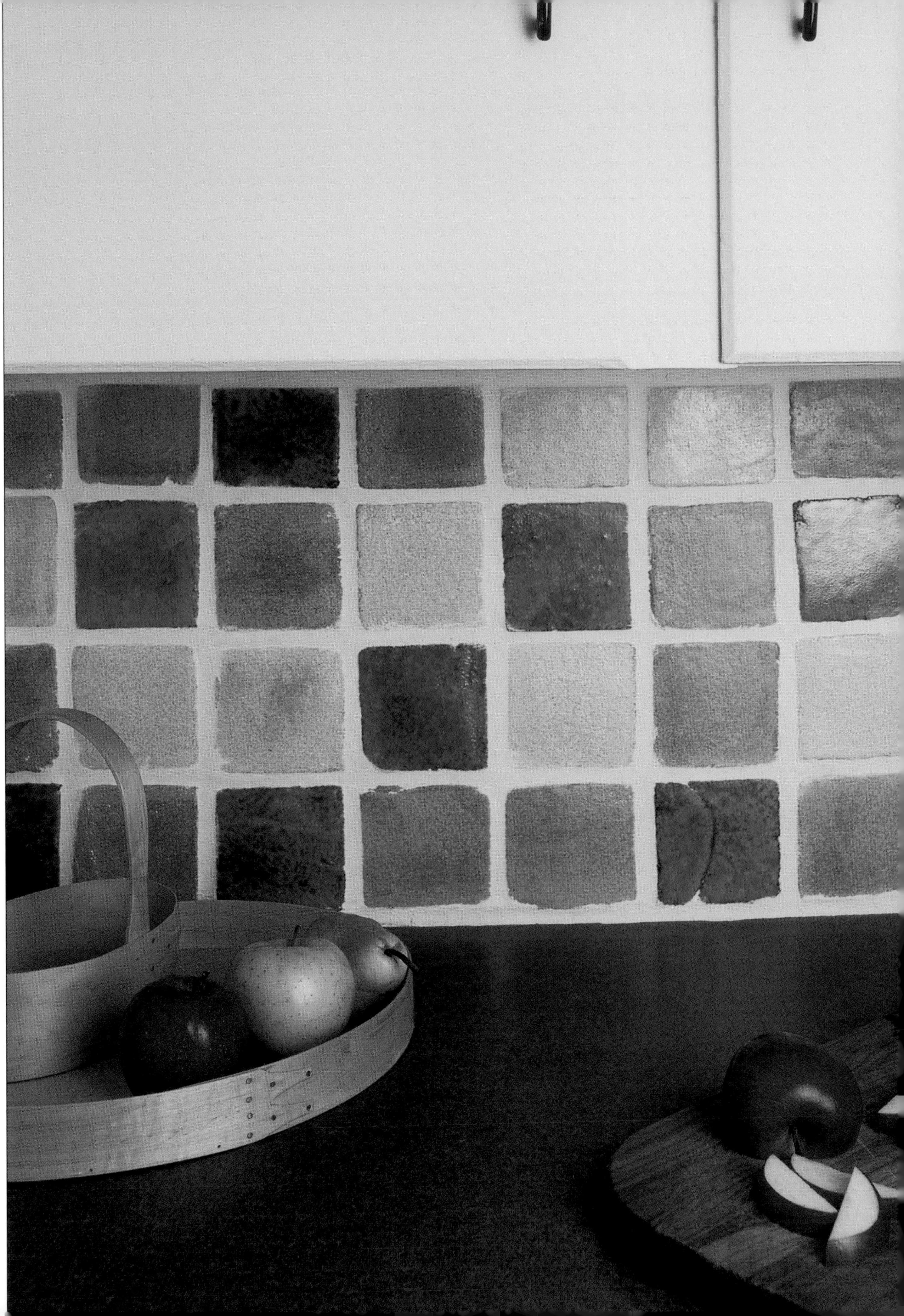

Tiling a Backsplash

Tile can provide a low-maintenance surface while adding a "splash" of color to your kitchen walls.

It seems to me that "backsplash" is a pretty accurate term. This area of the kitchen takes an especially hard hit, day after day, collecting splatters that wallpaper and painted drywall weren't intended to handle.

By covering the wall above the counter with tiles, you make cleanups far easier. After a quick sponging, the tiles look as good as new. So why aren't tiled backsplashes more common? Homeowners tend to shy away from tile work. There is the prospect of all that gooey adhesive, all those tiles to stick into it, and then some mysterious substance called grout.

But even if you are without experience, tiling a backsplash will go easily. There's not much that can go wrong, because the area—just a few square feet—is so modest.

And a backsplash is a great way to add color and texture to your kitchen. The variety of tile shapes, sizes, and designs is staggering—the biggest challenge to this job may be selecting the tile! A note about size: To keep everything in proportion, I recommend smaller tiles (2" to 4") for a backsplash. The smallest tiles are often called mosaic tiles and come in 1' square sheets with a nylon-reinforced backing. The advantage of this is that the tile spacing is preset—which makes for a quick and easy installation.

Tools

Sanding block
Tile cutter (can be rented)
Trowel with smooth and
  notched edges
Plastic tile spacers (if tiles
  don't have spacing tabs)
3' or 4' level
Rubber mallet or hammer
  and pad
Rubber grouting float
Sponge

Materials

60-grit sandpaper
Acetone or denatured alcohol
Grout sealant
Adhesive
Tile adhesive primer (to seal
  porous surfaces before apply-
  ing adhesive)
Grout
Cheesecloth

Preparation

Measure the wall to calculate how many tiles you'll need. If you are using a mix of tiles, lay out a pleasing pattern along the countertop, running along just as you want them on the wall above.

Protect the countertops from the job ahead by covering them with drop cloths or a couple layers of a strong paper, such as kraft or builder's paper.

LEVEL OF DIFFICULTY
Moderate

TIME REQUIREMENT
2 days

COST ESTIMATE
$100 to $200

KITCHENS

1 PREPARE SURFACE

Installing tiles can add significant weight to a wall. It's imperative that the surface to which you'll be adhering the tiles be structurally sound and well prepared.

- Sand the walls with coarse-grit paper for a better bond. A sanding block makes the job go more easily.
- Wipe down the surface with either acetone or denatured alcohol to remove oils that might interfere with adhesion.
- For porous surfaces, apply a coat of tile adhesive primer.

2 APPLY ADHESIVE

- Apply the adhesive to the wall, using the flat edge of a trowel.
- Create ridges in the adhesive by running over it with the notched edge of the trowel (see the manufacturer's directions for proper notch size).

3 PLACE THE TILES

If an area of wall does not have a counter-top or trim along its lower edge, tack on a temporary strip of wood (such as a 1 by 3) to support the weight of the adhesive and the tiles.

- Press the tiles into place. Use a level to maintain a horizontal line. If the tiles don't have tabs to determine the spaces between them, use plastic spacers to maintain an even gap.
- To set the tiles, give each tile a rap with a rubber mallet; for thin tiles, cushion the blow with a scrap block wrapped with a cloth (*inset*).

KITCHENS

4 APPLY GROUT

- Allow the adhesive to set up per the manufacturer's instructions.
- If you are using a grout mix, prepare it according to the directions. Plan on working on no more than 10 square feet at a time.
- Spread grout over the tiles with a rubber grout float. Move the float on diagonals to force grout between the tiles.

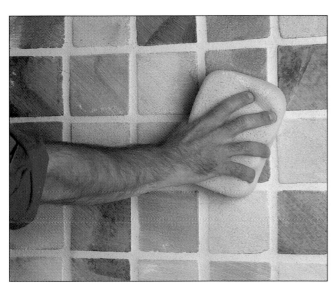

5 REMOVE GROUT HAZE

- After the grout partially sets up, wipe it off with a damp sponge, being careful to avoid pulling grout out from the joints.
- After the first pass, use the sponge to form a level joint between tiles.
- When the grout has dried, remove the thin haze from the tile faces by rubbing with cheesecloth.
- Apply a sealer to the grout after waiting the specified time (typically 2 to 4 weeks).

TOOL
KNOW-HOW

Motorized Tile Saw

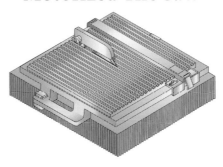

You can cut tiles in a few ways, ranging from low- to high-tech. The simplest method is to score the face with an ordinary glass cutter, then snap it over a nail as a fulcrum. That works well if the tiles are thin and glazed smooth. But for thicker tiles and those with a rough finish, you'll have an easier time of it by renting a manual tile cutter. Another option is to purchase an inexpensive motorized saw (*above*). It cuts with a diamond-encrusted blade that runs in a water bath to keep it cool. The saw is easy to use and includes a rip fence that allows you to quickly trim tiles to identical width.

PROJECTS

Replacing a Vanity 60

Installing
a Pedestal Sink 66

Upgrading
a Medicine Cabinet 70

Replacing
Bathroom Lights 74

Upgrading a Toilet 78

Installing
a Whirlpool Tub. 84

Installing a Bathroom
Exhaust Fan 90

Installing
Shower Doors. 94

Installing
Bathroom Tileboard. 100

BATHROOMS

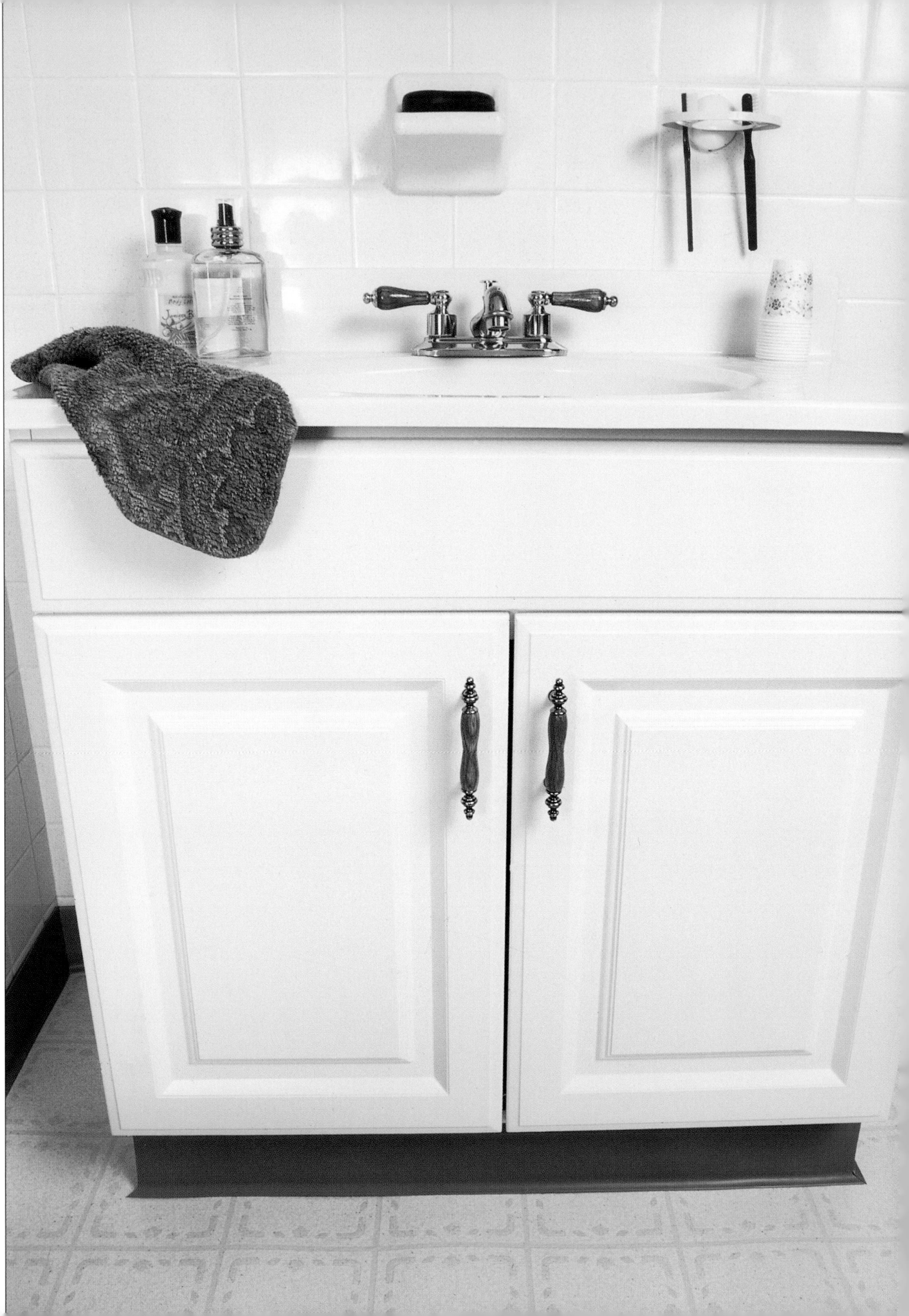

Replacing a Vanity

Unlike a kitchen, you can give a bathroom a totally new look by replacing just one cabinet— the vanity.

Bathroom vanity cabinets receive a lot of wear and tear, especially with young children in the house. Even if it's in decent shape, an older vanity cabinet may just look tired and outdated. In many cases, if the sink and faucet are in good shape, consider replacing just the vanity. Or you can upgrade the whole set.

If the existing cabinet is a stock size (24", 30", 36", and 48" wide are typical), the simplest approach is to replace it with one the same size. If you have the room, you can upgrade to a larger size. On the other hand, switching to a smaller cabinet to gain some room may expose unfinished patches of wall or floor. Cabinets priced at the bottom of the range may be fine, but avoid cabinets in which the exposed parts—doors, drawer fronts, and sides—are made of fiberboard, because it will damage easily from contact with water.

Installing a new vanity is quite simple, while replacing (or reinstalling) the sink and faucet set is only slightly more challenging. If the plumbing makes you nervous, you can still replace the vanity cabinet and hire a plumber to make the connections.

Tools

Adjustable wrench
Channel-type pliers
Wide-blade putty knife
Stud finder
Pry bar
3' level
Electric drill and bits
Phillips-head and flat-head
  screwdrivers
Caulking gun
Utility knife
Hole saw and saber saw
  (optional)
Fine-tip permanent marker
  (optional)

Materials

New vanity
Sink (if replacing)
Faucet set (if replacing)
Supply tubes
Teflon tape
Wood shims
Wall anchors and screws
Silicone caulk
Cove base molding and
  adhesive

Preparation

Turn off the water supply before disconnecting the faucet.

LEVEL OF DIFFICULTY
  Moderate

TIME REQUIREMENT
  1 to 2 days

COST ESTIMATE
  $100 to $250

1 DISCONNECT THE PLUMBING

- Turn off the supply valves for the sink. If there are no shutoff valves right at the sink, turn off the main water inlet valve for the house. Drain the water in the lines by turning on the faucet.

- Disconnect the supply lines with an adjustable wrench.

- Disconnect and remove the P-trap—have a bucket and towels handy, as there will be water in the trap.

2 REMOVE TRIM AROUND BASE

- Use a pry bar to remove any wood trim from around the base of the vanity.

- Use a wide-blade putty knife to remove vinyl cove base molding from the adjacent wall if necessary.

3 REMOVE OLD VANITY TOP

Even if you're discarding the entire vanity and sink, you'll probably have to remove the sink to get access to the screws holding the vanity cabinet to the wall.

- Remove any screws that hold the sink top to the vanity.

- Some sink tops are held in place with silicone adhesive; if yours is, simply pry the sink top up from the cabinet.

Ron's
**PRO
TIPS**

Routing Plumbing through Cabinet Floor

When you shop for a new vanity, you'll notice that most of them are built with an open back. If your supply and waste lines come in through the bathroom wall, then there's no cutting or drilling needed to route the pipes into the cabinet. But if your pipes come up through the floor (or if your vanity does have a back), you'll need to drill holes in the cabinet for the pipes. These holes need to be accurately located and drilled.

With the cabinet positioned level, mark the wall and floor along one side of the cabinet *(top right)*. Use these marks to measure and record the locations of the pipes, relative to the side of the cabinet. Then transfer the marks onto the cabinet floor or back, whichever you're drilling through. Use a

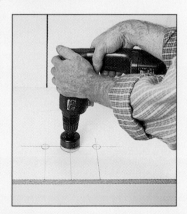

2" hole saw to drill the hole for the waste pipe *(bottom right)*. Use a ⅞" or 1" spade bit to drill the holes for the supply pipes. Then slide the cabinet over the pipes and into final position against the wall.

4 LEVEL THE NEW VANITY

- Set the vanity in place against the wall.
- With a 3' level, check the vanity for level, both side-to-side and front-to-back.
- Insert wood shims under the base as needed to level the cabinet.
- Once level, draw lines on the floor and wall so you can easily reposition the vanity after completing the next step.
- Note: After the cabinet is screwed to the wall, cut off the excess shims flush with the base of the cabinet.

BATHROOMS

TOOL
KNOW-HOW

Stud Finders

When installing new cabinets, shelves, and other fixtures, it's important to anchor them securely to the wall studs. Drywall and plaster just don't have any holding power by themselves.

There are two types of stud finders that will pinpoint those invisible studs for you. The magnetic stud finder *(left)* seeks out the metal nails or screws holding the drywall to the studs. Just slide it slowly in a zigzag pattern over the wall until the magnetic rod pivots, indicating a screw or nail. These cost just a couple bucks, and no homeowner's toolbox should be without one.

The more sophisticated electronic stud finder *(right)* emits electronic waves that detect changes in the density of the wall. It's just about foolproof and works more quickly than the magnetic stud finder above. It costs around $10 to $15 and is well worth the money.

5 MARK STUDS AND SCREW CABINET TO WALL

- Locate and mark the wall studs behind the vanity *(see Tool Know-How, left)*.
- Drill holes through the vanity back rail, then screw the cabinet to the wall *(inset)*.
- On tiled walls, it may be difficult to detect the wall studs. Use a masonry bit to drill the holes, and insert plastic wall anchors *(see page 175)* to receive the screws.

6 CONNECT FAUCET AND SUPPLY TUBES

It's a lot easier to connect the faucet set and the supply tubes to the sink before installing the faucet set on the new cabinet.

- Install the faucet set and the pop-up drain—follow the specific instructions supplied by the manufacturer.
- Connect the supply tubes to the threaded supply inlets on the faucet.

BATHROOMS

7 ATTACH VANITY TOP TO CABINET

- For cultured-marble vanity tops, apply a generous bead of silicone caulk to the top edge of the vanity cabinet, then position the vanity top and press down.
- Some vanity tops may require screws or other mechanical fasteners driven up through corner blocks in the cabinet.

8 CONNECT SUPPLY AND WASTE LINES

- Connect the supply lines using an adjustable wrench.
- Connect a new P-trap to the tailpiece *(inset)*. Tighten the slip nuts snug by hand, then give each a quarter-turn with a pair of channel-type pliers.

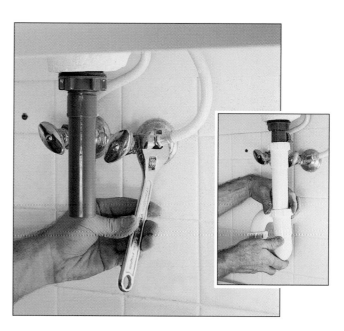

9 ADD TRIM TO BASE

Apply trim to the base of the cabinet to match the trim in the room. Vinyl cove base is clean and easy to work with on tile walls.

- Cut cove base molding to length with a utility knife.
- Glue molding to the cabinet and walls with vinyl cove base adhesive.

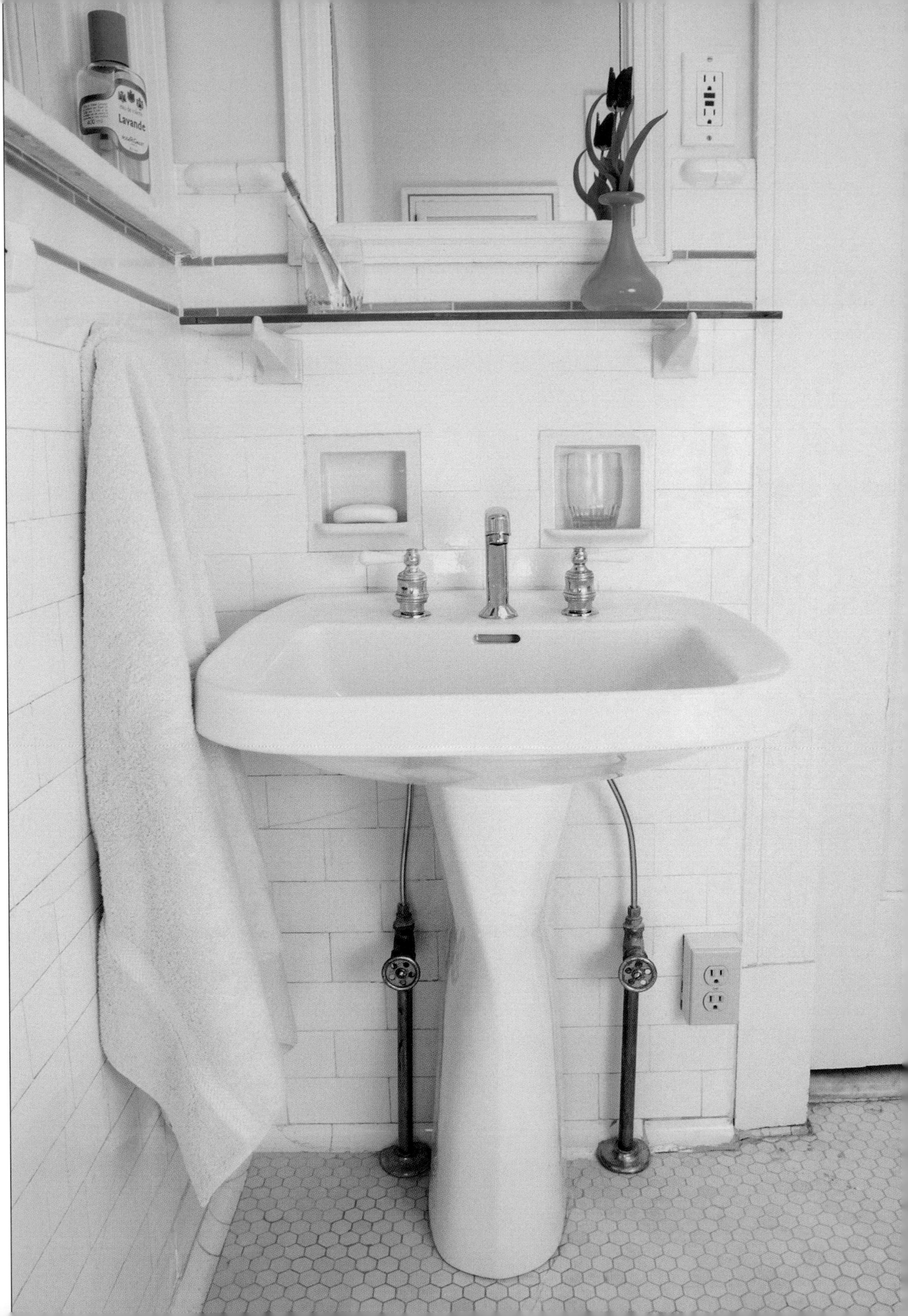
Lavande

Installing a Pedestal Sink

Install a sink that deserves to be put on a pedestal.

Bathroom sinks are among the hardest-working objects in the home. And once upon a time, sinks looked important, with their cast-iron construction, their sturdy pedestals, and basins big enough to wash a baby in. Then something happened to the bathroom sink: It got smaller and plainer, until we ended up with that familiar unlovable dish perched on spindly chrome legs. Nobody liked these sinks except plumbers, who appreciated their light weight and all that open space in which to spin a wrench.

Traditional designs like the pedestal sink are on their way back. They typically are made of porcelain and come in two pieces, so you won't find them difficult to handle. (Nevertheless, installation will go far easier if you have someone to help hold parts and share the lifting.) If your decorating leans toward the traditional, have a look at these retro sinks, along with traditional hardware to match.

Here's a tip if you're thinking about shopping at a store that sells mainly to the plumbing trade. Their sinks and faucets may not come with directions—a potential nightmare for the weekend do-it-yourselfer. You can count on home-center models to include at least minimal step-by-step instructions.

Tools

Tape measure
Channel-type pliers
Adjustable wrench
Putty knife
Phillips-head and flat-head screwdrivers
Electric drill and masonry bits
Hacksaw
Flexible-tubing bender (for chrome-plated supply lines)
Caulking gun

Materials

Pedestal sink
New faucet (optional)
Toggle bolts to fit wall bracket
Teflon tape
Bucket and rags
Silicone caulk
Chrome-plated or flexible supply lines

Preparation

Check to see whether built-in toothbrush and soap trays will limit the height of the new sink you choose.

Close the two shutoff valves under the sink. Then open the faucets to drain the water in the lines. If a faucet continues to drip after a minute or so, one or both shutoff valves may need to be replaced.

You might have to remove the trap when you dismantle the old sink. If you do, have a bucket and rags handy to catch the water from the trap.

LEVEL OF DIFFICULTY
 Moderate to Challenging

TIME REQUIREMENT
 1 day, with occasional assistance from a helper

COST ESTIMATE
 $180 to $400 for a sink, and $75 to $150 for a faucet set

1 LOOSEN THE OLD SINK'S CONNECTIONS

- Use channel-type pliers to loosen the nut at the top of the trap directly below the drain; use an adjustable wrench to loosen the nuts securing the supply lines at the shutoff valves.
- If there is caulk around the perimeter of the sink where it meets the wall, use a putty knife to break the seal.
- Wall sinks typically hang on a concealed metal wall bracket and also are attached directly to the wall by screws on both sides of the sink's back. They may rest on two legs as well. Remove the screws.

2 REMOVE OLD SINK

- Arrange a spot to place the sink, and clear a path to it.
- Bending at the knees to take the weight, lift the sink straight up a couple of inches to disengage it from the wall bracket, then carry it away.
- Stuff a damp rag in the top of the drain-pipe to block sewer gasses and to prevent objects from falling in.
- Remove the old wall bracket.

3 ATTACH WALL BRACKET

The wall bracket for the new sink should be centered on the drainpipe and located at the height given by the manufacturer.

- Measure up from the floor, hold the bracket in place, and mark the wall through the center of the two mounting slots. These slots permit adjusting the basin once it is placed on the pedestal.
- Drill holes with a masonry bit, and insert toggle bolts.
- Attach the wall bracket with the screws supplied, placing the bracket as high as the slots will allow and tightening the screws only slightly. In the next step, the weight of the basin will press down the bracket to its proper position.

4 POSITION THE SINK

- Position the pedestal over the drainpipe and the proper distance from the wall, as noted in the manufacturer's instructions.
- Lower the basin onto the pedestal so it engages the wall bracket.
- Mark the floor through the holes in the pedestal base; mark the wall through the anchor holes in the basin's back.
- Lift off the basin and remove the pedestal. Tighten the bracket screws.
- Drill another two holes through the bracket's holes into the wall, and install toggle bolts.

5 ASSEMBLE BASIN HARDWARE

- Install the faucet and drain to the basin following the manufacturer's directions.
- Wrap Telfon tape around the faucet tail-pieces and attach the supply lines. Flexible lines *(see page 27)* are easy to install, but chrome-plated tubes may look better; cut them to length with a hacksaw, then bend with a flexible-tubing bender.
- Insert the tailpiece into the drain hole, then thread on the flange from the top.
- Assemble the pop-up drain as directed.
- Attach the trap to the tailpiece at the bottom of the sink.

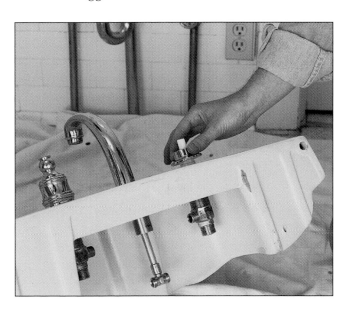

6 INSTALL SINK

- Set the pedestal in place. Position the basin on the pedestal against the wall, then lower it to engage the wall bracket.
- Drive screws through holes in the back of the basin and the pedestal base. Over-tightening may break the porcelain.
- Again using Teflon tape, attach the supply lines to the shutoff valves.
- Remove the aerator from the faucet to flush debris from the pipes and hardware. Open the shutoffs and test your work, looking for leaks. Tighten components as necessary. Reinstall the aerator.
- Apply silicone caulk around the edge of the sink.

BATHROOMS

Upgrading a Medicine Cabinet

Replacing the medicine cabinet is an easy way to spruce up a dreary bathroom.

A lot of homeowners that I visit suffer from what I call the "all or nothing syndrome." Let's say they tired of an old, increasingly dingy bathroom, but year after year they kept on living with it. It wasn't for lack of money; it was because they just couldn't push themselves into a complete remodeling project, with all the inconvenience that that would bring. They assumed that upgrading the bathroom is an "all or nothing" proposition.

But it's not. Replacing just one fixture or another can go a long way toward making a bathroom not only tolerable, but pleasant again. And medicine cabinets are one of the easier things to upgrade.

You'll find the current stock of medicine cabinets in most home centers to be varied and versatile. Many are designed so they can be surface-mounted or recessed. Many come with lighting fixtures attached. And just because your current medicine cabinet is recessed doesn't mean you can't upgrade with a larger surface-mounted design, as this project shows.

Tools

Electic drill and twist bits
Masonry bits (if drilling into tile)
Phillips-head and flat-head screwdrivers
3' level
Tape measure
Claw hammer
Wire-stripping pliers (optional)

Materials

Medicine cabinet
Wall anchors (if necessary)
$\frac{1}{4}$" plywood strips to match cabinet (optional)
Construction adhesive (optional)
Lightbulbs (if needed)

Preparation

Before buying a new cabinet for recessed installation, carefully measure the old one. You may have to temporarily remove the old one to get an accurate measurement of the opening.

Safety

If your medicine cabinet includes a light fixture, be sure to turn off power at the service panel while working on the electrical connections.

LEVEL OF DIFFICULTY
Easy

TIME REQUIREMENT
$\frac{1}{2}$ to 1 day

COST ESTIMATE
$30 to $200, depending on the cabinet features

1 REMOVE OLD CABINET

If it's removable, consider salvaging the mirrored door from the old medicine cabinet.

- Turn off the power at the service panel if there is a light fixture attached to the old medicine cabinet. Then disconnect the wiring.
- Using a screwdriver, remove the screws that hold the medicine cabinet to the wall.
- Carefully pull the cabinet from the wall.

2 MARK LOCATIONS OF ANCHORS

Recessed cabinets can be screwed directly into the wall studs on either side of the opening, but surface-mounted cabinets are likely to need wall anchors. (Note that the wood face frame and light fixture have been removed from the cabinet.)

- Position the cabinet in place on the wall, and check that it is level.
- Mark the wall through the mounting holes in the back of the cabinet.

3 DRILL HOLES AND INSERT ANCHORS

Choose a wall anchor for the job; *see Choosing Materials on page 175.* Plastic inserts, used here, may not be sufficient for a larger cabinet, especially in a drywall wall.

- Drill holes specified by the manufacturer for the wall anchors. Use a masonry bit to drill through tile.

4 MOUNT CABINET TO WALL

- Position the cabinet on the wall so the holes line up.
- Drive screws through the cabinet back into the wall anchors. Don't fully tighten any of the screws until all of them are started into the wall anchors.

Ron's
PRO TIPS

Adding Wood Sides to a Metal Cabinet

Many of the medicine cabinets available today are designed so you can mount them either recessed into a wall pocket or on the surface of the wall. Some of these (like the one shown here) have a nice oak face frame, with less attractive white metal sides. If surface-mounted, the white metal sides might not work with your décor.

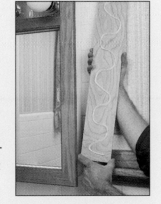

But you can easily cover the metal sides with ¼" oak plywood, converting it into an all-wood cabinet. Small strips are often sold in the kitchen accessory area for cabinet refacing, and many home centers sell oak plywood in quarter-sheet sizes. Just cut the plywood to size (or have it cut), brush a couple coats of polyurethane onto the face sides, and glue them onto the cabinet with construction adhesive or contact cement.

5 CONNECT WIRING

Unless you're familiar with basic wiring techniques, call an electrician in to do the job. In all cases, make sure the power is turned off at the service panel before disconnecting or connecting electrical wires.

- Route the supply wires into the cabinet and secure them with a cable tie (usually supplied with the fixture).
- Connect the ground wire to the cabinet, and the fixture wires to the supply wires (black to black, and white to white) with the wire nuts supplied with the fixture.

Replacing Bathroom Lights

You'll see better— and look better— in the mirror.

A lot of detail work goes on in the bathroom—applying make-up, flossing, shaving—and good task lighting is a must. And the more candlepower you have bouncing around, the better you're able to clean up all those nooks and crannies. Because bathrooms tend to be light in color and modest in size, it doesn't take a half-dozen halogens to get the job done. You may need nothing more than updated fixtures that can take 100-watt bulbs.

Avoid mounting the new fixtures directly above the mirror; two fixtures mounted on each side work best. When choosing fixtures, look for those that will diffuse the light rather than cast harsh shadows. Frosted globes, like those in the new fixtures shown here, do a good job. Make sure that the fixtures can handle a bulb of sufficient wattage; less-expensive models may be rated at a maximum of 60 watts.

Tools

Phillips-head and flat-head screwdrivers
Electrical tester
Wire-stripping pliers

Materials

New light fixtures
Lightbulbs
Wire nuts (if not provided with the fixture)

Preparation

Because you will be working with bare wires, check that the bathroom's current is turned off at the service panel before beginning.

LEVEL OF DIFFICULTY
Easy

TIME REQUIREMENT
Less than ½ day

COST ESTIMATE
$20 per fixture and up

BATHROOMS

1 REMOVE OLD FIXTURES

- Shut off the power to the bathroom. Try the light switch to make sure there is no current to the fixtures. Or use an electrical tester to determine that the power is off; see Tool Know-How, below.

- Remove the mounting screws and pull the old fixture(s) from the wall or ceiling, untwist the wire nuts, and separate the wires.

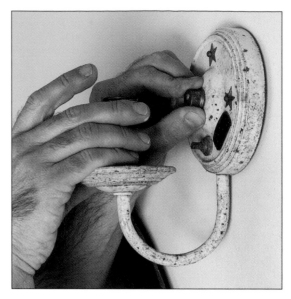

2 STRIP WIRES IF NECESSARY

- Use wire-stripping pliers to strip insulation from the wires coming from the electrical box or the new fixtures.

- To prevent any wires from breaking when twisted, be careful not to nick the wires with the pliers as you remove the insulation.

TOOL KNOW-HOW

Electrical Testers

You can tell whether wires or electrical terminals are "hot" by using an inexpensive tester. One of its elements is touched to the bare end of a hot wire (look for black insulation) and the other to either a neutral wire (white insulation) or a ground wire (indicated by green insulation or paint). If there's current flowing through the circuit, the tester's light comes on. Some testers have only a single probe that requires you to simply touch a wire to detect current flowing. Testers are handy for preventing you from touching live wires when doing electrical work; they also tell whether or not a troublesome device is getting current.

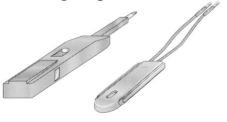

3 INSTALL MOUNTING HARDWARE

• Attach any mounting hardware (typically a universal mounting bracket) to the electrical box with the hardware supplied, as specified in the manufacturer's directions.

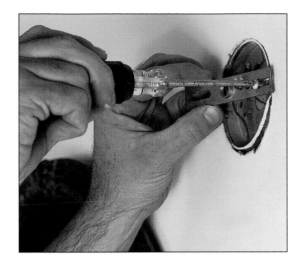

4 CONNECT WIRES

Use wire nuts to connect the fixture wires and the wiring from the electrical box.

• To make a sturdier connection, use pliers to grasp the bare ends of paired wires and twist them together clockwise (looking down on the ends).

• Twist on the wire nuts, then carefully press the wiring into the box.

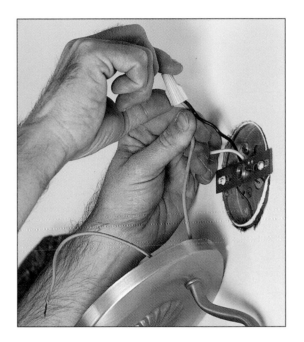

5 ATTACH NEW FIXTURES

Following the manufacturer's directions, attach each fixture to its electrical box.

• In most cases, this means first installing a threaded nipple into the mounting bracket, then slipping the fixture over the nipple and threading on a cap to secure the fixture.

• Screw in lightbulb(s) and attach the globe(s).

• Restore power to the fixtures.

Upgrading a Toilet

Whether it's in need of repair or a facelift, upgrading a toilet is an afternoon's job.

It may be among the least glamorous projects around the house, but replacing a toilet can also be one of the more urgent projects that you need to tackle. When a toilet leaks or otherwise stops functioning, many homeowners understandably panic and automatically call in a plumber. If there's only one toilet in the house, you can't exactly be casual about the situation when it breaks down. But it's actually one of the easier plumbing jobs you can do.

You may also want to replace a toilet as part of a larger bathroom remodeling effort. If you're putting down new flooring, for example, it's best to remove the toilet and run the flooring all the way under it. Sure, you can put the old toilet back, but perhaps it's time for an upgrade. All new toilets sold today use less water than their predecessors of 10 years ago, so saving water is one of the bonuses of replacing an older toilet.

Tools

Putty knife
Adjustable wrench
Socket wrench set
Channel-type pliers
Phillips-head and flat-head
  screwdrivers
Caulking gun

Materials

New toilet
New seat (optional)
Toilet flange bolts
Clean rags
Wax ring
New toilet supply tube
  (optional)
Teflon tape
Silicone caulk

Preparation

Turn off the water at the shut-off valve and flush the toilet. Remove the remaining water in the tank with a sponge.

LEVEL OF DIFFICULTY
Easy to Moderate

TIME REQUIREMENT
½ day

COST ESTIMATE
$80 to $200

BATHROOMS

1 REMOVE TANK AND BOWL

- Using an adjustable wrench, disconnect the supply tube from the toilet tank.
- Unbolt the tank from the bowl using a screwdriver on the bolt heads inside the tank, and an adjustable wrench on the nuts under the tank.
- Lift off the tank and set it aside.
- Remove the nuts holding the bowl to the flange on the floor, and lift off the bowl *(inset)*. Set the bowl on its side to drain out any water in the internal trap.
- Stuff a damp rag in the flange opening to prevent sewer gas from escaping.

2 REMOVE OLD WAX RING

A wax ring seal prevents water and sewer gas from leaking out from the waste line. Don't try to reuse an old wax ring, even if it looks fairly new.

- Carefully scrape off the old wax ring with a putty knife from the underside of the toilet and the closet flange on the floor. It's messy stuff, so avoid getting it on your clothes and even on the floor.

3 INSTALL NEW FLANGE BOLTS

The old flange bolts may be usable (and surprisingly, new toilets don't always come with the new bolts), but use new bolts anyway. The last thing you want is to have one of the bolts get stuck after setting the bowl in the new wax ring.

- Slide the flange bolts into the slots in the closet flange and position them opposite one another and parallel with the wall behind the toilet.
- Slip on the plastic retainer washers that hold the bolts in place.

BATHROOMS

4 INSTALL NEW WAX RING

- Turn the toilet bowl upside down and place the new wax ring around the horn at the base.
- If the wax ring has a plastic flange, the flange should face up. If the ring doesn't have a flange, then the flat side of the wax ring should face up; *see Choosing Materials, below.*

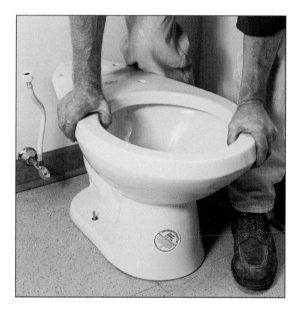

5 POSITION NEW BOWL

- With a new wax ring installed, lift the bowl and carefully lower it down onto the flange bolts (a helper is invaluable in lining everything up). If the bolts are positioned properly, the wax ring will correctly contact the floor flange.
- Apply sufficient downward pressure to the bowl so it meets the floor. Avoid swishing the bowl side-to-side in an effort to depress the wax ring: If you compress it too much, it won't seal properly.

CHOOSING Materials

Wax Rings

When you go to buy a wax ring, you'll find two basic types available. One has a molded plastic flange inside the wax ring, and the other does not. The plastic flange helps direct the flow of water into the waste pipe, and generally it's worth using a flanged wax ring. But there are two different sizes to match the different sizes of closet flange openings.

There are also special wax rings available that are designed to make up for differences in floor height created when you install a new floor. Otherwise you'd have to raise the closet flange itself, which can be difficult. If you install a new tile floor, for example, the special "extender kit" wax ring will span the increased distance between the toilet and the closet flange.

BATHROOMS

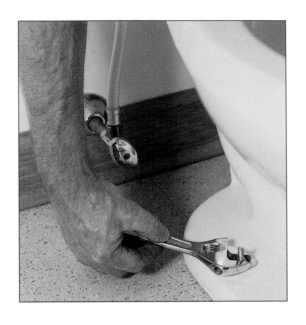

6 TIGHTEN FLANGE BOLTS

Before tightening the flange bolts, be sure to install the washers—a metal one first, then a larger plastic one that will receive the decorative cap covering each nut.

- Install the washers, then tighten the nuts with an adjustable wrench. Don't overtighten. If the base does not contact the floor completely, the gap can be caulked, as shown in Step 11.
- Some flange bolts are longer than necessary and are designed so you can snap off the excess after tightening. Use a pair of pliers to snap off the excess length on the bolts.

7 INSTALL NEW SPUD WASHER

A spud washer is the soft rubber washer that fits over the flush valve—the threaded tube coming out of the bottom of the tank.

- Turn the new tank over and rest it on its top edges on a towel or cloth.
- Make sure the large nut is tight around the flush valve.
- Fit the rubber spud washer over the flush valve with the tapered end up.

8 INSTALL TANK AND TIGHTEN TANK BOLTS

- Set the tank onto the back of the bowl with the spud washer seated in the opening in the opening in the back of the bowl.
- Insert the tank bolts, with a large rubber washer on each, through the inside of the tank and then through the holes in the back of the bowl. You may have to shift the tank a bit to get the holes aligned.
- Install a washer and nut on each bolt. With a screwdriver inserted into the head of the tank bolt, use a socket wrench or adjustable wrench to tighten the nuts. Tighten each side a little at a time to keep the tank level on the bowl.

9 TIGHTEN SUPPLY LINE TO TANK

Supply tubes are available to fit most existing plumbing installations. The top end that connects to the toilet is a standard size, while the other end varies to match your shutoff valve.

• Tighten the supply tube onto the shutoff valve with an adjustable wrench.

• Then wrap a few turns of Teflon tape around the threads of the shutoff valve and thread the nut on the other end of the supply tube; tighten with an adjustable wrench or channel-type pliers.

10 INSTALL SEAT

• Assemble the hinge if it's not already connected to the seat.

• Position the seat with the hinges over the seat holes, install the seat bolts, and secure the locking nuts from under the seat. Tighten the bolts by hand, using a screwdriver to keep the bolts from spinning.

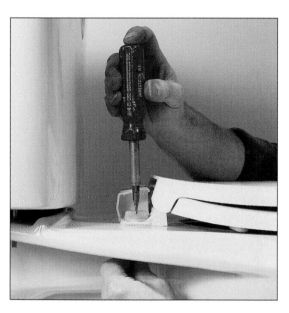

11 CAULK AROUND TOILET BASE

Chances are that the toilet base won't sit perfectly flat against the floor around the entire perimeter of the base, but the gaps can be caulked to keep dirt from gathering there.

• Apply a bead of silicone caulk around the perimeter of the base.

• Run a finger moistened with water over the caulk bead to smooth it out and press it into the gap.

• Remove any excess caulk with a clean, damp rag.

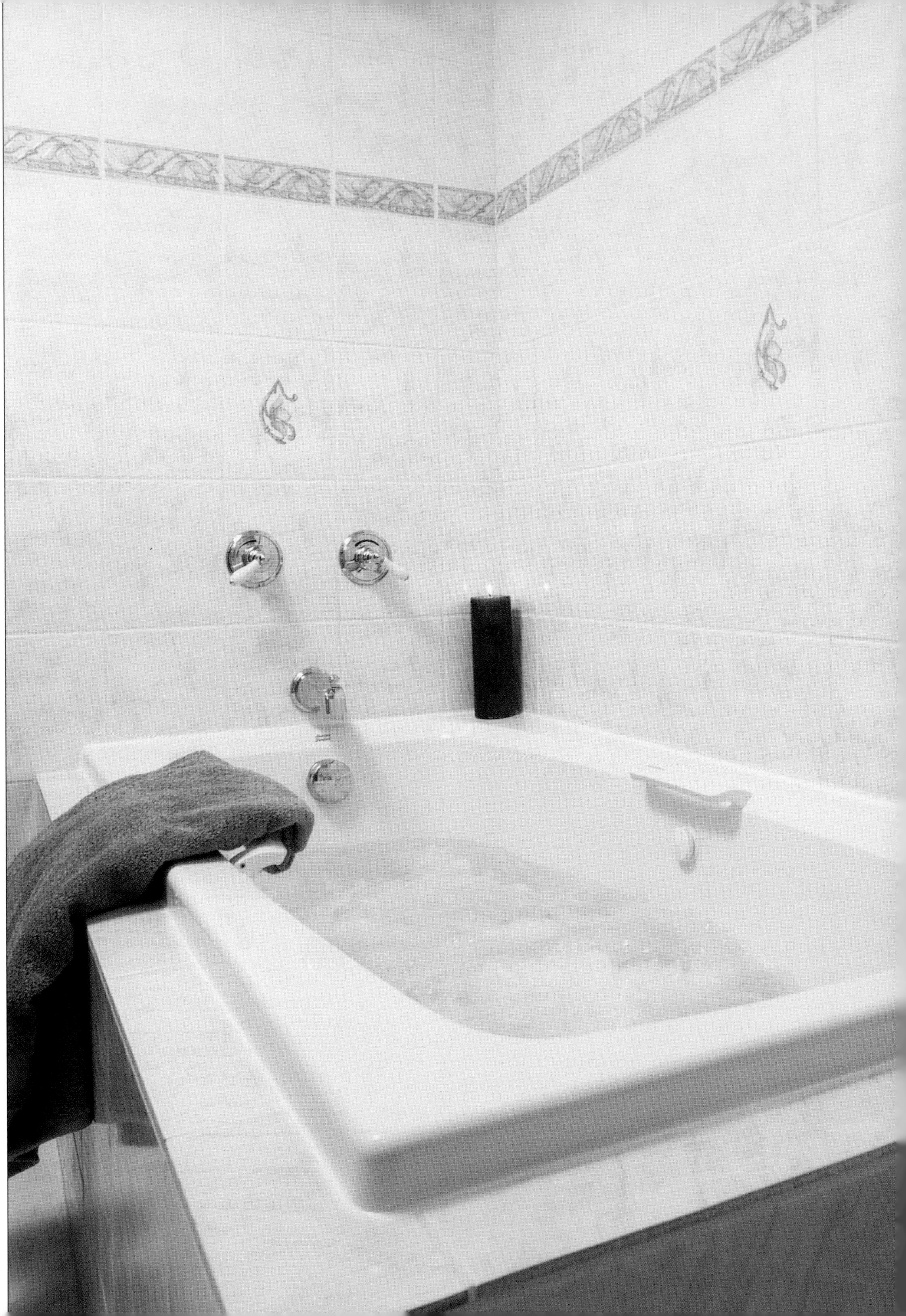

Installing a Whirlpool Tub

Turn your bathroom into a home spa with a luxurious whirlpool tub.

Taking a long hot bath is a treat we afford ourselves less and less in today's busy world. But that seems to be changing with the advent of whirlpool tubs for the home bathroom remodeling market. Costs have dropped as their popularity has risen. So if you're planning on upgrading your bathroom, consider adding a whirlpool tub—just make sure that the increased tub size is not a problem for your existing framing. If in doubt, check with the local building inspector or consult a plumbing expert.

You can replace an existing tub with a whirlpool without tearing up the rest of the room. But check the sizes of whirlpool tubs first, and consider carefully how the one you choose will meet the existing floor and walls.

Installing a whirlpool tub is no more difficult than installing a regular tub. But you do need to run a designated GFCI electrical line for the motor. Because of the hazards possible where electricity and water come together, consult an electrician on this part of the job. Also, the plumbing for a whirlpool tub can be more variable than for regular tubs—the faucet can be mounted on the wall in conventional fashion, or it can be mounted on a deck that surrounds the tub. Like conventional tubs, whirlpool tubs can include a shower.

Tools

3' or 4' level
Claw hammer
Electric drill and twist bits
Channel-type pliers
Masonry trowel
Utility knife
Leather gloves and safety mask

Materials

Whirlpool tub
Carpenter's shims
Mortar mix
Drywall (optional)
Waste-overflow assembly
P-trap assembly
#10 nails
Wiring, GFCI outlet, switch
3½"-thick fiberglass insulation
Cement board or tile backer
2" galvanized deck screws
Tile, thin-set mortar, and latex-modified grout (optional)

Preparation

Have a designated GFCI electric line run before installing the tub.

Safety

It's important to meet all code requirements for whirlpool tubs—consult an electrician or a building inspector. Also, consider installing a switch so the outlet for the motor can be switched off when the tub is not in use. That way, curious hands can't turn on the whirlpool when the tub is empty—which can damage the motor.

LEVEL OF DIFFICULTY
Challenging

TIME REQUIREMENT
2 to 3 days

COST ESTIMATE
$600 and up, depending on the tub

BATHROOMS

1 DRY-FIT AND LEVEL THE TUB

Before you can build the frame that will support the perimeter of the tub, you'll need to position the tub level in its final location.

- Set the tub in place and level it in both directions. The top deck of the tub slopes inward, so rest the level only on the outside edge of the deck. If your level is too short, span the tub with a straight-edged piece of wood.
- Insert carpenter's shims under the base of the tub to make it level *(inset)*.

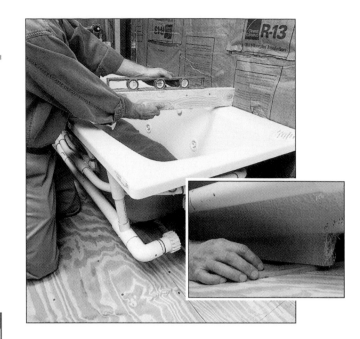

Adding a Sound Barrier

Ron's
PRO
TIPS

As you stretch out in your whirlpool tub, the swooshing water soothes tired muscles and calms frazzled nerves. But if someone's bedroom is adjacent to the bathroom, their experience may be less than pleasurable. That's because whirlpool tubs make a good bit of noise. Heard from the room below or next door, it sounds like a loud dishwasher. This can be a special problem if there are babies or young children trying to sleep while you're enjoying the tub.

To reduce sound transmission, apply one or more layers of drywall to shared walls that the tub will butt against. If you have enough space, you can increase the sound-absorbing capacity of the wall significantly by screwing the second layer of drywall over ½" wood spacers. The space between the two layers of drywall deadens the sound more than two layers one against the other.

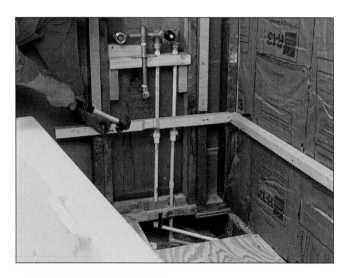

2 BUILD THE TUB FRAME SUPPORT

On this project the tub butts against inside walls on two sides, and rests on a stud frame on the other two.

- Screw or nail a cleat on the inside walls. The edge of the tub will rest directly on the cleats. (Note: Allow for optional mortar base; *see Step 4.*)
- Build a 2 by 4 stud frame to support the remaining sides of the tub. The edge of the tub will sit above the stud wall, allowing space for cement board and finished tile; *see Step 10.*
- Leave an opening in the stud wall for an access panel to the motor; *see Ron's Pro Tips on page 89.*

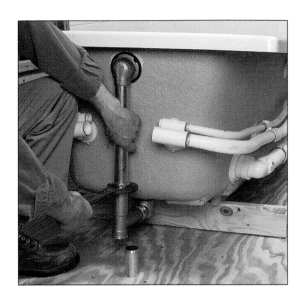

3 ATTACH WASTE-OVERFLOW ASSEMBLY

The waste-overflow assembly is not supplied with the tub but comes as a complete kit in either brass or PVC. The assembly, including the tailpiece, needs to be completely installed before the tub can be set permanently in place.

- Assemble the waste-overflow unit according to the manufacturer's directions.
- Before attempting the final tub installation, dry-fit again to make sure the tailpiece engages the P-trap correctly. You may need to cut the tailpiece or purchase a slightly longer one than provided.

4 SET TUB IN MORTAR BED

Although a mortar bed is not required, it will give the tub a more solid footing, reducing vibration and sound transmission.

- Mix enough mortar to provide a ½"-thick layer where the tub base meets the floor. Many tubs have skid-like runners molded into the fiberglass, and the edges of these skids are what rest on the floor.
- Trowel out a ½"-thick level pad to receive the base of the tub.
- Apply a bead of silicone caulk to the top edge of the cleats on inside walls.
- Set the tub in place, making sure the tailpiece slips into the P-trap. Stand inside the tub to press it down into the mortar.

5 CONNECT P-TRAP

The P-trap *(inset)*, which connects the tub tailpiece to the drain line, will have a slip nut that can be hand-tightened. This is necessary since it's usually impossible to fit a wrench or pliers into the space available.

- Make sure the tailpiece is aligned straight into the P-trap; if it's at an angle, it will be difficult to tighten completely.
- Once in position, hand-tighten the slip nut as tight as possible.

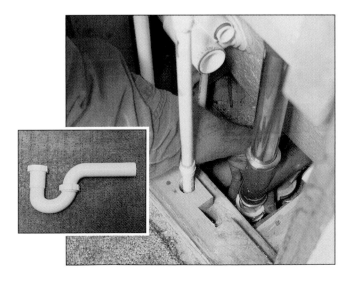

BATHROOMS

6 BUILD OUTSIDE STUD WALLS

Most tubs have optional apron pieces available for the side of the tub. In this project both the side and back are framed out with stud walls and then tiled.

- Build stud walls using 2 by 4s. The walls should extend equally at the side and back. Also, be sure to allow space for cement board, the finished tile, and a ⅛" expansion gap for silicone sealant.
- Nail or screw the stud wall sections together.
- Level the stud walls and screw them to the floor and wall.

7 MAKE ELECTRICAL CONNECTIONS

- Install a GFCI (ground fault circuit interrupter) outlet inside the access panel area of the stud wall close to the motor (or have an electrician do this).
- Plug in the pump motor.

8 FILL TUB AND TEST WHIRLPOOL

Typical manufacturer's instructions advise you to fill the tub and run the pump before closing off the walls around the tub.

- Fill the tub till the water covers all the jets, then turn on the whirlpool.
- Check all the PVC pipes and fittings for leaks.
- Drain the tub and check the connections at the P-trap.

BATHROOMS

9 INSULATE TUB WALLS

Insulating the outside walls around the tub will help reduce heat loss and noise transmission.

- Wearing gloves and a fiberglass-specified mask, cut lengths of fiberglass insulation to fit in the wall cavities.
- Tuck the insulation into the wall cavities with the kraft paper facing inward; this will prevent the fiberglass fibers from getting pulled into the motor.
- Add staples if necessary to hold the insulation in place.

Fitting an Access Panel

Ron's **PRO TIPS**

Here's an easy way to make an access panel that will blend seamlessly with the rest of a tiled tub wall, as shown in the opening photograph of this project. First tile around the access opening you built in the stud walls.

Then cut a piece of plywood to fit comfortably inside the opening. Nail or screw strips of 1 by 2 around the inside of the opening so that when tiled, the access panel will be flush with the surrounding wall. Next, with the access panel in place, mark the grout lines from the surrounding tile, then apply tile to the panel. Hold the panel in place with two finish-head screws driven through the lip around the edge of the panel into the blocking strips.

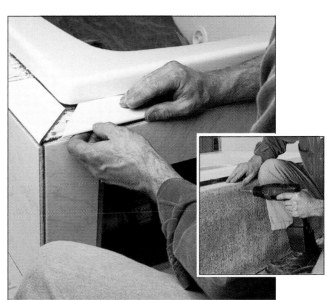

10 APPLY TILE BACKER AND TILE

If you're going to apply tile to the outside walls and deck around the tub, you'll first need to install tile backer. Tiling around a tub is similar to tiling a floor; *see page 202.*

- Cut the tile backer to size with a utility knife or special cement board cutter.
- Screw the tile backer to the studs with galvanized drywall or deck screws, making sure they sink below the surface of the material *(inset).* Then apply fiberglass tape and thin-set to the joints.
- Apply thin-set mortar to the tile backer and position the tiles in place with spacers. When dry, apply grout; see page 202 for more on working with ceramic tile.

Installing a Bathroom Exhaust Fan

An exhaust fan will keep your bathroom both looking and smelling fresh.

While most newer homes have exhaust fans in every bathroom, plenty of older homes are not equipped with these moisture- and odor-reducing accessories. And it's surprising how often I see freshly completed remodeling jobs where no one thought to put an exhaust fan in when it would have been easiest to do so. But that's not a problem—adding an exhaust fan can be done after the fact.

In some cases, it's possible to install a fan in the ceiling, routing the duct between the joists to an outside wall. If you've got easy access to the joists from above, this may be the way to go. But often the only way to get access is to tear up the ceiling. An alternative I often suggest is to mount the fan in an exterior wall, like the one shown here. The only catch to this type of installation is that the exterior wall must be a stud wall (unless you're willing to cut into masonry) and there must be access to the exterior where the vent will be mounted.

There are a wide variety of fan designs available, and many incorporate a light or even a heater. Check with an electrician before you buy the fan to see whether it's possible to add these options. Besides features to consider, you'll also need to select a fan that is sized for the square footage of your bathroom.

Tools

Claw hammer
Stud finder
Stepladder
Utility knife and keyhole saw
Saber saw (optional)
Electric drill and twist bits
Phillips-head and flat-head screwdrivers

Materials

Exhaust fan
Dryer vent kit
Duct tape (or hose clamps to fit flexible ducting)
Wire nuts

Preparation

You (or an electrician) will need to run power to the fan and install a switch, ideally adjacent to the light switch. Also, loosely assemble the exhaust duct to the fan to gauge the relationship between the inside opening for the fan and the exterior opening for the vent.

Safety

Turn off the power at the circuit breaker or fuse box whenever you're working with electric wiring. Apply a piece of tape over the breaker switch or empty fuse socket as an extra precaution.

If the walls you're cutting into were built prior to 1978, lead paint may have been used; see the Safety note on page 287 before beginning work.

LEVEL OF DIFFICULTY
Moderate to Challenging

TIME REQUIREMENT
1 to 2 days

COST ESTIMATE
$30 to $100 for the fan; $10 to $20 for the vent kit; $100 to $200 for wiring done by an electrician

BATHROOMS

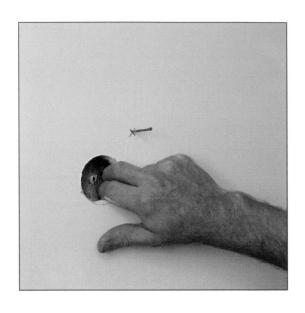

1 LOCATE WALL STUDS

Exhaust fans need to be screwed to a wall stud, so the first task is to find the stud closest to where you want to mount it.

- Use a stud finder *(see page 64)* to locate the studs.
- Drill an exploratory hole next to the stud where the opening will go, to locate the edge of the stud exactly; or cut a small hole with a keyhole saw.
- Push back any insulation and probe into the stud space to make sure there are no wires or plumbing where the opening will be cut.

2 MARK OUTLINE OF FAN ON WALL

The most accurate way to define the opening you'll need to cut for the fan is to use the fan as a template.

- Hold the fan next to the stud it will be fastened to, and in the desired location.
- Then trace around the perimeter to define the opening.

3 CUT OPENING

- For cleaner cuts in the drywall or plaster, carefully score the surface first with a utility knife.
- Plunge a keyhole saw through the drywall at one corner. Then saw along the line. Repeat for the remaining sides.
- Once the drywall is removed, cut through the insulation, if any, and remove it.

4 MARK OPENING ON EXTERIOR

The fan's exhaust duct will determine the location of the opening in the exterior wall; it's typically offset toward the top, connected to the fan via flexible ducting.

- Temporarily connect the fan, ducting, and vent to determine where the vent can be located. Then drill a hole through the wall from inside as a reference.
- Position the supplied flange so the hole you drilled is centered in the opening.
- Mark the opening using the supplied flange (or the vent) as a template.

5 CUT OPENING IN EXTERIOR

- Drill a ⅜" starter hole, then cut the opening with a saber saw fitted with a wood-cutting blade, or by hand with a keyhole saw.
- After connecting the flexible ducting to the vent with duct tape, attach the vent cap to the exterior wall with the screws provided (or use 1½"- to 2"-long galvanized deck screws).

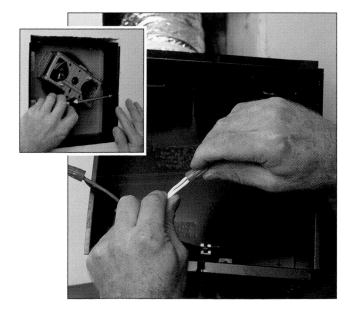

6 CONNECT DUCTING AND WIRES

Since the ducting, fan, and vent are all shoehorned into the wall, this final stage can be awkward—have a helper hold the fan while you make the connections.

- Remove the fan unit from its metal box and connect the flexible ducting, and secure it with a hose clamp or duct tape.
- Connect the black and white wires with wire nuts, and connect the ground wire to the fan box as shown in the fan assembly instructions.
- Replace the fan in the box and secure it to the stud *(inset)*. Then mount the exhaust cover and turn the electricity back on.

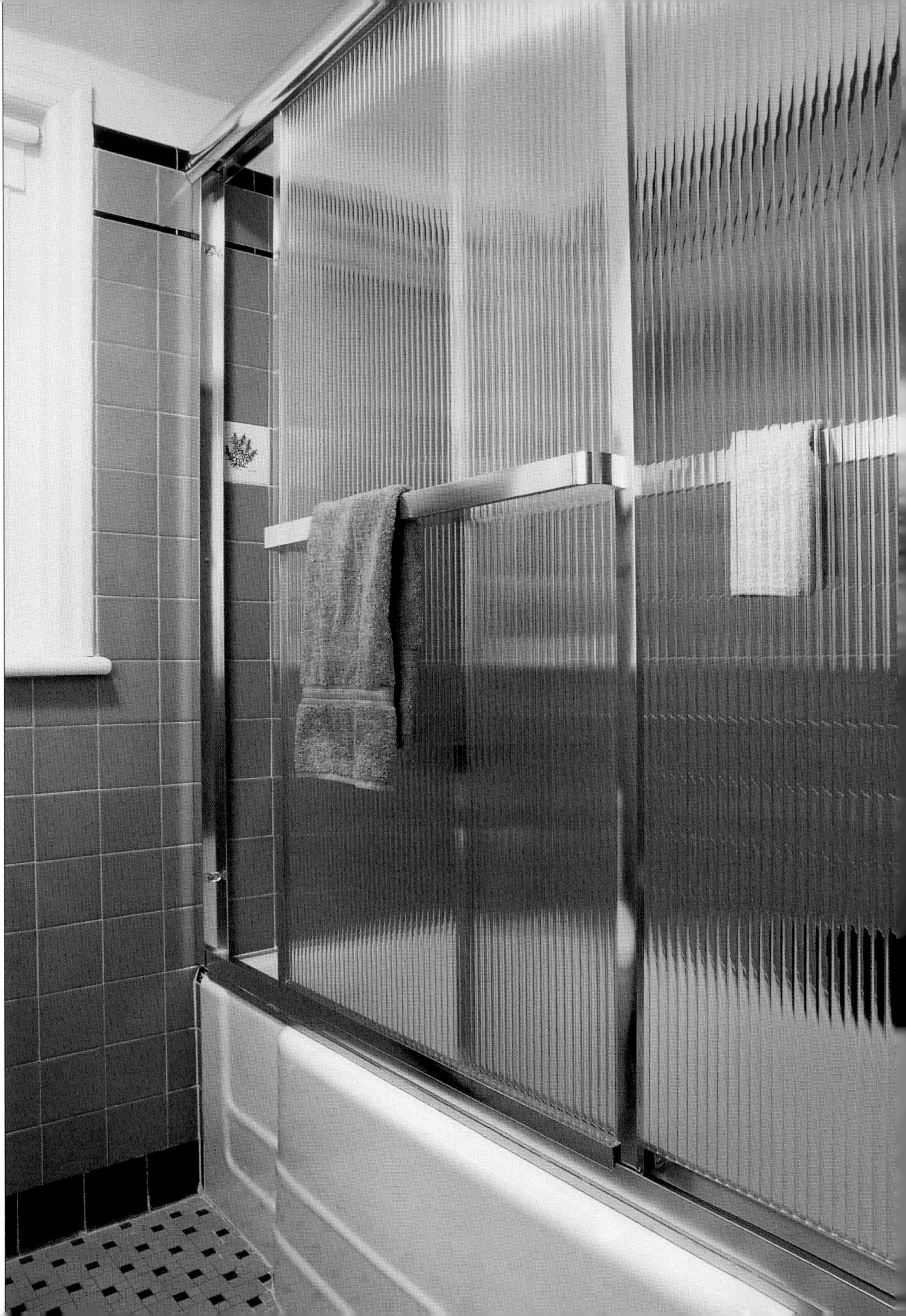

Installing Shower Doors

Doors work better than a curtain— and look better, too.

There are attractive shower curtains, and there are expensive shower curtains. But to my eye, no shower curtain on the market looks nearly as good as a pair of mid-priced glass shower doors. The patterned or frosted glass can transform a modest bathroom. And the installation isn't that challenging. The shower door sets I've seen are well thought out, leaving little guesswork even for homeowners with relatively little DIY experience. Just remember that you are working with big sheets of glass in a room with a lot of hard surfaces. Keep the floor clear of tools to avoid losing your footing at a crucial moment. You shouldn't need a helper except for lugging the boxed unit into your house; individual doors aren't that heavy.

The doors are set within a four-part frame. There are two upright jambs along the walls, a track that sits on the rim of the tub, and a header from which the doors hang. Models are available with silver or gold frames; you'll want to base your choice on the color of the existing bathroom fixtures.

Tools

Tape measure
Carpenter's level
Safety glasses
Hacksaw with 32-tpi blade
Miter box
6" mill file
Center punch (if working with
  ceramic tile)
Claw hammer
Phillips-head and flat-head
  screwdrivers
Electric drill and masonry bits
Caulking gun
Caulking tool

Materials

Shower door kit
Standard masking tape or
  duct tape
Painter's masking tape
Silicone caulk
Denatured alcohol

Preparation

Check to see whether towel racks on the end walls will interfere with the installation.

It's easy to remove a towel rack anchored with screws, but you will have to fill the holes with grout or silicone, matching either the tiles or the existing grout.

To remove a rack with brackets set into the tile, carefully chip out the brackets with a chisel, then fill in the spaces with tiles. Either use matching tiles or substitute decorative tiles such as the botanical designs used in this project.

LEVEL OF DIFFICULTY
Moderate

TIME REQUIREMENT
1 day

COST ESTIMATE
$175 to $600

BATHROOMS

1 MEASURE FOR THE UNIT

Before purchasing the unit, first measure your tub.

- The maximum horizontal size of the unit must be at least as great as the distance between the walls at each end of the tub. You will be cutting the bottom and top pieces (the track and header) to length to fit the opening exactly.

- Vertically, the unit must fit between the top of the tub side and the ceiling.

2 CHECK WALLS FOR PLUMB

- Use a carpenter's level to make certain the walls at each end of the tub are reasonably plumb—straight up and down, with no dips or bumps.

- If they are not, you may have to caulk a substantial gap in order to seal the wall jamb, which must be plumb for the unit to work properly.

3 CUT TRACK TO LENGTH

- Measure the distance between the walls at the ends of the tub. Following the manufacturer's instructions, subtract the specified clearance for the jambs from this measurement and then mark one end of the track.

- Wearing safety glasses, cut the track to length with a hacksaw and a miter box.

- Center the track on the edge, and use standard masking tape to temporarily hold it in place. With a soft pencil, mark the track's position on the tub.

4 MARK JAMBS FOR INSTALLATION

- Hold one of the jambs in position, with its lower end engaging one end of the track.
- Plumb the jamb with a carpenter's level.
- Use a soft pencil to outline the position of the jamb on the wall.
- To mark the position of the jamb's anchor holes on a tub surround, use a soft pencil. On ceramic tile, place a center punch through each hole in turn, and tap gently with a hammer to avoid cracking the tiles. (The resulting dimple will help keep the drill bit from skating over the glazed surface.)
- Repeat for the other jamb.

TOOL
KNOW-HOW

Hacksaws

A hacksaw is typically used to cut materials other than wood. The saw's frame prevents the blade from flexing and helps to ensure a precise cut. Blades can easily be replaced when dull, or whenever you want to switch to coarser or finer teeth. The number of teeth per inch (tpi) commonly ranges

from 16 to 32; to make a smooth cut in the aluminum track and header, use a 32-tpi blade. And to keep the saw perpendicular, use a miter box. A simple shop-made wooden model with slots in its sides will help guide the cut.

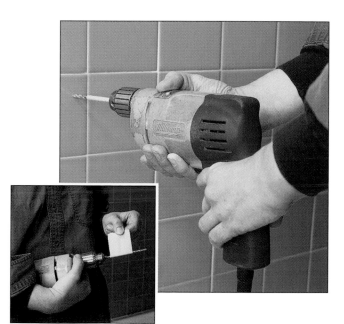

5 DRILL HOLES FOR JAMBS

- Choose a drill bit diameter as directed in the instructions; use a masonry bit for ceramic tile, or a standard bit for a tub surround that is not backed up by tile.
- Wrap a bit of masking tape around the bit to serve as a simple depth gauge *(inset)*.
- Drill the holes for the jambs and clean them out.
- Insert plastic anchors that come with the unit, gently tapping them in with a hammer until flush with the surface.

BATHROOMS

6 ATTACH TRACK

- Remove the track, turn it over, and apply silicone caulk along its underside, following the instructions. (If your kit didn't come with caulk, make sure to buy a type that's compatible with aluminum—not all silicones are.)
- Put the track in position as guided by the pencil marks.
- Again tape the track to the tub to keep it from shifting.

7 ATTACH JAMBS

- Hold the jambs in position, aligning their holes with the holes in the wall.
- Attach the jambs by driving screws into the plastic anchors. Note that some of these screws may also serve to secure bumpers against which the doors slide.
- Remove the tape securing the track.

8 CUT AND ATTACH HEADER

- Measure between end walls to determine the length of the header, and make adjustments in the measurement as directed in the manufacturer's instructions (as you did in Step 3).
- Wearing safety glasses, cut the header to length.
- Install the header over the jambs, following the instructions.

9 HANG DOORS

- Assemble the roller hardware as per the manufacturer's instructions.
- Install both doors by hanging their rollers from the rails of the header.
- Adjust the rollers as necessary so that the doors align with the jambs.

Tape Before You Caulk

Ron's PRO TIPS

Silicone caulk is one of those miracle products that it's hard for me to imagine living without. The stuff is durable, flexible, and waterproof. As for its ease of application, caulk goes on like toothpaste—but it can be tough to do a precise job. That's where a roll of painter's tape comes in. It is made to peel off easily, without lifting paint or leaving behind a gummy residue. Before caulking, carefully place a strip of tape along both sides of the joint and about 1/8" away from it. Then caulk away.

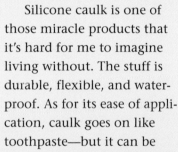

Go over the wet bead with a caulking tool or, in a pinch, a plastic picnic spoon. Lift the tape strips, and you've got a thin, consistent line of caulk. Clean up any smears with denatured alcohol and a soft cloth.

10 ATTACH HARDWARE AND APPLY CAULK

- Attach the inside guide to secure the inner door, as well as any seals in the frame or doors. Attach the doors' towel racks, if not pre-installed.
- Remove dust, debris, grease, and soap before caulking the bottom track, the corners where the inside of the jambs meet the walls, and the gaps at both ends of the track.
- Run a plastic caulking tool along joints for best results. To make the job look professional, see Ron's Pro Tips *(left)*.
- Allow the caulk to set at least 24 hours before using the tub, or as directed on the caulk container.

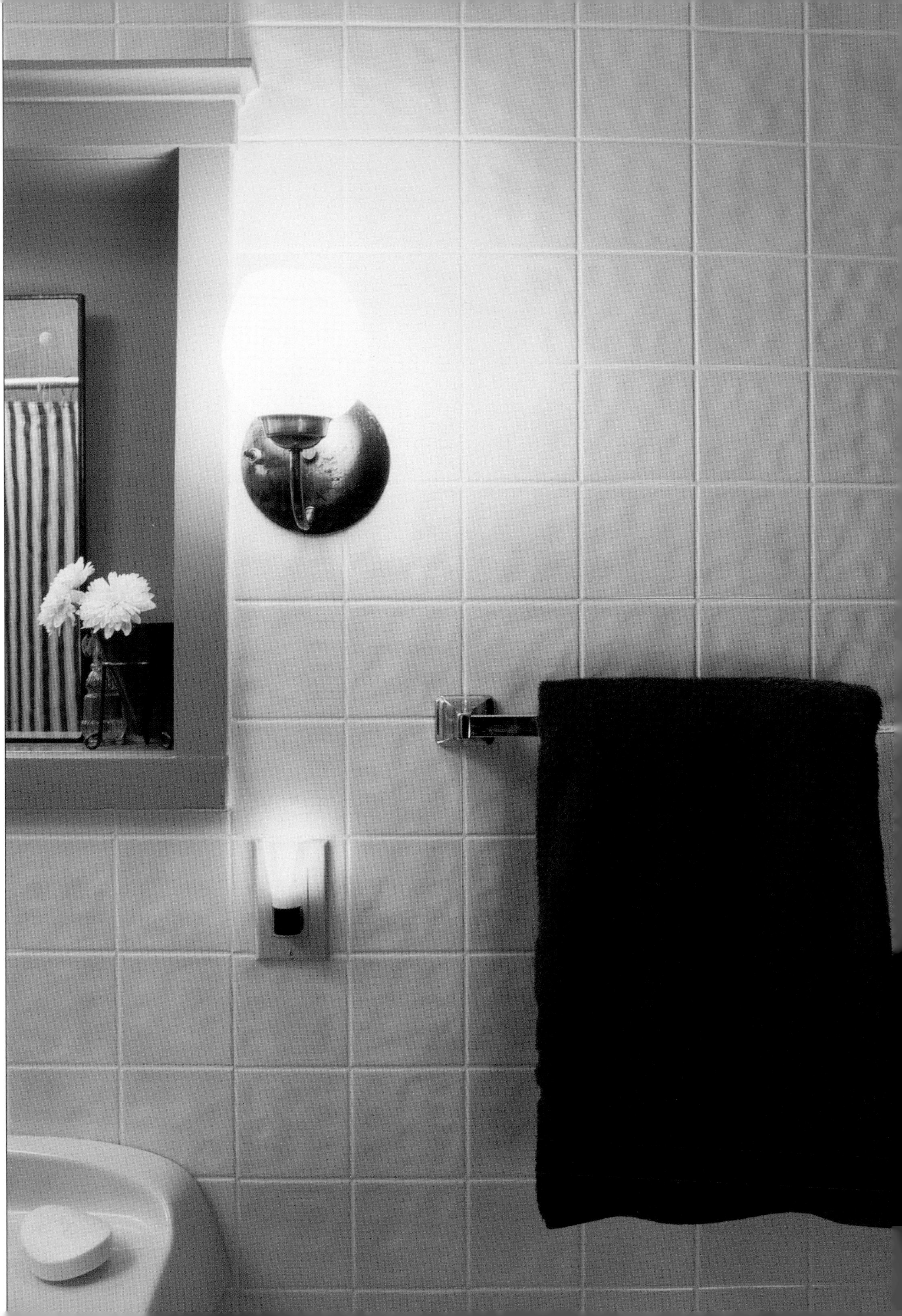

Installing Bathroom Tileboard

Tileboard

has all

the advantages

of real tile

but is

much easier

to install.

I get a lot of calls from home-owners whose bathroom walls are a constant problem. The plaster walls in older bathrooms suffer cracks from years of excess moisture. You can patch and repaint, but the cracks seem to open again sooner or later. And even on solid walls, the paint often peels from the bathroom's high moisture level.

Tiling the walls is a good but expensive solution. Tileboard is less expensive, and for the beginner do-it-yourselfer it's a great alternative to real tile. Sold in 4 by 8 sheets, tileboard is basically ⅛"-thick fiberboard (Masonite) with a surface layer of impermeable material that mimics tile. The joints and corners get caulked to look like grout. Once installed, tileboard looks like the real thing.

Other forms of tileboard are designed to look like vinyl wallpaper or plain plastic wallcovering. These require plastic connector strips at the seams and corners.

Tools

Circular saw
Saber saw
Straightedge
Tape measure
¼" notched trowel
Caulking gun
Hammer
Rubber roller or grout float
Putty knife
Dust mask and eye protection

Materials

Tileboard
Construction adhesive
Silicone or acrylic latex caulk
Wood or plastic trim
1" finish nails
Putty to match the trim
Varnish or paint (for wood trim only)
Spackling compound

Preparation

Patch any loose areas of plaster and fill large holes and cracks with spackling compound.

LEVEL OF DIFFICULTY
Moderate

TIME REQUIREMENT
2 to 3 days for an average-sized bathroom

COST ESTIMATE
$200 to $300, depending on the size of your bathroom

1 MEASURE AND CUT TILEBOARD

Plan the tileboard layout so all the cut edges will fall at areas that will get caulked or trimmed, and all visible seams will be factory edges.

- Measure the wall and mark the tileboard face with a straightedge.
- Wearing a dust mask and eye protection, cut the tileboard with a circular saw.
- Measure and mark openings for outlets, switches, and light fixtures, and then cut them out with a saber saw.

2 APPLY ADHESIVE

Use adequate ventilation and apply a general-purpose construction adhesive with a trowel or caulking gun. Before applying adhesive, check the wall with a straightedge. If there are broad depressions, apply more adhesive in these areas.

- Apply adhesive generously in one direction with a ¼" notched trowel.
- If using a caulking gun, apply a ¼" bead of caulk around the perimeter of the panel area, and a zigzag pattern every 6" in the interior area.

3 PRESS PANEL TO WALL

This is the most critical part of the job. The larger the panel, the harder it is to apply pressure over the whole panel until the adhesive takes hold. The key is to go back over a glued panel every five minutes for about a half hour, making sure the adhesive has grabbed.

- Apply pressure to the tileboard with a rubber roller *(see page 31)* or grout float.
- Use nails or screws wherever they will be covered by trim.

4 APPLY TRIM

Most home and building centers stock plastic or polyurethane trim that matches the tileboard. Or, if you prefer, you can use wood trim and paint it to match.

- Apply a coat of varnish or paint to the wood trim before installing it.
- Attach the trim with 1" finish nails.
- After installing the trim, fill the nail holes with matching putty.

5 CAULK SEAMS AND JOINTS

Pure silicone caulk is the best, but it can be hard to work with and clean up. Some acrylic latex caulks have added silicone and are easier to work with.

- Apply a bead of caulk at all exposed edges—at seams, along trim, and in corners.
- Smooth the caulk bead with a fingertip moistened with water.

CHOOSING
Materials

Tileboard

There is a wide variety of tileboard to choose from, though many home centers stock only a small selection of these. If you don't like what you see on the shelves, ask at the custom order counter. Two basic types of tileboard predominate. Those that look like conventional wall tile are butted one to the next, and the seams are filled with silicone caulk that matches the "grout" joints in the tileboard. Those that

appear like vinyl wallpaper require plastic strips at the seams and in corners. All varieties of tileboard are made with a thin but sturdy fiberboard panel and are attached to walls with construction adhesive.

Windows & Doors

HOW TO FIX IT Kitchen & Bathroom Plu

Stenciling Walls 106

Painting Walls 110

Stripping Wallpaper 114

Hanging Wallpaper 118

Adding a Wallpaper Border . . . 124

Installing Wainscoting 128

Installing Chair Rail 134

Installing Wall Paneling 138

Refinishing Trim 146

Building
a Fireplace Surround 150

Making a Built-In
Window Seat 156

Installing Bifold Doors 160

A Faux Wall Finish 164

Finishing Off
a Basement Wall 168

Installing Simple Shelves 172

WALLS

Stenciling Walls

Stenciling is a quick and easy way to add color and interest to any room.

The art of stenciling has been around for a long time, and recently it has enjoyed a rise in popularity. I suspect it has a lot to do with the prevalence of "country" decor that I see in so many people's homes. But stencils come in a wide range of patterns and, used wisely, can enhance any style of room. You can even design and cut your own stencils. And applying stenciling to a wall couldn't be easier.

Typically, stenciling is applied around all the walls in a room at a specific height—at the ceiling, above the base molding, or at chair-rail height. In a room with a high ceiling, the stencil can be applied at a height that breaks up the large expanse of wall—between 6' and 8'. Or you can use an architectural feature of the room—a door or window, for example—to establish the height of the stencil.

Going further, many people highlight doors and windows by surrounding them with a stencil pattern or create a semblance of wainscoting around the bottom of a room with panel patterns. I've even seen accent stencils around the corners of a wall-hung picture. Your creativity is the only limit in the colorful world of stenciling.

LEVEL OF DIFFICULTY
  Easy

TIME REQUIREMENT
  ½ to 1 day for an average-sized room

COST ESTIMATE
  $20 to $50 for stencils, paints, and brushes

WALLS

1 ESTABLISH LAYOUT LINES

You can run a stencil around a room at any height, but it's best to use a physical feature of the room as the starting point.

- When stenciling along the ceiling or base molding, use the ceiling or base molding itself as the layout guide.
- On other parts of the wall, strike a very light pencil line using a 2' or longer level. Work out from a corner, connecting the lines as you go.

2 TAPE STENCIL IN PLACE

You can start the stencil pattern randomly and simply wrap it around the corners wherever it falls. Or you can have it end evenly at corners by determining the right spacing for each wall.

- Tape the stencil flat on the wall using masking tape or painter's tape.

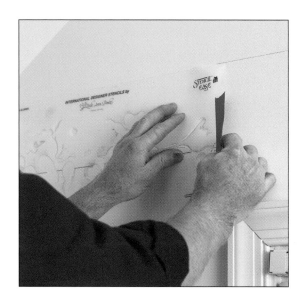

CHOOSING
Materials

Stenciling Paint and Brushes

The materials required for stenciling are few and inexpensive. Next to the stencils themselves, paint and brushes are the most important ingredients. Stenciling paints are almost exclusively water-based acrylic, which dries very quickly. If you can't find the exact color you want, try mixing colors. Acrylic paints clean up with water.

The best brushes are made with densely packed bristles that are securely bound with metal ferrules to wood handles. There is a range of brush sizes to correspond to the range of stencil sizes. Plan on using a separate brush for each color in any stencil.

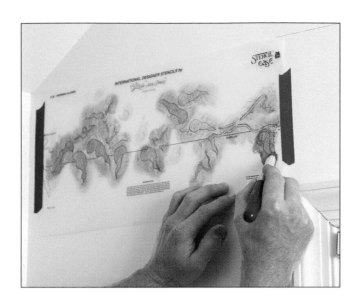

3 APPLY PAINT

There are two basic techniques for stenciling. Swirling—moving the brush in a circular motion; and stippling—tapping the tip of the brush against the wall. Try them both on a scrap of paper before you begin, to decide which will look better. Or use them both on different parts of the stencil.

- Spread a dollop of each color paint on a paper plate, dip the brush tip into the paint, and apply paint lightly to the wall.
- Press the stencil against the wall as you apply the paint to prevent paint from bleeding behind the stencil.

4 MOVE STENCIL TO SECOND POSITION

- If you are spacing the stencil pattern, measure along the level line from the end of the first stencil and mark where the edge of the second stencil should be located.
- For a continuous stencil pattern, overlap the registration marks to locate the stencil in the second position.
- Tape the stencil to the wall, and paint.

5 CLEAN STENCILS AND BRUSHES

It's important for future use to clean all the paint from the stencils and brushes.

- Rinse the stencils with warm water over the sink and rub them gently to remove paint.
- Dab the brush tips against your hand while running warm water over the brush (*inset*).
- Dry the brushes on a soft, clean cloth. To keep the brush bristles tight and clean, wrap a small rubber band around each at the base of the bristles after drying.

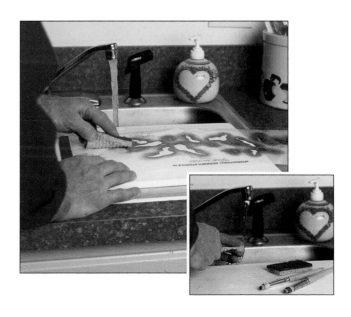

Windows & Doors

HOW TO FIX IT **Kitchen & Bathroom Plumbing**

Painting Walls

Paint is the fastest way to give a room a beauty makeover.

There is no easier way to change the looks and atmosphere of a room than applying a coat of paint. (That's after you've lugged furniture out of harm's way and covered everything that can't be moved, of course.) Even the scent of fresh paint can make me feel like I've got a new lease on life.

One of the things I like best about painting a room is that it's so ecomonical to do. A couple gallons of paint, and you're in business. (Note: Pre-1978 homes may have been decorated with lead paint, see the Safety note on page 287 before beginning work.) Since your only real investment is the paint, don't skimp on quality. Invest in a brand name you can trust. You'll be amazed the difference that only a few dollars per gallon can make.

To make sure that you'll continue to be happy with a paint job, look after the details. Neatness counts, because the eye seems irresistibly drawn to little blunders in that otherwise seamless field of color.

Tools

Rubber gloves
Sponge
Trim brush or pad applicator
Roller frame and cover
Paint tray
2" to 3" sash brush

Materials

120-grit sandpaper
Trisodium phosphate (TSP)
Masking tape or painter's tape
Kraft paper or newspaper
Drop cloths
Interior primer
Interior paint

Preparation

No matter how careful you try to be, stray paint will find its way onto exposed surfaces. Take the time to either remove furniture or cover it. The painting will go that much more quickly, and you won't have the nagging worry that one slip could ruin the day.

Plan to do the ceiling first, if it is to be painted, and then the walls. You should do the trim last to avoid marring it with drips and splatters from a roller.

LEVEL OF DIFFICULTY
Easy

TIME REQUIREMENT
½ day

COST ESTIMATE
$15 to $30 per gallon

WALLS

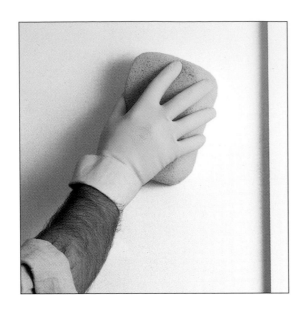

1 PREPARE WALLS

- Remove outlet and wall switch covers and other wall-mounted fixtures.
- Sand the walls with 120-grit sandpaper if they have a gloss or semi-gloss finish to allow the new coat to adhere better.
- Vacuum cobwebs and dust.
- Wash the walls with a solution of TSP (a cleanser available from hardware stores) and warm water, especially if they have been exposed to cooking grease and soiling from hands. Rinse well.

2 MASK AND COVER SURFACES

- Use masking tape or painter's tape to edge areas you don't want to be painted.
- Use newspaper, kraft paper, or drop cloths to cover baseboards, windowsills, and floors; hold them in place with masking tape.

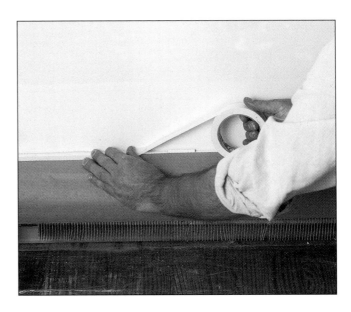

3 PAINT EDGES

- With a narrow trim brush or the applicator shown here, paint around the edges and corners of the room.
- Take special care in cutting in around trim, because these places tend to be highly visible and show off mistakes.

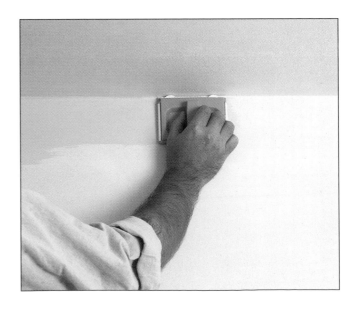

4 ROLL LARGE SURFACES

Use a roller cover with a short nap (⅜")
for smooth walls, and a longer nap (¾" or
more) for textured walls.

- Stir the paint well and pour some into a
  paint tray.
- Dip the roller into the paint and run it
  along the bottom of the pan to disperse
  the paint evenly.
- Apply the paint with large, overlapping
  W shapes, taking care to catch any
  rivulets before they can dry. Make those
  big Ws from right to left, then go over
  the area again in the opposite direction.

5 TOUCH-UP TIME

- Inspect your work under a strong light,
  and apply a second coat if necessary.
- Roll or brush any areas you might have
  missed.
- Clean up paint spatters before they
  harden.
- Then move on to the trim with a sash
  brush, masking the freshly painted walls
  with painter's masking tape (it's less
  likely to pull up not-quite-cured paint).

Ron's
PRO
TIPS

Painting a Ceiling

Painting walls is kid stuff,
compared with ceilings.
They're harder to reach, requiring a person of standard
height either to work from an
elevated place (a stepladder
or boards on sturdy supports)
or to use a roller with an ex-
tended handle. The roller shown here is small
and nimble, better
suited for working
overhead than the
standard full-sized
model. Start by
painting the peri-
meter and around
ceiling fixtures, then
roll the rest.

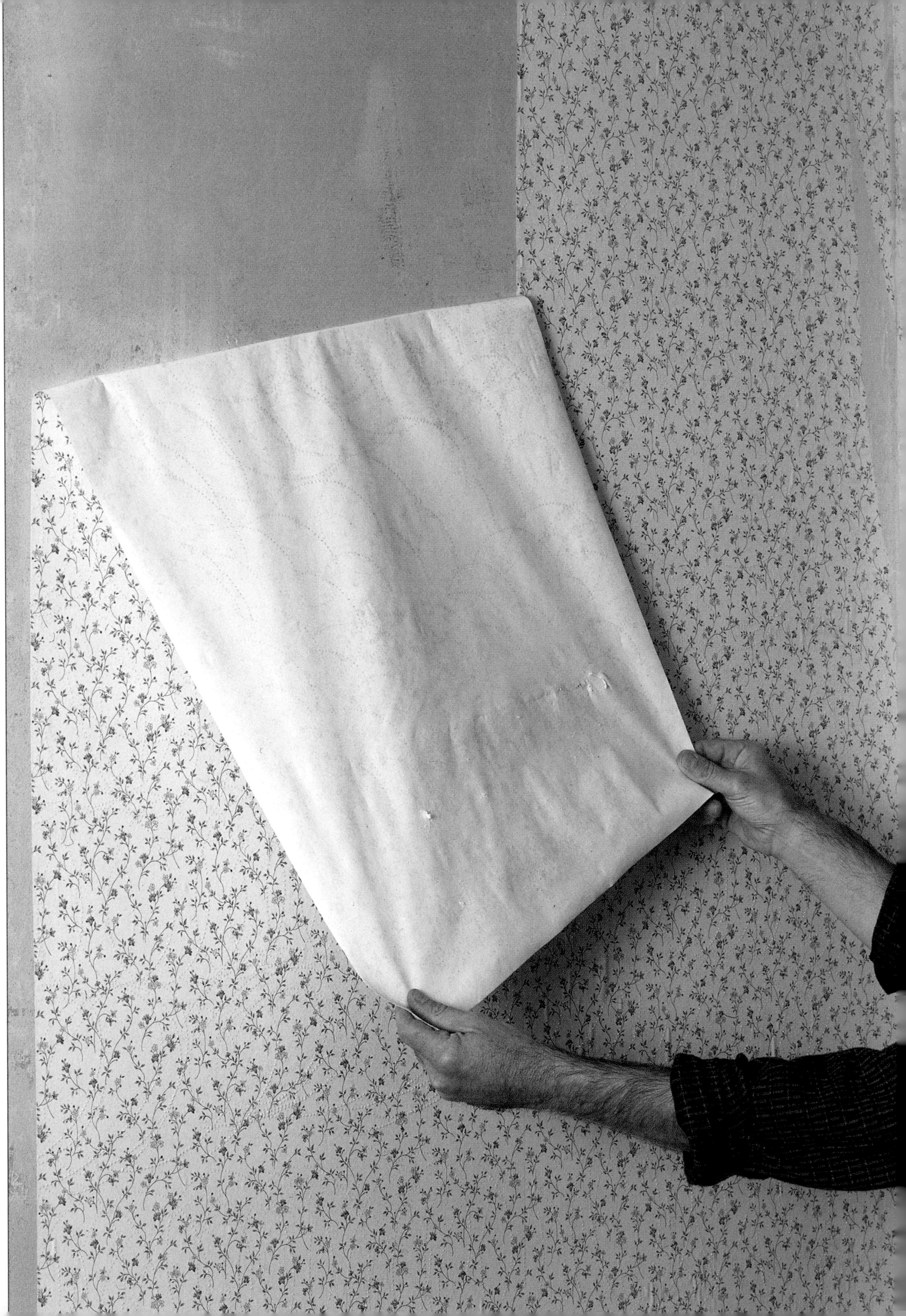

Stripping Wallpaper

Stripping away outdated wallpaper is not as difficult— or messy— as you might think.

Nothing looks quite as old and fussy as outdated wallpaper. Trouble is, the stuff won't leave your house willingly. It has to be coaxed off the walls, and it can make a mess on its way out. The traditional tool for the job, a wallpaper steamer, turns your place into an indoor rain forest.

I favor another way, one that keeps the mess very manageable. You may even find yourself enjoying the act of helping a room shed its old look. The trick is to use a spray-on enzyme solution that soaks through the paper and loosens the grip of the paste. An elegantly simple gadget called a perforating tool helps the solution to penetrate.

Those long, unsightly sheets will peel off neatly, and all that's left to do will be to sponge away excess paste from the naked wall. (Note that steaming remains the more efficient way to strip several layers of wallpaper.) There are no tools to rent, nothing to plug in. All remodeling chores should be this easy and satisfying.

Tools

1-gallon pressurized garden sprayer
Perforating tool
Sponge
Putty knife
Rubber gloves
Eye protection

Materials

Drop cloths or old towels
Enzyme-action wallpaper stripper

Preparation

Get the wall ready by removing cover plates from light switches and outlets.

Take down drapes from windows.

Push back furniture that might be misted when you spray on the stripper.

Safety

Many enzyme-based wallpaper strippers can cause skin and eye irritation. Be sure to put on eye protection when spraying and wear rubber gloves whenever you handle the solution.

LEVEL OF DIFFICULTY
Easy

TIME REQUIREMENT
$\frac{1}{2}$ day

COST ESTIMATE
$10 to $30, depending on the amount of wallpaper to be stripped

WALLS

1 PROTECT THE ROOM

- You'll be spraying lots of liquid, so cover the immediate area with drop cloths or old towels to minimize cleanup.

- Cloths can be tucked behind baseboard radiators with a broad-bladed putty knife.

2 PERFORATE WALLPAPER

Have a look at the perforating tool before you start work. Its toothed wheels bite through the paper to help the enzyme solution penetrate.

- Run the tool over the wall in spirals, applying very little pressure.

- Give particular attention to perforating the paper along the top of the wall, where the streaming solution will have less time to penetrate.

- Check your work, making sure you have made perforations at a minimum of one per square inch across the entire wall.

3 SPRAY ON THE STRIPPER

- Mix up a batch of enzyme solution in the conventional garden sprayer, following the manufacturer's directions for amounts and water temperature.

- With the nozzle about 1' from the wall, begin to spray. Because the solution runs down, you should give particular attention to the tops of the wall and the area just under windowsills.

- Continue wetting down the wall every 10 minutes or so for a half hour to make sure the enzyme does its work; otherwise, you may only be able to peel away the top surface of the paper, leaving a lower layer and the paste.

4 PEEL OFF PAPER

If the paper doesn't come off easily, it's an indication that you need to spray on more enzyme solution and then give it time to work.

- Start peeling at a top corner of a strip, using a putty knife as needed.
- If areas begin to dry before you get to them, wet them again.

Wallpaper Perforators

As helpful as it is, the enzyme solution tends to just run off your walls unless you encourage it to penetrate the paper. A perforator is an inexpensive tool that makes thousands of tiny holes in the paper in minutes. This step of the job is easier than it sounds—the tool needs little pressure to do its work.

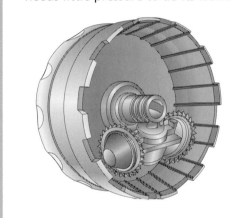

5 SPONGE AWAY PASTE

- Wearing rubber gloves, remove the remaining paste from the bare walls with a sponge soaked in the enzyme solution.
- Coax off stubborn patches of paste with a putty knife.
- Rinse the wall well with a sponge dipped in clean, warm water; this step is especially important if you will be painting the wall rather than repapering.

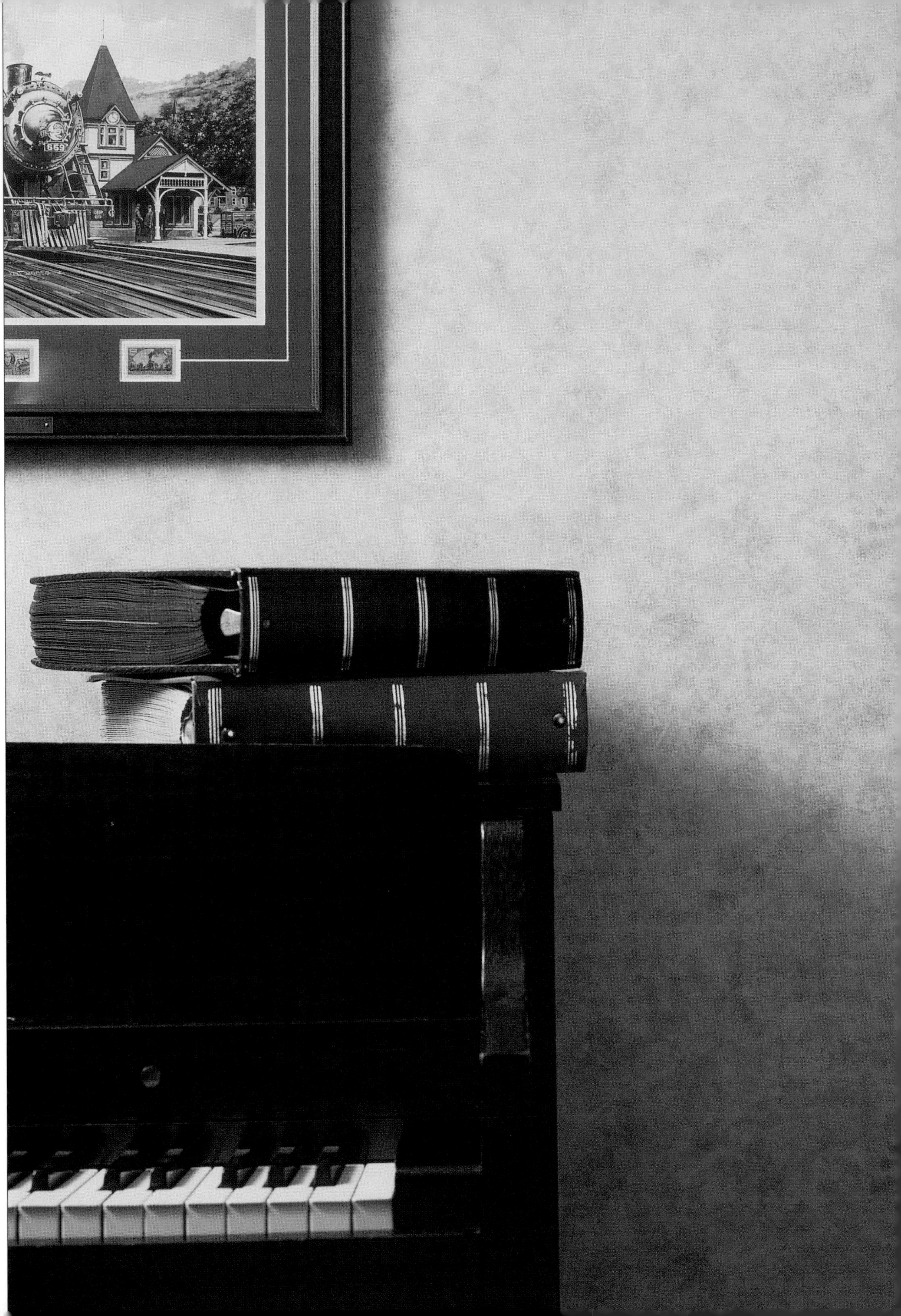

Hanging Wallpaper

Wallpaper

can add

color,

depth,

and texture

to any

room.

I can't think of a bolder way to change the atmosphere of a room than papering the walls. Depending on the pattern you choose, you can turn almost any rectangular space into an intimate nook for gathering, a parlor with Victorian formality, or an exotic retreat. Wallpaper also has a practical side: It conceals the wall's history of cracks, spackling, patching, and stomach-turning paint schemes.

Still, many homeowners tend to shy away from hanging paper. They may have heard the line that the only thing you'll see are your mistakes—and there's some truth to that. But take heart: If you make a mistake, you can do what the pros do—peel the botched strip off and try again. It's encouraging to watch the experts work, because even they have to stretch and coax those long, gooey sheets into place. So relax, and enjoy the transformation of your room!

Tools

Phillips-head and flat-head screwdrivers
Stepladder
Tape measure and 3' level
Scissors and a utility knife
Water tray (if pre-pasted paper)
Paint roller or brush (for paste)
Wallpaper brush and sponge
Wide-blade putty knife

Materials

Wallpaper
Paste (if unpasted paper)
Spackling compound
Mesh tape
150-grit sandpaper
Newspaper or drop cloths

Preparation

Strip old paper for best results; see page 114.

If you're planning on painting the ceiling and trim, do this before hanging the paper.

When shopping for paper, know the room dimensions, ceiling height, and number of doors and windows.

Although wallpaper can hide wall problems, defects may show through. Patch cracks with spackling compound, using mesh tape to span larger gaps, then prime spackled areas. Lightly sand walls with 150-grit paper to remove bumps and lessen the sheen of glossy walls.

LEVEL OF DIFFICULTY
Moderate

TIME REQUIREMENT
1 day for an average-sized room

COST ESTIMATE
$90 to $220 for a 12' by 12' room with 8' ceilings (18 single pre-pasted rolls)

WALLS

1 REMOVE COVER PLATES

- Use a screwdriver to remove the electrical cover plates.
- Since water from the wet wallpaper can creep into the electrical boxes, make sure to shut off the power to the room at the service panel before hanging the paper.

2 DRAW A PLUMB LINE

Most walls aren't straight up and down, so align the first strip along a plumb line.

- Begin at the least-conspicuous inside corner in the room (the patterns of the first and last strips won't meet dead-on).
- Measure from the corner a distance equal to the width of the paper less ½".
- With a pencil, draw a plumb line at this point, using a 3'level.
- To determine the length of the paper strips, measure from the top of the baseboard to the ceiling, and add 4" to allow a 2" overlap at top and bottom.

3 WET OR PASTE THE PAPER

Unpasted papers require you to brush or roll on wallpaper paste. Pre-pasted papers are soaked and then applied to the wall. Note that certain pre-pasted papers should be "booked" before applying *(see page 224)*, while others go up without this step; consult the instructions for your paper.

- Cut the first strip of paper to length.
- To soak the strip, reroll it with the paste side out and place it in a tray of warm water as instructed by the manufacturer.
- Or, to apply paste, lay the strip face down on a drop cloth and use a brush or a roller.

4 HANG FIRST PIECE

- Identify the top edge of the rolled strip to make sure it will be installed properly.
- Begin hanging at the ceiling, allowing a 2" overlap at the top and bottom and a ½" overlap at the corner.
- Align the sheet with the pencil line, adjusting it by pressing with your palms as needed.

5 SMOOTH THE SHEET

- Smooth the sheet with downward strokes of a wallpaper brush.
- Brush air pockets toward edges.
- If wrinkles can't be removed or if the alignment is off, peel off the entire strip and rehang it.

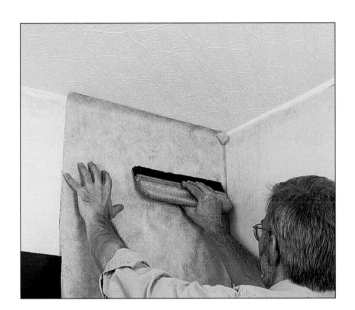

CHOOSING
Materials

Wallpaper Choices

Compared to looking at a chart of paint colors, shopping for wallpaper is a stimulating experience, with a wide range of textures and materials. Fabric-backed pa- pers are especially durable; vinyl papers are reasonably priced and have become the most popular choice; grasscloths, with their woven nat- ural fibers, are expen- sive and difficult to clean, but their textures are distinctive; and paintable embossed pa- pers do a good job of covering up uneven or cracked walls and can be painted any shade to match the rest of the room.

6 TRIM AT CEILING

- To trim the paper at the ceiling, first peel the edge of the paper down and cut along the crease.
- Press the paper back in place with a wallpaper brush or sponge.

Utility Knives

Traditionally, people who were handy with wood always carried a lovingly honed jackknife in a back pocket. Utility knives don't get that kind of affection, but they are extremely sharp, making them all but indispensable for many household projects. The simplest *(top)* is nothing but a handle with a holder for a single-edged razor blade. A utility or carton knife *(middle)* is a sturdier and safer choice. The blade can be retracted into the handle. When the edge gets dull, there's another edge on the concealed half of the blade, and the handle also holds several replacement blades. A less expensive alternative *(bottom)* has a scored blade that can be snapped off to provide a fresh, sharp edge.

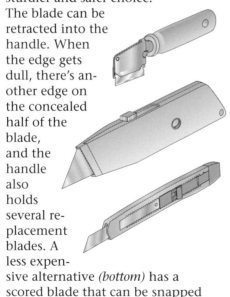

7 TRIM AT BASEBOARD

You have two options when trimming the lower end of the wallpaper sheet.

- Trim the overlap at the bottom of the strip as you did at the top.
- Or, tuck the paper into a gap between the baseboard and wall. Use a wide-blade putty knife to press the paper behind the baseboard. Trim away any excess with a utility knife *(see Tool Know-How, left).*

WALLS

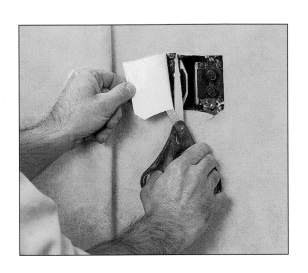

8 CUT AROUND ELECTRICAL BOXES

Double-check that the power to the boxes is shut off at the service panel before trimming paper around them.

- Hang the wallpaper strip over each box.
- Use scissors or a utility knife to cut out a rectangular area no larger than will be concealed by the cover plate.

9 TRIM AROUND WINDOWS AND DOORWAYS

- Hang a full-length strip right over the window or door.
- At each corner of the window or door, cut a diagonal slit from the opening to the outer corner of the trim; you will do this at the top two corners of a door, and at all four corners of a window.
- As with baseboards, you have two trimming options: trim with a utility knife guided by a putty knife; or, if there is a slight gap between the trim and wall, press the paper into this corner with the brush, then cut along the resulting crease with scissors, leaving at least ½" extra to tuck behind the trim.

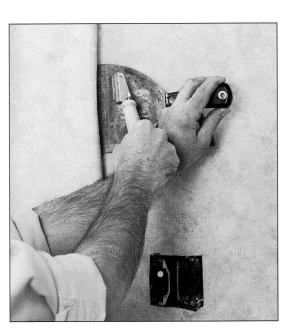

10 CONTINUE AROUND ROOM

- Align each strip of paper so that its pattern matches that of the preceding strip.
- Butt edges of strips so that they meet evenly, without gaps or overlapping.
- Plan on making a seam at each inside corner. Cut the first sheet to overlap the corner by ½"; on the adjacent wall, align the next sheet with a plumb line and cover the overlap.
- Run a full-width strip around an outside (projecting) corner to avoid a seam along the exposed edge.
- Sponge each strip with clean water to rinse away excess adhesive.

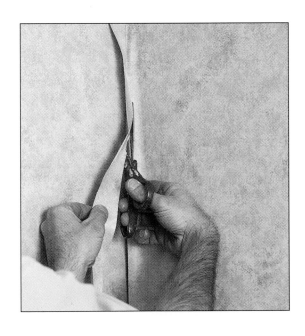

Adding a Wallpaper Border

Borders are the quickest and easiest of papering jobs.

A wallpaper border, whether on papered or painted walls, looks as impressive as wood molding—and those paper strips are a lot simpler and cheaper to put up. If you can wrap a package with tape, then you can run a border around a room. Another thing I like about wallpaper borders is that you can try them out to judge the effect. Just ask for a sample or a buy a strip, put it up temporarily with double-sided tape, and then stand back and have a look.

As with full-width wallpapers, borders come either pre-pasted or without paste. (If you will be pasting a vinyl border over vinyl paper, note that you should use a special vinyl-to-vinyl adhesive.) You also can buy borders with peel-off backing to make the job still easier. Borders come typically in 15' spools, so most walls can be done with a single strip.

If I haven't already convinced you that there's a wallpaper border in your future, here's another plus: A border will cover up any unevenness along the top ends of the strips after you've papered the walls.

Tools

Carpenter's level or straight-edge
Tape measure
Chalk line
Scissors
Wallpaper tray (for pre-pasted paper)
Wide-blade putty knife
Utility knife
Sponge
Wallpaper brush

Materials

Wallpaper borders
Wallpaper paste (for nonvinyl surface)
Vinyl-to-vinyl adhesive (for vinyl border on vinyl paper)

Preparation

If the ceiling and trim are to be painted, do so before hanging the border.

To determine how much border you'll need, measure the perimeter of the room. Note that you also can run borders around doors and windows, or use them as a visual chair rail.

LEVEL OF DIFFICULTY
Easy

TIME REQUIREMENT
½ day

COST ESTIMATE
$40 to $80 for a border around a 12' by 12' room

WALLS

1 CHECK CEILING FOR STRAIGHTNESS

If your ceiling is extremely wavy, you might not want to install a border—this bold visual feature will call attention to the area. In most rooms, the border will follow the contour of the ceiling without a problem.

- Butt a level or straightedge up against the ceiling at various points. To minimize any waviness, snap a chalk line along the top of the wall and align the border with it.

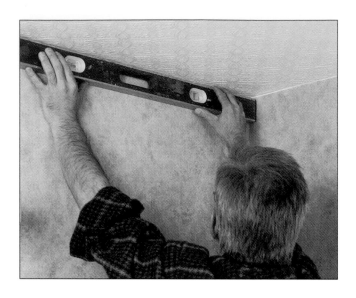

2 HANG FIRST PIECE

- Measure the wall for the length of the first strip.
- Cut the strip to length, allowing ½" overlap at each corner.
- Brush paste onto the strip or soak it, unless the border has a peel-off backing.
- To handle the strip more easily (and to allow the adhesive to activate if the instructions call for it), fold it into a "book" with pasted sides facing each other *(see Ron's Pro Tips on page 224)*.
- Press the strip in place, beginning with a ½" overlap at the first end and continuing along the wall.

3 SMOOTH OUT WRINKLES

- Use a damp sponge or wallpaper brush to work out any wrinkles in the strip.
- Press any bubbles out toward the edges with the sponge.

4 FIT CONSECUTIVE PIECES

- If strips must meet between corners, temporarily place the new, dry strip over the end of the strip on the wall and align the patterns.
- Using the blade of a broad putty knife as a straightedge, double-cut through both strips at once with a utility knife to make a common end with an uninterrupted pattern.
- Soak or paste the new strip, and put it in place.

5 TURNING CORNERS

As with papering walls, inside and outside corners require different treatment.

- Have strips meet at inside corners. Allow ½" of overlap when the first strip is applied, as in Step 2. Before soaking or pasting the next strip, tuck it into the corner so that the pattern is continued, make a crease in it, and cut off the strip along this fold with scissors.
- Run the border around outside corners if possible, to avoid having a seam along an exposed edge.
- As you apply border strips, use a sponge and clean water to remove excess adhesive from them.

Ron's PRO TIPS

A Wallpaper "Return"

When a wallpaper border butts up against a piece of wood trim, the transition is often abrupt. You can give it a more finished appearance by borrowing a trick used in finish carpentry—adding a "return" (*see page 154*). But instead of wood, this return is cut from a scrap piece of the border. Look at the border to see if it has a stripe of some sort along one edge. (The return shown here was taken from the border's lower edge.) Cut a

return roughly as long as the border is wide. Then cut off the lower end of the strip at a 45-degree angle. This makes an attractive transition so that the return will look like a part of the border's design. Finally, paste the return on the end of the border.

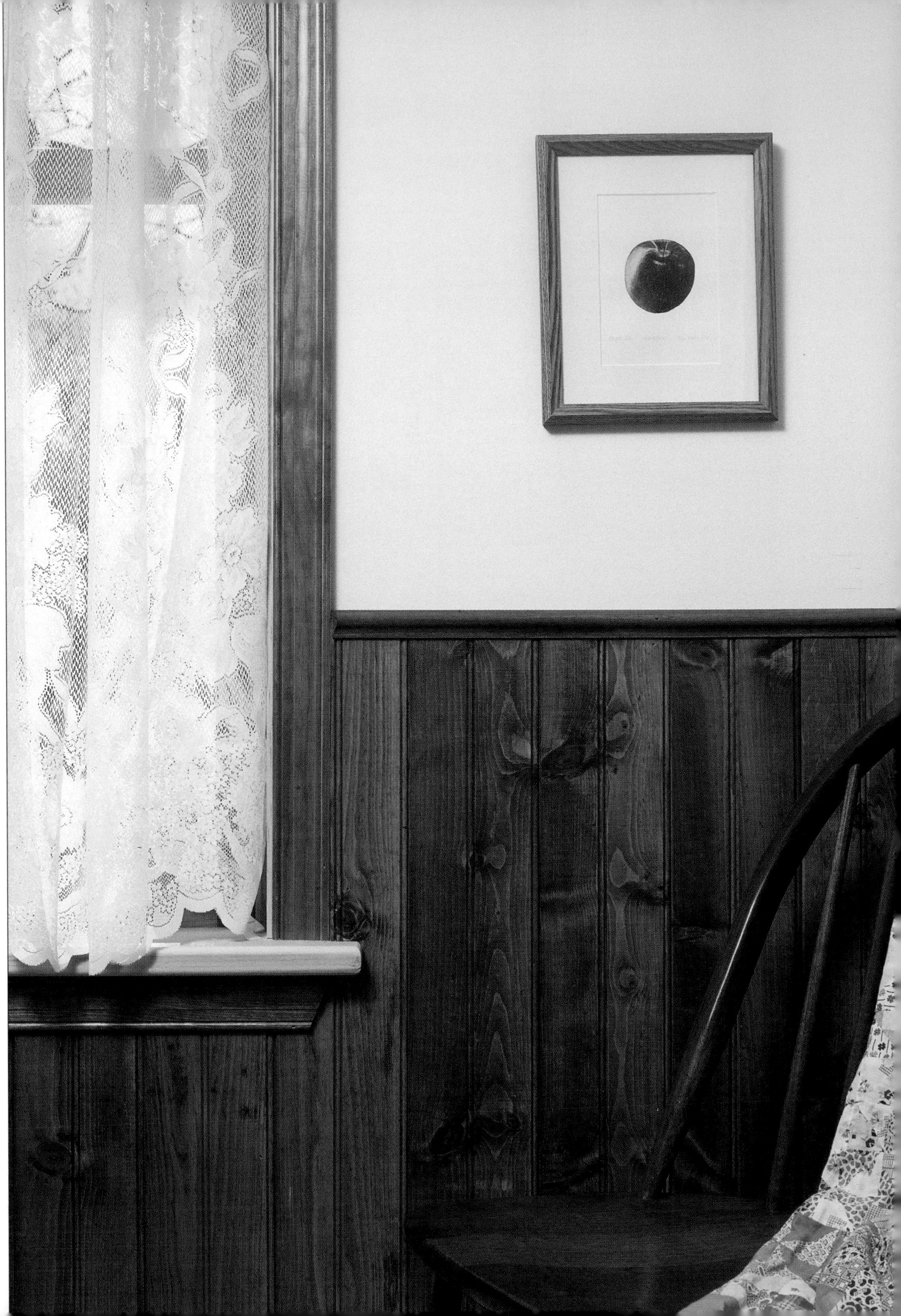

Installing Wainscoting

Wainscoting can make a room look formal or country casual.

Wainscoting was once attached to walls to protect them from the hard knocks of heavy furniture. Although this still holds true, today it's used mostly for looks. Wainscoting can make a room seem more formal (if you paint it) or countrified (if you stain it).

You can special-order wainscoting in a frame-and-panel style, which looks something like a traditional door laid on its side. The type shown here is simpler to install. Its tongue-and-groove vertical boards are trimmed at bottom and top by a baseboard and a cap rail. The boards often have a decorative "bead" along one edge, as well as others down the center to make a single board look like two or more. Home centers sell all the pieces you need, ready-cut as kits, in both pine and oak.

Even though wainscoting is thought of as mostly ornamental, I recommend it where the lower walls will take a beating—playrooms and bathrooms in particular. If finished with a paint or polyurethane with some gloss to it, the wainscoting will clean up well and hide scuff marks.

Tools

Wide-blade putty knife
Tape measure and 4' level
Stud finder
Hand saw or power miter saw
    (can be rented)
Saber saw or coping saw
Caulking gun
1/4" disposable notched trowel
Hammer and pry bar
Nail set or pin punch
2" paintbrush

Materials

Vertical boards
Baseboard
Cap rail
Construction adhesive
Mineral spirits
1¼" and 2" finish nails
Wood putty
Electrical box extenders
Paint, stain, or varnish

Preparation

Check to see whether windowsills have to be extended to project beyond the thickness of the wainscoting.

Wainscoting can be stained or painted before installation, as was done in the project shown here. This spares you the trouble of masking adjacent areas when applying finish and ensures that you won't see bare-wood tongues peeking out between boards.

LEVEL OF DIFFICULTY
Moderate

TIME REQUIREMENT
2 to 3 days for an average-sized room

COST ESTIMATE
$5 to $7 a square foot for pine wainscoting, baseboard, and cap rail; $10 to $25 for hardwood, depending on the species

1 REMOVE BASEBOARDS AND COVER PLATES

- Use a wide-blade putty knife to coax the baseboards from the wall. Switch to a pry bar for more leverage. You also can free the baseboards by punching through their finish nails with a nail set or a small pin punch.
- If you will be reusing the baseboards, see Refinishing Trim on page 146.
- Remove any electrical cover plates that will be covered with wainscoting.

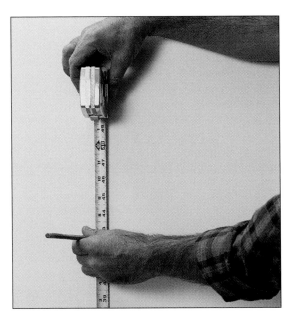

2 ESTABLISH THE HEIGHT

Generally, the lower the ceiling, the lower the wainscoting should be. To judge the effect, mock up wainscoting with panels of cardboard carton or sheets of inexpensive poster board. Consider raising or lowering the wainscoting to avoid awkward meetings with window trim and wall switches.

- Mark the wall at the desired height, then measure down for the margin that will be added by the cap rail to establish the top end of the vertical boards.

3 LAY OUT TOP EDGE

- Extend the top edge around the room with a level and a pencil.
- Go around the room again with a stud finder, and mark the location of studs.
- Draw a vertical line along the center of each stud to just above the height line; you will be face-nailing wainscoting to studs where possible, and eventually nailing the baseboards and cap rail to them as well.

WALLS

4 MEASURE AND CUT VERTICAL BOARDS

- Starting in a corner or at the edge of door trim, measure for the length of the vertical boards.
- Cut the boards to length with a power miter saw.
- Use a saber saw or coping saw to cut the boards for windows and outlets. (To locate cutouts, see Ron's Pro Tips on page 142.)
- Continue to measure the height as you proceed around the room, to allow for any changes caused by an uneven floor.

Ron's PRO TIPS

Box Extenders

The additional thickness that wainscoting adds to a wall creates a problem with the electrical outlets and switch boxes. If you can access the nails or screws that fix a box to the wall studs, you can remove them, leverage the box out so it's flush with the wainscoting, and fasten it in place. More likely, you won't have access. That's where box extenders come in. Simply purchase the appropriate thickness of extender and attach it to the electrical box to bring the outlet or switch out so it ends up flush with the wainscoting.

5 APPLY ADHESIVE

Install the vertical boards one at a time, beginning at a corner or door.

- Apply a bead of construction adhesive along the back of a board (make sure to provide adequate ventilation).
- Spread the adhesive with a ¼" notched blade of a disposable trowel.
- Position the board with its grooved edge facing the corner or door frame; slide it into place to help distribute the glue.
- Use mineral spirits to clean up any glue that ends up where it shouldn't.

WALLS

6 CHECK BOARDS FOR PLUMB

- Use a level to make sure newly glued boards are plumb. Any slight adjustments you have to make will be concealed by the tongue-and-groove joint.
- Do not force boards together; leave roughly 1/32" between them to allow the wood to expand and contract with changes in humidity.
- To rip the last board in a run, use a hand saw or a saber saw with an edge guide.

7 NAIL THE BOARDS

- Face-nail each board just above the floor, into the plate behind the wall. (Some thin wainscoting ends in a rabbet along the top of the baseboard and can't be nailed into the plate.)
- Blind-nail the top end into the wall, angling the nail into the corner made by the tongue. Use a nail set to avoid damaging the tongue.
- Face-nail boards into studs where possible; recess the heads for puttying.

8 MITER CAP RAIL PIECES

Where cap rail pieces meet at inside and outside corners, their ends are cut at 45-degree angles with a power miter saw or a hand saw.

- If you suspect a corner is not a true 90 degrees, make test cuts in two scraps of rail stock and hold them in place; adjust the saw setting until you get a good fit.

9 INSTALL CAP RAIL

- Attach the cap rail *(see Choosing Materials, below)* with 1¼" finish nails, driving them into the wainscoting.
- Wherever it's possible, nail into the studs as well.
- Recess the heads with a nail set.

10 INSTALL BASEBOARDS

- In corners, miter the baseboards as you did the cap rail *(see Step 8)*.
- Attach the baseboards with 2" finish nails; the nails should be long enough to drive through the wainscoting and into studs and plates.
- Recess the heads with a nail set.
- Putty nail holes in the baseboards, cap rail, and vertical boards.
- Touch up any areas with the same finish that you applied before you installed the wainscoting.

CHOOSING
Materials

Cap Stock Profiles

The exposed tops of wainscoting boards are trimmed with a cap rail to hide the tongue-and-groove joints. Typically, rails have a squared notch or "rabbet" along their lower back edge to fit over the top of the wainscoting. They come in many different profiles, some simple (like the one in this project) and others elaborate. Try to choose rails and baseboards that will match in terms of visual weight and complexity.

Installing Chair Rail

Chair rail dresses up a room the way a tie does an oxford shirt.

Putting up chair rail is something like bracketing your windows with shutters: You don't really need either of them, but these holdovers from an earlier time can affect the appearance of a home more than their modest size would suggest. Chair rail is a great antidote to the blandness of drywall, adding personality to rooms that look a little too perfect and office-like.

As with other types of molding, the scale of the chair rail should be in keeping with the room. Larger spaces can handle something on the beefy side, such as the two-piece style shown here; smaller, lower rooms are better off with slimmer stock. The height should be right, too; because the original purpose of chair rail was to prevent chair backs from marring dining room walls, this trim logically should be placed between 32" and 36" from the floor.

You can use chair rail along the border between two wall treatments, such as a wallpapered lower section and paint above. It can also be used to make a transition between paneling below and paint or wallpaper above; see Installing Wainscoting on page 128.

Tools

Tape measure
Chalk line
Claw hammer
Hand saw or power miter saw
(can be rented)
Stud finder (optional)
Electric drill and twist bits
Caulking gun
2" trim brush
Putty knife

Materials

Primer and paint or varnish
2" finish nails
Acrylic latex caulk
Wood putty to match the
finished chair rail

Preparation

If you will be using custom-milled molding, order it well in advance.

Decide on how to treat molding that will be thicker than the door and window casing it meets: You can make a square cut; or bevel the exposed edge; or back-cut the protruding portion at an angle so it extends a bit beyond the casing, as shown on the opposite page.

Consider applying paint or a clear finish to the molding before nailing it up, especially if walls and ceiling are not due to be repainted. In either case, prime the back of each piece to prevent warping.

LEVEL OF DIFFICULTY
Easy

TIME REQUIREMENT
$\frac{1}{2}$ day, with helper to hold long stock for marking and nailing

COST ESTIMATE
$50 (pine) to $125 (oak) for 1-piece molding in a 12' by 12' room

WALLS

1 LOCATE AND MARK THE HEIGHT

- At each corner of the room, measure down from the ceiling to the desired height and make a mark.
- With a helper or a tacked nail anchoring an end of a chalk line in one corner, hold the other end at the mark in an adjacent corner and snap the line *(inset)*.

2 CUT RAIL AND ATTACH AT CASINGS

For casings that are the same thickness as the molding, end the molding with a simple square cut. If the molding is thicker than the casings, bevel or back-cut its protruding portion, as shown on page 134.

- If the stock isn't long enough to span a wall, scarf two or more pieces as described on page 229.
- Locate the studs with a stud finder, hold the chair rail in place, and transfer stud locations to it.
- Drill pilot holes in the molding at each stud, and tack the molding in place with 2" finish nails.

CHOOSING
Materials

Chair Rail

Chair rail molding is available in a wide variety of profiles and materials at most home centers and lumberyards. The profiles shown here are some of the more commom. If you can't find the profile you're looking for, a full-service lumberyard or a local cabinetmaker may be able to custom-make molding for you. Another way to come up with a unique profile is to "build" the profile by stacking up separate moldings. Simply nail the separate pieces together as you attach them to the wall.

3 MAKE CUTS FOR FIRST PIECE

- Low-profile molding meets at the corners with 45-degree cuts, as for the base of the two-piece rail in this project.
- Or, for molding with a higher profile, use a combination of square and coped cuts; *see page 230 for more on coping.* Both ends of the first rail are cut square, as shown here.

4 MAKE CUTS FOR REMAINING PIECES

- For low-profile molding, continue to work around the room, making 45-degree cuts at each corner.
- On high-profile molding, the second piece meets the square end of the first with a coped cut *(see page 230).* The other end of the second rail has a straight cut. The third rail is treated the same way. The fourth has two coped cuts.
- When each rail is properly installed, drive the nails home, countersink them, and putty the holes.
- Brush on primer and paint or varnish.

Ron's
PRO
TIPS

Blind-Nailing

The standard way to conceal nail holes on wood that will be finished clear is to plug them with putty. That works well enough; but even if you get an excellent color match, the wood may change in hue over time, making the putty more obvious. A sly old way of hiding nail heads is to carefully lift a sliver of wood with a knife or chisel, drive the nail through the exposed wood, then glue the sliver back in place. If done right, this bit of sneakiness is

all but undetectable. To make sure the hammer doesn't flatten the chip and destroy the effect, use a nailset for the last few blows.

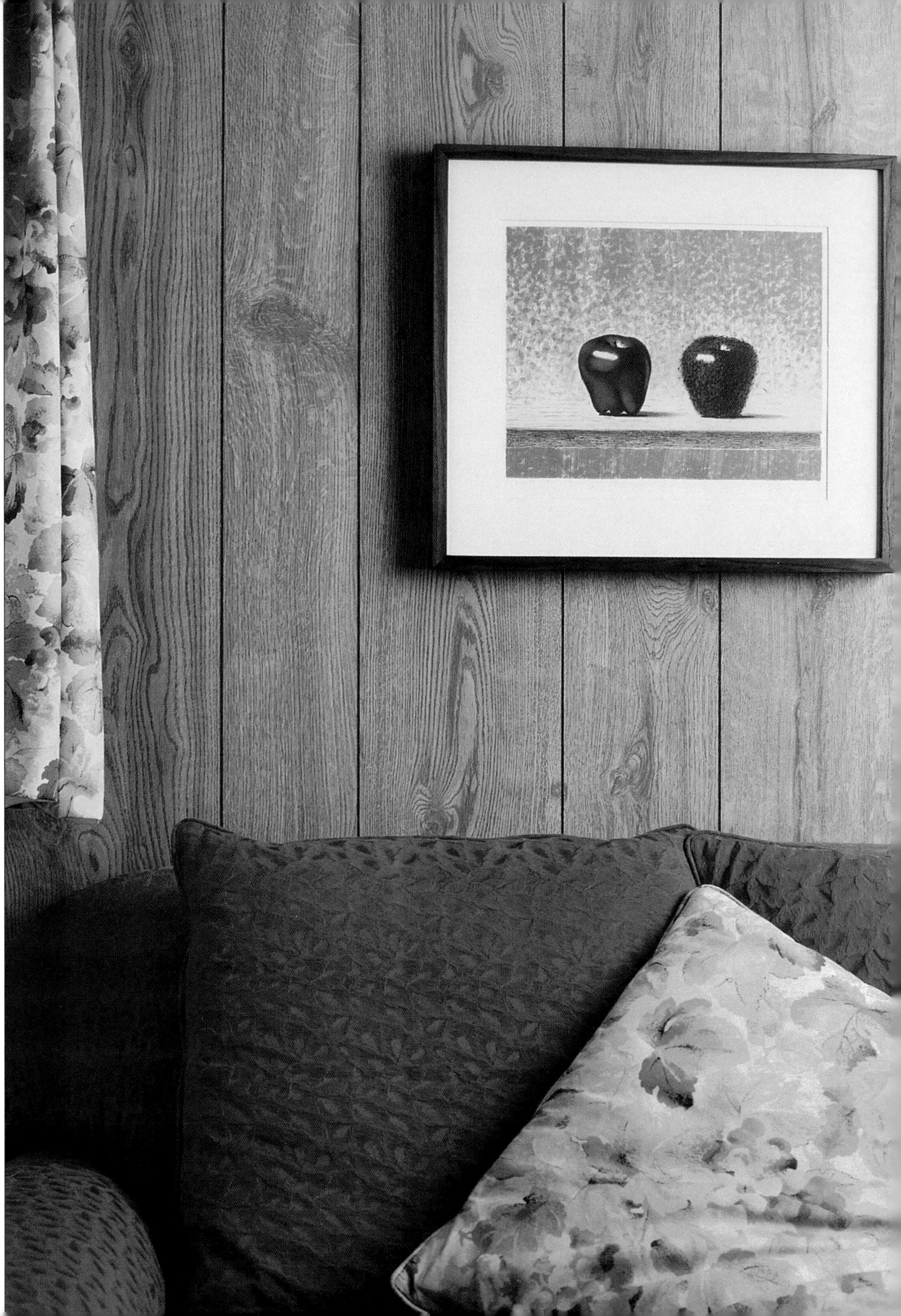

Installing Wall Paneling

Paneling is one of the easiest ways to finish a room.

To a lot of people, wood wall paneling has a bad reputation. Dark, ugly, knotty, fake looking—the criticisms are many, and in some cases at least partially valid. Nevertheless, paneling remains one of the most often used materials in home remodeling. The reasons are pretty simple. Paneling goes up very easily in 4 by 8 sheets; matching trim is readily available; and it's already finished, so once it's up, the job is just about done. Better-quality paneling is made of real wood, and it will last for decades. This longevity makes paneling a good lead-abatement procedure when used to cover up lead-based paint on walls (abatement is considered any covering that will last 20 years).

If you're planning on finishing a room and are looking for alternatives to drywall, give paneling a second look. But don't settle for the stock offerings on display at your local home center. A lot of them are flimsy and cheap-looking. These represent just the tip of the paneling iceberg. Ask for selections that can be custom-ordered, or find a supplier who can provide a wider range of colors and styles. You'll be surprised at the broad range of colors, patterns, and styles that are available today.

This project shows paneling installed on newly constructed stud walls in a basement. But you can apply paneling over existing wall materials like plaster or drywall.

Tools

Tape measure
Claw hammer and nail set
Electric drill and twist bits
Masonry bit
Utility knife
Staple gun
Circular saw or hand saw
Straightedge
Keyhole saw or saber saw
Caulking gun
Leather gloves and safety mask

Materials

10d framing nails
Carpenter's shims
3" drywall screws
Masonry screws
$3/8$" heavy-duty staples
$3\frac{1}{2}$"-thick fiberglass insulation
Paneling
Outlet and switch boxes (optional)
Construction adhesive
Wood stain
1" paneling nails
Base molding
Corner trim (inside and outside)
$1\frac{1}{2}$" finish nails
Matching wood putty

Preparation

If you're covering walls in a basement with paneling, use the procedures detailed in Finishing Off a Basement Wall shown on pages 168–171—just substitute paneling for drywall in the final stages.

LEVEL OF DIFFICULTY
Moderate

TIME REQUIREMENT
2 to 4 days

COST ESTIMATE
$300 to $500

WALLS

1 BUILD STUD WALLS

For preexisting walls, skip to Step 5. For basement walls, see pages 168–171 and then proceed to Step 5.

- Measure between the floor and the joists and subtract 3" for the combined thickness of the top and bottom plates.
- Cut enough studs to length with a circular saw or hand saw to make an 8'-long section.
- Mark centerlines on the top and bottom plates 16" apart.
- Nail the studs between the top and bottom plates with framing nails.

2 ANCHOR WALLS

- Slide carpenter's shims under the bottom plate to plumb the wall sections and to lift them snug against the ceiling joists.
- Nail through the bottom plate to anchor the wall sections to the floor. On concrete floors, drill through the bottom plate and into the concrete with a masonry bit, then drive concrete screws in.
- Drive 3" drywall screws up through the top plate into the ceiling joists.

3 CUT INSULATION

On new walls, you may want to add kraft-faced fiberglass insulation to reduce heat loss and sound transmission.

- Measure the height of the wall cavities.
- Wearing gloves and a proper mask, roll out the insulation. Place a scrap piece of thin plywood underneath, then condense the insulation with a straightedge and cut through it with a utility knife.

4 STAPLE INSULATION TO STUDS

- Pack the insulation firmly into the wall cavities.
- Pull the paper flange on the edges of the insulation onto the studs, and staple every 8" to 10".

Clamp-On Straightedges

When cutting sheet goods like paneling or plywood with a circular saw, you can get straighter and smoother cuts by using a straightedge to guide the saw. Any straightedge will work—I often use the factory edge on a scrap piece of ¾" plywood and a pair of C-clamps to hold the straightedge in place.

Commercial saw guides eliminate the need for separate clamps because the clamps are built right into the bar. Just lay the bar onto the workpiece, make sure it's parallel to the cut line and the right distance away, clamp it on, and make your cut. Saw guides are available in a variety of lengths at hardware stores and home centers.

5 CUT PANELING TO LENGTH

You can cut paneling with a variety of tools—a hand saw, a saber saw, or a circular saw. Thin plywood paneling can even be cut with a sharp utility knife.

- Measure the height of the wall space to be covered. If the height varies across the 4' section where the paneling is going, cut the paneling to the shortest height.
- Mark the height right on the paneling with a marker and straightedge.
- To guide a circular saw, clamp a straightedge onto the paneling, parallel to the cut line. (Cut with the face side down to avoid chipping the face of the paneling.)

WALLS

6 INSTALL ELECTRICAL BOXES

When building new stud walls, you may want to add some electrical boxes for outlets or switches. Check with an electrician or your local building inspector first regarding code requirements.

- The face of the outlet box should protrude from the stud a distance equal to the thickness of the paneling. Use a scrap of paneling to set the box out the correct distance.

- Position nail-on outlet boxes against studs at the correct height (again, check your local code), and drive in the attached nails.

Ron's
**PRO
TIPS**

Locating Cutouts on Panels

One of the more frustrating tasks when putting up paneling (or any wallcovering material, for that matter) is making cutouts for electrical boxes. The conventional approach is to measure carefully from the adjacent panel and from the floor or ceiling to the box, and transfer the dimensions onto the panel. No matter how careful I was when using this approach in the past, something always went slightly wrong. And being off just ¼" can ruin a panel.

Here's a better approach. Use the box itself to transfer its location to the panel. Rub some vibrant lipstick or chalk against the outside face of the box *(below)*. Then carefully place the panel into position, aligning the edge with the panel that's already in place, or with the corner. Once you've got the panel perfectly in place, just press up against the area where the box is located behind the panel. The lipstick or chalk will leave an impression that is ready to be cut out *(right)*. And the fit should be perfect.

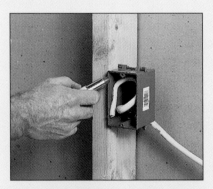

7 DRILL PILOT HOLES FOR CUTOUT

Cutouts for electrical boxes can be cut with a keyhole saw or a saber saw. But first you need to drill starter holes in one or more corners.

- Drill the starter holes in the corners with a ⅜" or larger drill bit. Be sure to support the face side of the panel so it doesn't chip out.

8 SAW CUTOUT

- Position the panel on a flat work surface.
- Place the blade of a saber saw or keyhole saw through one of the starter holes, and saw to the opposite corner.
- Continue like this until the cutout is complete.

9 APPLY CONSTRUCTION ADHESIVE

Although you'll use nails to secure the paneling *(see Step 10)*, I suggest the added insurance of construction adhesive along with the nails. The adhesive helps hold the panel along the entire length of the studs, so fewer nails are needed.

- Use a caulking gun to apply a bead of adhesive along the full length of the studs.
- Press the panel against the studs, then pull it away and let the adhesive get tacky for a few minutes. When you press it back in place, it will have more grab.

WALLS

10 NAIL PANELS TO STUDS

Most "wood" paneling has irregularly spaced vertical grooves, but two of the grooves are spaced 16" on center to coincide with standard stud framing patterns. That way the nails are concealed inside the grooves. Using color-matched nails will make them less noticeable.

• Drive 1" paneling nails into the grooves every 8" or 10".

• Use a nail set to drive the nails flush with the bottom of the groove. There's no need to countersink the nails into the groove.

Ron's PRO TIPS

Invisible Seams

Although most paneling is well made, with good straight edges, in practice the edges don't always butt together perfectly. It's easy to start at one end of the panel with things aligned just right, but have the other end out of alignment by the time you tack in the last nail. The result is a gap along the seams, which can show up as a light strip of color on an otherwise unbroken expanse of darker wood. So if you're using medium- to dark-colored paneling, try this trick.

Right before putting up each new panel, apply a quick coat of wood stain to the center of the stud where the seams will fall. The stain need not be a perfect match, just in the same range or slightly darker. Apply adhesive only to the outside edges of the stud's front so it won't squeeze out over the stain. Then tack up the panel as usual. Any gaps that do occur will be invisible.

WALLS

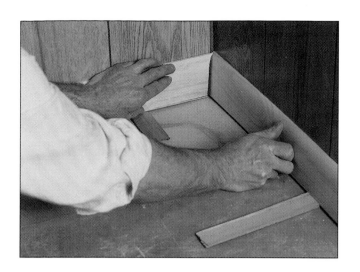

11 FIT BASE MOLDING

Base molding that matches your paneling may be available, or you can choose unfinished molding and paint or stain it.

- Cut molding to fit the wall sections. Miter the molding at outside corners, and cut a coped joint at inside corners; see Crown Molding on page 230.
- Nail the molding in place with 1½" finish nails. (If your basement floor is uneven, insert shims under the molding to level it before nailing it to the wall.)

12 APPLY INSIDE CORNER TRIM

At the inside corners, the paneling will rarely fit perfectly, one piece to the other. Various styles of molding (often a cove or bead) are available to finish off these corners. Typically, you'll want to finish the ceiling before applying the corner trim.

- Measure and cut the inside molding to length, and nail it in place with 1½" finish nails.
- Countersink the nails and apply a matching putty.

13 APPLY OUTSIDE CORNER TRIM

The area where the paneling meets at a corner also needs to be treated to cover the exposed edges. Corner trim shaped like a V is just the ticket.

- Measure and cut the outside molding to length, one piece at a time.
- Nail the molding in place every 6" to 8", countersink the nails with a nail set, and fill the holes with matching putty.

Refinishing Trim

Make tired trim look like new.

Rooms get a good bit of their personality from trim, especially if the wood has an interesting profile or is finished clear. But trim takes a beating because of its location, and it tends to be repainted so often that it get lost under a thick, unappealing coat.

You can refresh the appearance of a room just by stripping off those layers, then painting or varnishing the restored surface. It's possible to do the job with the trim in place, but I've found that everything goes smoother if the trim is removed first. This does a couple of things. First, it eliminates the bending that can make this job a real pain; once the trim is removed, I set it on a pair or sawhorses at a comfortable working height. Second, regardless of whether you use a chemical stripper or a heat gun, refinishing trim can be messy; removing the trim allows you to work on the trim someplace where the mess won't be a problem—like a basement, a workshop, or even a patio on a nice day.

Safety note: Pre-1978 trim may have been decorated with a lead-based paint; see the Saftey note on page 287 before you begin refinishing.

Tools

Chisel or putty knife
Pry bar
Sawhorses
Leather and/or rubber gloves
Heat gun
Paint scraper
Claw hammer
Nail set or pin punch
Brush for paint or varnish

Materials

Paint stripper (optional)
Wood putty
100- and 220-grit sandpaper
1¼" and 2" finish nails
Masking tape
Paint or varnish
Clean rags

Preparation

Set up a stripping area, preferably with a pair of sawhorses on several layers of newspaper.

Leather work gloves are best when using a heat gun; also protect your hands with gloves when applying chemical stripper. Carefully clean up all old paint for disposal.

Provide ventilation to avoid inhaling concentrated fumes from either chemical or heat stripping; work outside if possible.

LEVEL OF DIFFICULTY
Easy

TIME REQUIREMENT
1 to 2 days to refinish trim (baseboard and door and window) of a small room

COST ESTIMATE
$6 per can for chemical stripper; heat guns sell from $25 to $60, and rent for $15 a day.

WALLS

TOOL KNOW-HOW

Heat Guns

There is no way to remove paint tidily. The stuff was intended to stick to wood, after all, and isn't easily coaxed off. But I've found that using a heat gun is an efficient way to remove paint. It works at temperatures high enough to degrade the paint without burning it (and creating clouds of noxious fumes). To prolong the life of the gun, before turning it off, always turn it to the COOL setting and let it run for several minutes. If you don't do this, you run the risk of damaging the heating element.

1 REMOVE TRIM

- Carefully pry the trim from the wall, using a hammer and chisel or stiff putty knife, then a pry bar for more leverage.
- If you can see the finish nails holding the trim in place, you may get better results by punching them through with a nail set or pin punch.

2 STRIP TRIM

- Place the trim on a pair of sawhorses.
- With gloves on, run a heat gun over a small area (but I don't recommend using heat to remove lead-based paints). As the finish softens, remove loosened material with a scraper. Move the heat gun constantly to prevent it from scorching the trim; this is particularly important if you'll be applying a clear finish.
- Or, use a chemical stripper (these work best for trim to be treated with a clear finish). Put on gloves, and brush on a generous layer over a small area. Wait for the paint to wrinkle, then scrape (*inset*) or lift off the paint with with a putty knife. Let the chemicals do the work. Apply more stripper as needed.

3 SAND TRIM

- Wipe the trim clean with a cloth.
- Fill nail holes with wood putty, and allow the putty to dry.
- Sand the surface with 100-grit sandpaper. If you are allowing some areas of finish to remain, feather the edges to smooth the transition to bare wood.

4 REINSTALL TRIM

- Put the trim back in place.
- Use 1¼" finish nails to attach the trim to the jamb; use 2" finish nails to attach the trim to the wall.
- Set the heads with a nail set, and fill the holes with putty.
- After the putty has dried, sand it flush with the trim using sandpaper wrapped around a scrap of wood.

5 PAINT OR VARNISH TRIM

- Mask surrounding surfaces, and apply the finish of your choice.
- Use multiple thin coats instead of one thick coat to cover the trim thoroughly.
- If you are applying a clear coat, sand lightly between coats with 220-grit sandpaper.

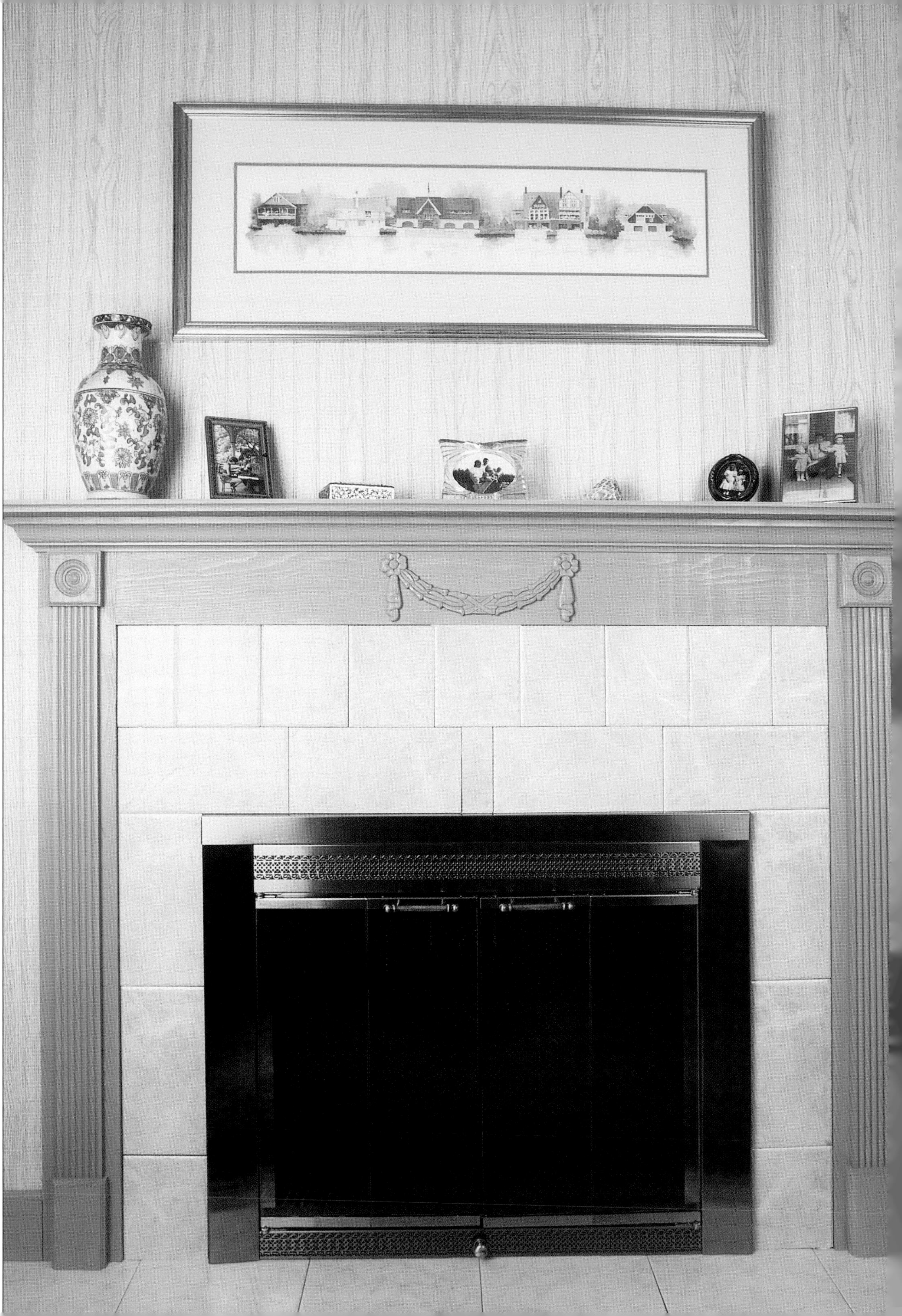

Building a Fireplace Surround

A fireplace can make a room warm and inviting— the fireplace surround can make it the center of attention.

A fireplace often serves as the centerpiece of a room. Whether it's an old-fashioned hearth or a modern gas fireplace insert, most people organize the room to take full advantage of the light and warmth a fireplace offers.

But many homeowners I've done work for complain that their fireplaces are too plain or austere looking to serve as a room's anchor. They're usually referring to a builder's special—a simple glass and brass screen, looking like it was just stuck in the wall, maybe with a course of tile around it. What they want is a wood fireplace surround topped off with a mantel.

The fireplace surround is a very traditional piece of American architecture and woodworking. While some of the best examples would be very challenging to replicate, you can make the one shown here using basic carpentry skills and stock materials available off the shelf at most home centers. Using the same procedure shown here, you can vary the details to come up with a unique fireplace surround that suits your tastes.

Tools

Tape measure
Hand saw and miter box
Combination square
Claw hammer
Portable router and profiling bit (optional)
Electric drill and twist bits
Nail set
Paintbrush
C-clamps and worktable

Materials

These materials are for a fireplace surround measuring 65" wide by 48" high.

Horizontal back board (1"×8"×6')
Vertical back boards (2) (1"×6"×10')
Mantel (1'×6"×6')
Fluted or beaded pilasters (2)
Plinth blocks (2)
Rosette blocks (2)
Decorative carved appliqué (optional)
2½" crown molding (6')
1½" and 2" finish nails
Wood glue
Masking tape or duct tape
150-, 180-, and 220-grit sandpaper
Wood putty or latex filler
Stain and/or varnish or paint

Preparation

Because it's combustible, the wood surrounding a fireplace must be set back a certain distance; check your local building requirements.

LEVEL OF DIFFICULTY
Moderate

TIME REQUIREMENT
1 to 2 days

COST ESTIMATE
$100 to $200 (not including fire screen or tile)

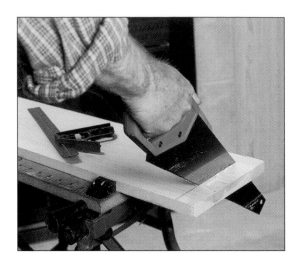

1 CROSSCUT HORIZONTAL BACK BOARD

The horizontal back board is a piece of 1 by 8 that will butt into the vertical back-boards *(see Step 3)*. Note: Because boards off the shelf rarely have square ends, cut both ends of each piece square.

- Mark each cut line with a combination square.
- Clamp the board to a worktable or bench (it's easier to guide the saw with two hands), and saw along the line.

2 NAIL HORIZONTAL BACK BOARD TO WALL

- Determine the location of studs *(see page 64)* and mark them on the wall.
- If there is no tile or brick edge that the back board will rest on, level the board.
- Nail the horizontal back board to the studs with 2" finish nails.

CHOOSING
Materials

Surround Components

All the ingredients for a fine fireplace surround can be found in most home centers. The back boards *(top center)* are 1 by 6 and 1 by 8 stock. Choose a select grade of pine if you plan on a natural or stained finish, or save money with #2 grade pine if you plan to paint.

Fluted pilasters *(bottom)* may be sold individually but are more likely to be found in a door trim package that includes the pilasters, as well as plinth blocks and two rosette blocks *(left)*.

Crown molding *(top right)* is a staple in every home center.

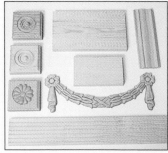

It's commonly stocked in both a finish grade and a less-expensive paint grade.

Finally, some of the larger home centers now stock a selection of laser-carved appliqués, like the garland shown here. These can add a real touch of elegance to the project.

3 CUT AND NAIL VERTICAL BACK BOARDS

Generally, you'll have less chance of measuring errors if you mark the cuts right off the pieces that they fit against.

- Position each vertical back board against the horizontal back board to mark the cut, then cut the boards as shown in Step 1.
- Nail the vertical pieces to the wall with 2" finish nails, holding them tight against the horizontal back board *(inset)*.

4 MARK AND CUT MANTEL TO LENGTH

The overall length of the mantel depends on the crown molding you've selected.

- Holding a small cutoff from the crown molding against the vertical backboard, position the mantel so it extends about an inch beyond the crown molding.
- Make a mark on the wall indicating the mantel overhang, add that same overhang to the other side, and that's the length of the mantel.
- Cut the mantel to length.
- If you have access to a portable router (or know someone who's handy with one), consider profiling the mantel edge with a round-over or chamfering bit.

5 NAIL MANTEL TO BACK BOARDS

The mantel rests on the back boards and is further supported by the crown molding, but you need the mantel in place first.

- Position the mantel so the overhang is equal on both ends.
- Drive 2" finish nails down through the mantel into the back boards.

6 CUT CROWN MOLDING

The crown molding is mitered at the ends where it turns the corner and returns to the wall. Carpenters call these short pieces "returns." Because it sits at an angle, the molding needs to be cut at a compound miter. The trick is to cut the molding upside down in a miter box.

- Hold the long piece of crown molding in place under the mantel, and roughly mark the direction of the miter cut. Then cut the first piece.

- Hold the piece in place again under the mantel, this time aligning the mitered end with the edge of the vertical back board. Now mark and cut the other end.

- To cut the returns, first cut a miter on a longer piece, then make the square cut that will butt against the wall.

7 ATTACH CROWN MOLDING

- Holding the molding in place so that it contacts the mantel and the back boards equally when viewed from the end, drive 1½" finish nails through the bottom of the molding into the back boards.

- The returns are too small to nail, so glue them in place. Apply a piece of masking or duct tape to hold the returns in place while the glue dries (inset).

Ron's
PRO TIPS

"Burnishing" a Miter Joint

The miter joint on this crown molding is a little tricky. Not only are the miters at a compound angle, but the return pieces are very small and you only get one chance to get each one right. If the joint is off badly, it may be worth cutting another small return piece. But if it's open just a little, here's a trick to close it.

Take a screwdriver with a round shank, and drag it across the miter with the shank perpendicular  to the corner, as shown. Press down fairly hard against the wood.

The goal is to slightly mash the wood fibers at the tip of the joint so they fill the gap. If one of the miters overlaps the other noticeably, press harder against that one. Repeat the process over each part of the joint that's open. Then lightly sand the joint.

8 LOCATE AND APPLY BLOCKS

- With the corner blocks positioned so they are centered on the vertical back boards, and tight up against the bottom edge of the crown molding, mark their locations on the horizontal back board.

- To prevent splitting, remove the block and drill holes for 1½" finish nails at least ½" in from each corner.

- Then nail the corner blocks in place.

- Repeat the procedure for the plinth blocks, setting them tight against the floor.

9 CUT AND APPLY PILASTERS

The pilasters are nailed in place between the corner blocks and the plinth blocks. You can also use a pilaster horizontally between the two corner blocks as shown here, or glue on a center decorative carving as shown on page 150.

- Cut one end of each pilaster piece, rest it squarely on the plinth block, and mark the length.

- Nail the pilaster in place with 1½" finish nails, centered on the plinth blocks. Repeat for the horizontal piece.

10 FILL, SAND, AND FINISH

A natural wood finish, either clear or stained, requires more sanding than a painted finish.

- Set all nails and fill the holes with wood putty. Latex wood fillers work well under most finishes, and they dry quickly.

- Sand all surfaces consistently, and round-over all the sharp wood edges. Once over with 150-grit paper is adequate under paint, but go over everything again with 180- or 220-grit when using a stain or clear finish.

- Mask off the wall and tile with tape, and apply the finish of your choice.

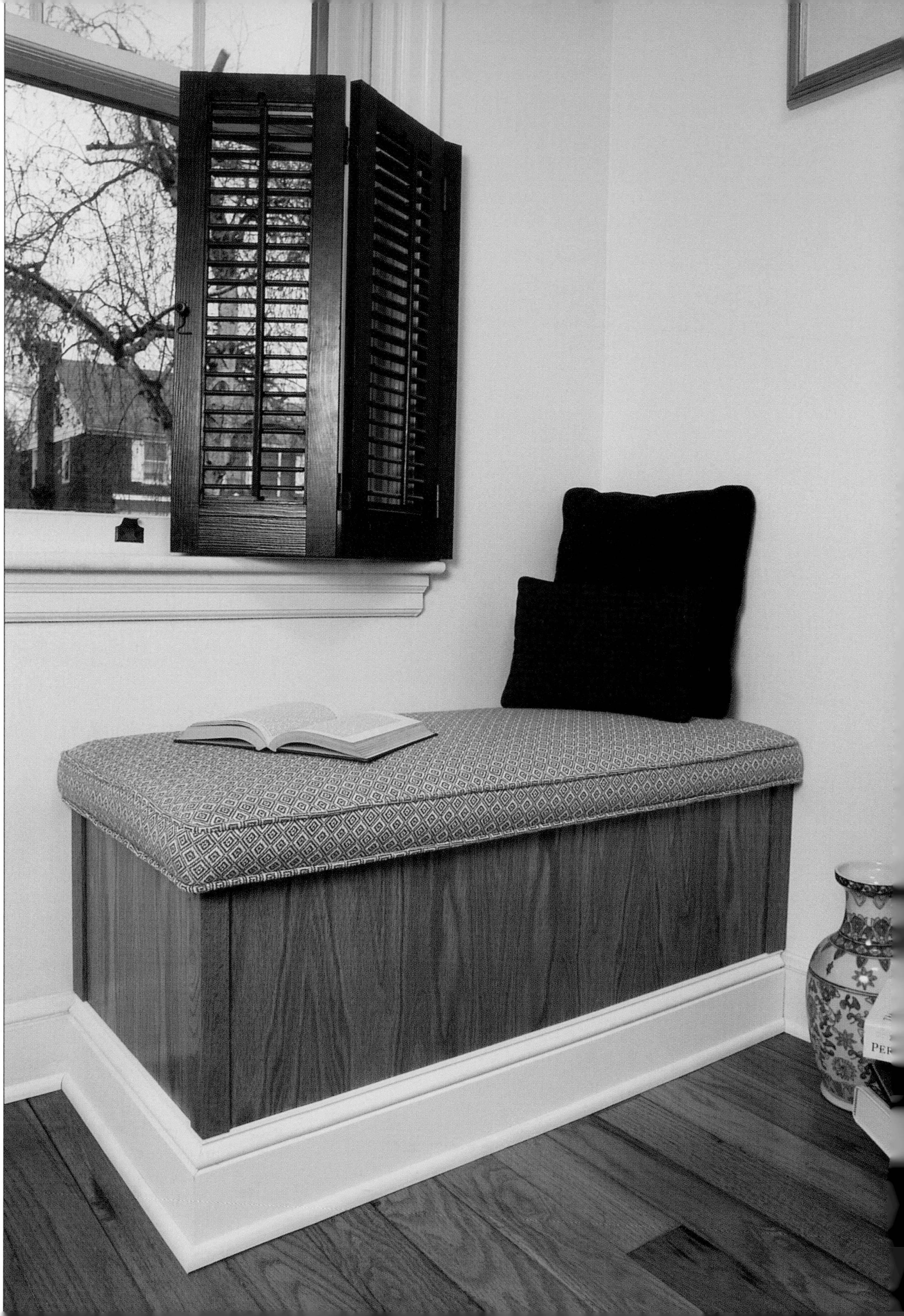

Making a Built-In Window Seat

A window seat is a great way to add a cozy nook to any room.

The homeowners I meet are always looking for ways to make their homes unique. They often succeed by creatively using standard store-bought materials, furnishings, and fixtures. After all, no two homeowners are likely to combine all the elements in a room in exactly the same way.

But sometimes you simply can't buy exactly what you want from any store or catalog. A window seat is a good example. Typically built right into the room, a window seat forms a cozy nook for reading or just watching the world go by. And no two are exactly alike.

You can build a window seat under just about any window, as long as the sill is between 15 and 30 inches above the floor. A window near the corner of a room is ideal because the seat is less likely to intrude into the room.

Using hardwood plywood, but no complicated joinery, you can make an attractive window seat and trim it to blend into the room. Make the cushion yourself, or have an upholsterer do that part of the job.

Tools

Sawhorses
C-clamps
Straightedge
Tape measure
Circular saw
Electric drill and twist bits
Countersink bit
Phillips-head and flat-head screwdrivers
Claw hammer
Nail set
Staple gun

Materials

½ to 1 sheet of ¾"-thick hardwood plywood
1⅝" and 3" drywall screws
Carpenter's wood glue
Duct tape
1" finish nails
Wood shims
Molding and trim to suit design
Polyurethane or similar finish
Upholstered cushion, or 1½"-thick foam and fabric
½" staples
Scrap wood blocks
Wood putty to match plywood

Preparation

Measure area for window seat carefully, especially if it will fit between two walls.

Seat height and depth should be between 14" and 18" (including cushion).

LEVEL OF DIFFICULTY
Moderate

TIME REQUIREMENT
2 to 3 days

COST ESTIMATE
$150 to $250, including the upholstered seat

1 CUT PLYWOOD TO SIZE

- Support the plywood on a set of sawhorses with the good face down to prevent splintering the veneer.
- Measure and mark each cut.
- Clamp a straightedge guide to the plywood. It should be set back from the cut mark a distance equal to the width of the saw's base.
- Cut the plywood to size.

2 SCREW PARTS TOGETHER

For a built-in seat like this, there's no need for complicated joinery; just apply wood glue and then screw the parts together with 1⅝" drywall screws. The screws and the plywood edges will be covered by trim.

- Hold the corners together with clamps. Use duct tape if you don't have clamps.
- Drill holes ¼" in from the edge for the screws and countersink them.
- Screw the parts together.
- When the box is assembled, check that it's square by measuring the diagonals—they should be equal.

CHOOSING
Materials

Hardwood Plywood

There are basically two kinds of plywood: the rough stuff you see at house construction sites, used for subfloors and roof sheathing; and a finer grade of plywood used for cabinetmaking and furnituremaking. The latter is usually referred to as hardwood plywood, because the face veneers are made of high-quality hardwoods like oak, cherry, and walnut (*shown left to right, top unfinished, bottom with a coat of varnish*).

Hardwood plywood is made to tighter tolerances than construction plywood. It has fewer voids, stays flatter, and is more consistent in thickness than construction plywood. It's perfect for making custom cabinets and built-ins.

Most home centers stock hardwood plywood in birch and oak, in full and half sheets, and in ¼" and ¾" thicknesses. Cherry and walnut can usually be ordered.

3 ATTACH SEAT TO STUDS

For convenience, you can apply a coat of finish to the seat box before installing it.

- Locate and mark the wall studs behind the seat.
- Where necessary, add wood shims between the seat cabinet and the wall.
- Drive 3" drywall screws through the seat cabinet and shims into the wall studs.

4 APPLY MOLDING AND TRIM

Use a variety of molding to conceal the plywood edges and screws and to cover gaps at the walls and floors.

- Cut and apply a base molding. It can (but need not) match the existing base molding in the room.
- Nail on L-shaped corner trim (available in oak and pine at most home centers) at the outside corners *(inset)*.
- Use thin, flat strips of matching wood molding to conceal the gap between the seat and the wall.
- Fill all nail holes with putty.

5 CUT PLYWOOD FOR SEAT

The seat is also made from plywood, but you can use lesser-quality material if you have it. Half-inch-thick plywood would be adequate, but I prefer ¾"-thick.

- Cut the seat so it overhangs the cabinet about ¼" on all exposed sides.
- Place the plywood seat on the cabinet, and scribe it to fit the walls if necessary.
- Cover the seat with a foam cushion and fabric, or have an upholsterer do the job.
- To keep the seat from sliding, nail wood blocks to its bottom. Set them in from the edges to fit just inside the cabinet.

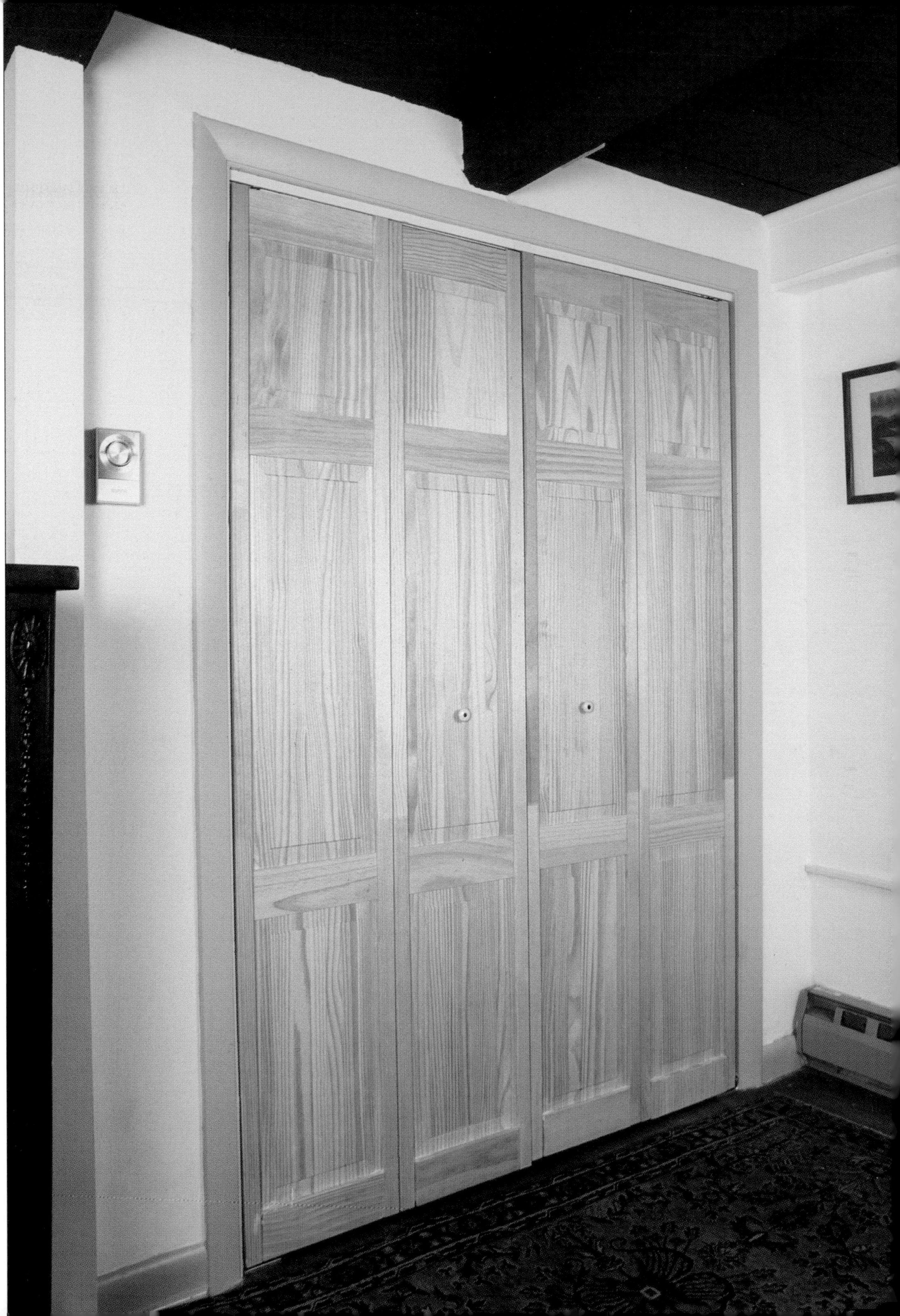

Installing Bifold Doors

These handy doors conceal closet contents when closed— and tuck out of the way when open.

Doors are doors, pretty much— they just haven't changed that much over the centuries. But one legitimate wrinkle is the bifold. Think of it as a single door that's sawed down the middle, then pieced back together with hinges. With its outer edge sliding along in an overhead track, this halved door folds neatly out of the way, rather than swinging out into the room. A single bifold can be used for a small opening, but the typical application is to mount a pair over a closet-sized opening.

Because they hang from above, bifolds tend to be made light in weight. They aren't as sturdy as standard doors, and you don't often see them between rooms. I recommend bifolds for storage areas where homeowners expect the doors to be open a lot of the time—to get at filing cabinets or a washer and dryer, for example.

One of the most familiar styles is the louvered door, but the project shown here uses a frame-and-panel model. You can find a hybrid, with frame-and-panel below and louvers above. And many home centers now carry bifolds with fancy etched-glass panes.

Tools

Tape measure
Phillips-head and flat-head
  screwdrivers
Electric drill and twist bits
Claw hammer
Putty knife

Materials

Bifold door(s)
Wood putty
Wood strips to fill hinge
  mortises (if necessary)

Preparation

Check that the opening is square—bifolds hang from tracks, and they may not operate properly if the opening is substantially out of plumb.

Bifolds come in a standard height—sized for an 80" opening—and in several widths. Measure at both the top and the bottom of the opening with a tape measure.

To fit doors to an opening of slightly less-than-standard height, you may be able to saw off small amounts from the top and/or bottom of each door, then bore new holes for the mounting hardware.

To fit doors to an opening that is slightly too wide, use pine strips to build out from the jambs on either side.

If the bifold doors you buy are unfinished, I suggest applying paint or varnish to them before mounting.

LEVEL OF DIFFICULTY
Easy

TIME REQUIREMENT
½ day

COST ESTIMATE
$125 to $200 for 2 bifolds

WALLS

1 REMOVE OLD DOORS

For openings where there is no existing door, skip to Step 2; otherwise you'll need to remove the old doors.

• Unscrew the hinges and remove the old doors. To fill in the hinge mortises in the jamb, see Ron's Pro Tips below.

• Remove any catches used to secure the doors, and putty the holes.

Ron's PRO TIPS

Filling Hinge Mortises

When you switch from conventionally hinged doors to bifolds, you're usually left looking at the mortises in the door frame where the hinges were. There happens to be a handy household object that will fill these gaps, and one that costs nothing—the familiar paint stirring stick. A length of it can be sawed off with a hacksaw (the small teeth make a tidy job of it) and then fit into place. Attach this plug with a thin layer of woodworking glue, and hold it in place with pushpins pressed firmly at its upper and lower edges until the glue has set. Then putty any cracks, allow the putty to dry, and sand the plug flush with the door trim. Stain or paint the plugs to match the trim.

2 ADD HARDWARE TO THE DOORS

Unlike a hinged door, a bifold is anchored at one point along the bottom and at two points along the top.

• With light blows of a hammer, tap the door's mounting hardware into the holes bored for them in the ends.

• Drill holes for the doorknobs and mount each one; the standard position for the knob is 36" from the floor, centered on the door panel.

3 INSTALL TRACK

The bifold's movement is guided by an overhead track.

- Hold the track in place and mark the doorjamb through the screw holes. Note that the track may need to be set out from the door stop so that the bifolds can move freely; check the manufacturer's installation instructions.

- Drill pilot holes in the frame where you marked. Slip door-mounting hardware into the tracks as directed, then attach the track with the screws provided.

4 ADD LOWER MOUNTING PLATES

- Position the bottom mounting plates provided in both lower corners, placing them the same distance out from the door stop as the track above. Mark for screw holes.

- Drill the holes, and drive the screws provided to mount the plates.

5 INSTALL DOORS

- Lift each door into place, engaging all three points at which it is mounted. On some models the top pivot pin is spring-loaded to make it easy to insert into the track hardware.

- Tighten the setscrew to anchor the door's top pivot. Or on some versions, you'll tighten the lower mounting pin to lock the door in place.

- Close the doors, checking for an even gap all around, including where the doors meet. Reposition as necessary to avoid binding.

SMARTEN UP — YEPSEN

A Faux Wall Finish

Paint walls with a sponge for special effects.

When you apply paint with a brush or roller, your goal is perfection. Consistency and evenness are everything. That's why sponging takes a little getting used to—and why it can be so much fun. It is an inexact craft, one that encourages you to experiment and find your own personal style. Once you see how quick and easy sponging is, I predict you'll have to restrain yourself from using this treatment on every surface in the house.

If the effect is to look natural, you need a genuine sea sponge with its random holes, big and little. Ordinary cellulose sponges are too uniform for good results. You can find the natural type at painting stores and home centers, along with cans of the colorless glaze used to add depth and texture to these finishes.

In the sponging technique shown here, there are two steps. The first is additive—you smear the paint over the wall with one sponge. The other is subtractive—you lift off some of the paint with a second sponge, creating a subtle pattern. For a simpler one-step technique, see Ron's Pro Tips on page 167.

Tools

Large natural sponges (2)
Paint tray
Bucket
Plastic cups for measuring
Disposable rubber gloves
Putty knife
Small artist's brush

Materials

Painter's masking tape
Drop cloths or newspapers
Disposable container
Latex wall paint
Latex glaze
Rags or old towels
Paintable caulk, or spackling compound and mesh tape
Primer

Preparation

Clean the walls with soap and water if they have been subjected to grease and dirt.

Patch thin cracks with paintable caulk, and wider cracks with spackling compound and mesh tape. Spot-prime the patched areas.

Practice the technique on posterboard or drywall scraps that have been rolled with wall paint.

Consider having a helper apply the paint, to allow you to use the second sponge before the paint can dry and become difficult to lift off.

LEVEL OF DIFFICULTY
Easy

TIME REQUIREMENT
½ day

COST ESTIMATE
For a small room, $30 for paint and glaze, and $10 for sponges

WALLS

1 MASK THE TRIM AND CEILING

This painting technique requires you to work freely and boldly, so do a good job of covering areas that aren't to be painted.

- Use wide strips of painter's masking tape; it won't lift paint from adjacent surfaces.
- Remove cover plates from outlets and light switches. Turn off the power to the room before sponging.
- Place a drop cloth or newspapers on the floor along the walls.

2 PREPARE PAINT MIXTURE

Although you can apply latex paint right out of the can, I like to mix in some latex glaze—it's an additive that adds depth and sheen to the paint. Glaze can be found in the paint section in most home centers.

- Use see-through disposable drinking cups to measure quantities; indicate levels on their sides as necessary with a permanent marker.
- In a disposable container, mix equal amounts of paint, glaze, and water. Stir this well.
- Pour a small amount of the mixture over the bottom of a paint tray.

3 DIP THE SPONGE

- Prepare both sponges by soaking in water and then removing any sand and shells that may be trapped in them.
- Squeeze the sponges well.
- Put on rubber gloves and dip one of the sponges into the paint.

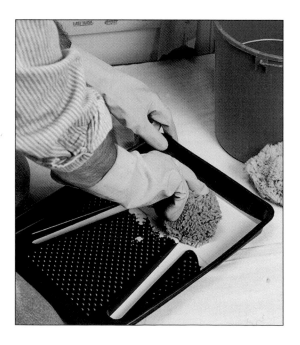

WALLS

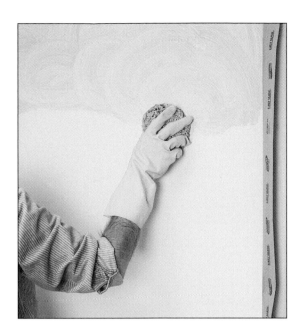

4 APPLY PAINT

- Beginning at the top of the wall, use the sponge to apply a thin layer of paint with varied, sweeping movements.
- Work downward in an area as wide as you can comfortably reach while standing in one place.
- Push the sponge into corners to make sure they get painted.

5 LIFT OFF PAINT

As soon as you've applied an area of paint, go over it with the second sponge.

- Work down from the top of the wall, pressing the sponge into the wet paint and lifting off. Keep turning the sponge for a natural-looking variation.
- Rinse the sponge frequently in a bucket of water, squeezing it well each time.
- Lift off the tape. Touch up around the edges with a small artist's brush dipped in the paint mixture.
- Flat- or drab-looking areas can be perked up by dipping a sponge in the paint mixture, blotting the excess on newspaper, then applying the paint as described in Ron's Pro Tips at right.

Ron's
PRO TIPS

Two-Color Sponging

For a one-step finish, you can simply dip a damp sponge in a shallow layer of the paint, glaze, and water mixture; remove any excess by blotting on newspaper; and lightly press the sponge onto the wall. This creates a highly textured-looking finish, and you may be happy with it. But here's a way to give walls a subtle, opalescent depth. Sponge on two (or more) colors with relatively the same value—that is, the same degree of lightness or darkness. For the wall shown here, I chose variations of the same color—one

"warm" and the other somewhat "cool." To ensure that the colors blend well together, I mixed a little of one in the other. I sponged on the warm paint first, allowing some of the white wall to show through. When that coat dried, I sponged on the cooler paint. Make sure you rotate the sponge each time you pat the wall with it, or you'll get a repetitive pattern that draws attention to itself.

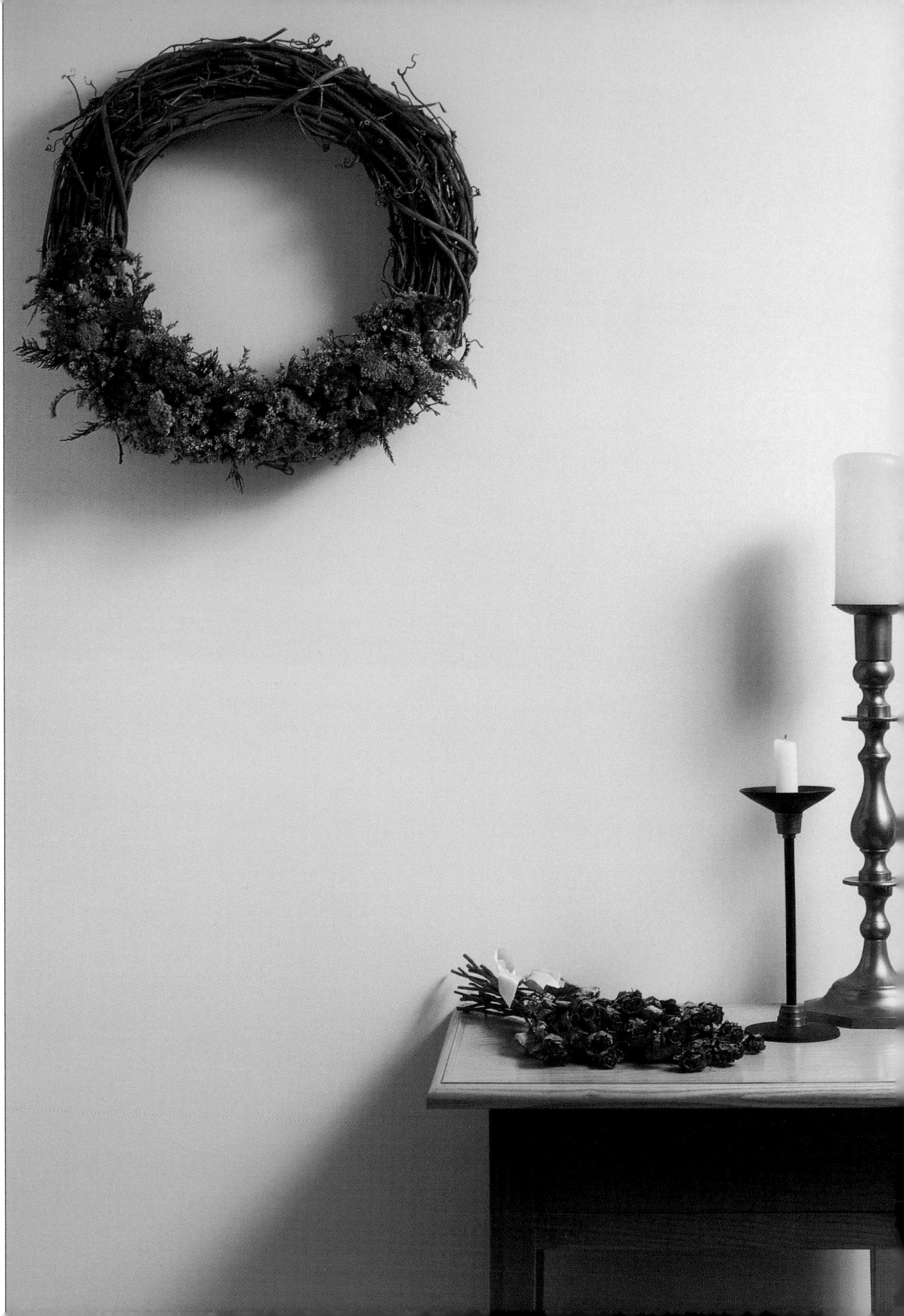

Finishing Off a Basement Wall

Applying drywall to basement walls can turn a dark and dank space into a bright and cheerful room.

Converting the basement into a usable space is one of the most common projects that I get calls about. There are a lot of variables to consider, but the first issue to look at is moisture: Is the basement relatively dry, or does it take in water through the walls or floor when the ground outside gets wet? If you do get water in the basement, there's no point doing any finish work until you solve the moisture problem. Consult a basement waterproofing specialist for ideas on eliminating water seepage.

Even if you never see water on the walls or floor, most basements tend to be very damp, which promotes mold and mildew on furniture and building materials. This project shows you how to finish basement walls with drywall, and at the same time reduce the moisture infiltration through the walls. So even if you don't plan to finish off the space completely with a finished floor and ceiling, you can still make it a drier and brighter space with painted drywall.

Tools

Electric drill and twist bits
Masonry bit sized for concrete screws
3' or 4' level and straightedge or drywall T-square
Staple gun
Utility knife
6" and either 10" or 12" drywall knives
Chalk line
Paint roller and tray

Materials

½" drywall panels
2" concrete screws
⅜" heavy-duty staples
1¼" drywall screws
Carpenter's shims
1×3 furring strips
¾"-thick foil-faced rigid insulation
Plastic vapor barrier
Drywall compound and tape
100-grit sandpaper
Paint

Preparation

To determine how many sheets of drywall and furring strips you'll need, first measure the perimeter of the section you're planning on finishing. Then for every 4' of width, you'll need one sheet of drywall and roughly four furring strips (this assumes a ceiling height of less than 8').

LEVEL OF DIFFICULTY
Moderate

TIME REQUIREMENT
2 to 4 days

COST ESTIMATE
$350 to $500 for a small basement

WALLS

1 SCREW FURRING STRIPS TO WALL

- Measure and cut the furring strips to length. It's best to raise them off the floor ½" in case of water seepage along the floor-to-wall area.
- Hold a furring strip in place (use a level to make sure it's plumb), and drill holes spaced roughly 16" apart through it and into the wall with a masonry bit *(inset)*.
- Drive the screws (hardened concrete screws only) with a screw gun or an electric drill/driver.

2 SHIM FURRING STRIPS

Basement walls are rarely flat, so you'll need to add shims to create a flat plane.

- Start with a strip closest to a corner, and use a long level to check that it's plumb. If you don't have a long level, hold a smaller level on a straight-edged board.
- Work out from the corner, making the other strips even with the first strip as well as possible by inserting shims between the furring strips and the wall.

3 ADD INSULATION AND VAPOR BARRIER

Rigid foil-faced insulation panels will add a small R-value (resistance to heat loss), and a plastic vapor barrier will minimize moisture penetration.

- Cut the insulation panels with a utility knife for a press-fit between the furring strips.
- Roll out the plastic vapor barrier and staple it to the furring strips, working from the top down. Use as few staples as possible.

4 CUT DRYWALL

- Measure and mark the face of the drywall. Plan to shim the drywall off the floor ½"; then if the floor ever does get wet, the drywall won't get damaged.

- Using a straightedge or drywall T-square, make a scoring cut along the marked line with a utility knife. You only need to cut through the paper facing.

- Snap the cutoff piece of drywall toward the back of the panel. The paper backing will act like a hinge. With the cutoff held at 90 degrees to the main piece of drywall, slice through the paper backing with the utility knife.

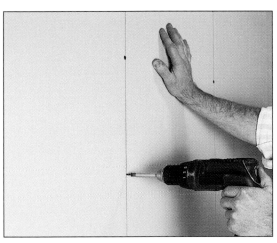

5 SCREW DRYWALL TO FURRING STRIPS

- Snap chalk lines on the drywall panels at each furring strip, except along the edges.

- Drive 1¼" drywall screws through the drywall and into the furring strips. The screw heads should sit below the surface of the drywall slightly—just make sure not to break through the face paper.

- Space the screws every 8" to 10".

6 TAPE AND FINISH THE DRYWALL

Finishing drywall isn't difficult, but it is messy. If you're not up for the dust and mess, hire a professional finisher after you've hung the drywall yourself.

- Apply a 3"-wide layer of drywall compound into the shallow trough formed where two sheets of drywall meet. Then press in a strip of drywall tape, and apply a thin coat of compound over the tape.

- Fill all the screw holes with compound.

- After the first layer dries (24 hours), scrape off any ridges with a 6"-wide knife and then apply a layer of compound with a 10"-wide knife at the joints *(inset)*.

- Sand smooth when dry, and then paint the walls.

Installing Simple Shelves

It takes just a few hours to install versatile, adjustable shelves on any wall in your home.

The request for shelving is something I commonly hear from homeowners—decorative shelves, utility shelves, shelves for books, shelves for toys. Every room in the house seems like it can use another shelf or two. The good news is that putting up shelving is one of the easiest projects you can tackle.

There are several types of ready-made shelving to choose from. The most versatile is the standard-and-bracket system. Two or more metal standards (thin, slotted channels) are mounted vertically on the wall, and adjustable brackets of various sizes are locked into the slots. The brackets hold the shelves.

This system is strong, adjustable, and available in a variety of finishes. Most retailers sell matching shelves, which are typically melamine-coated particleboard. Or you can supply shelves of your own choice. The light-duty standards and brackets are suitable for most household storage needs, while heavy-duty varieties for the shop or garage can be found at more specialized hardware stores.

Tools

Rubber mallet
Tape measure
3' level
Claw hammer
Electric drill and twist bits
Phillips-head and flat-head screwdrivers

Materials

Shelving standards and shelf brackets
Shelves
Mounting screws (if not provided)
Hollow wall anchors (if necessary)

Preparation

Clear off the wall where the shelves will go.

Patch any holes with spackling compound.

LEVEL OF DIFFICULTY
Easy

TIME REQUIREMENT
½ day

COST ESTIMATE
$30 to $100, depending on the number of shelves

1 LOCATE WALL STUDS

Ideally, you want to anchor one or more of the standards directly to wall studs. Where the standard does not align with a stud, use hollow wall anchors *(see Choosing Materials on the opposite page).*

- If you don't have a stud finder *(see page 64)*, tap the wall gently with a rubber mallet to find a stud location. The sound will change from hollow to solid.

- Measure in each direction from the stud to confirm stud spacing—typically 16" on center for interior walls.

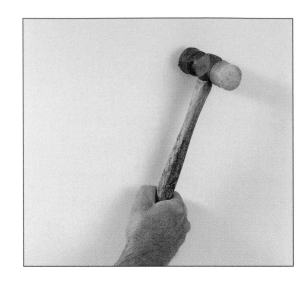

2 POSITION FIRST STANDARD

It doesn't matter which standard in a group you mount first—the left, right, or middle.

- Consider how high and low you'll want any of the adjustable shelves, and position the standard accordingly.

- Hold a level against the edge of the standard and position it plumb.

- Mark lightly along the edge of the standard with a pencil *(inset).*

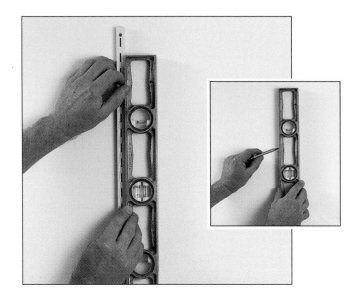

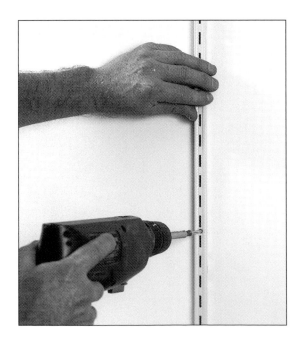

3 SCREW FIRST STANDARD TO WALL

- Hold the standard on the mark and drive screws through the mounting holes in the standard into a stud or hollow-wall anchor. (The screws may or may not be supplied with the standards.)

- Drive in one screw, then double-check that the standard is plumb before driving in the remaining screws.

4 MARK FOR SUBSEQUENT STANDARDS

In order for the shelves to be even and level, each of the standards must be mounted at exactly the same level.

* Hold a level against the bottom edge of the mounted standard, and make a level mark where the next standard will be located.
* Repeat Steps 2 and 3.
* Make sure the standards are positioned uniformly—most have a directional arrow indicating the "up" end.

5 INSTALL BRACKETS AND SHELVES

You can mount as many brackets and shelves as you like on a set of standards.

* Tap the brackets securely into the standards with a mallet or hammer.
* Make sure brackets for each shelf are at the same level.
* Place the shelves on the brackets and adjust them so they're centered *(inset)*.
* To remove a bracket, tap sharply up on the bottom edge, close to the standard.

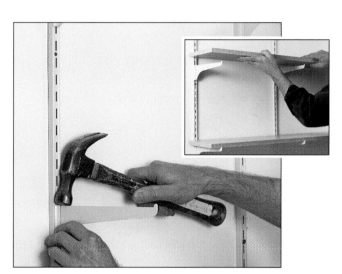

CHOOSING
Materials

Hollow-Wall Anchors

When you can't secure shelving standards to wall studs, use one of the following hollow-wall anchors: *(shown left to right)* plastic inserts, self-tapping aluminum inserts, "Molly" bolts, and toggle bolts.

* Plastic inserts are the least expensive and work for light-duty applications. Simply drill a hole so the insert is snug, tap it in with a ham-

mer, and drive in a screw.
* Self-tapping aluminum inserts can be driven right into drywall without first drilling holes. Then you can screw directly into them.
* Expanding Molly bolts are inserted into a hole that you first drill in the wall. A machine screw driven into the insert forces wings on the back side of the wall to expand. Molly bolts work well but are size-specific—each is designed for a specific wall thickness.
* Toggle bolts are

one of the strongest anchors, but they require a relatively large hole to pass the spring-loaded wings through. Once inserted through the drywall, the wings spring open and a machine screw pulls the wings tightly against the back face of the drywall.

Resilient Sheet Flooring 178

Installing a "Floating"
Laminate Floor 186

Installing Floor Tiles 192

Refinishing
a Wood Floor 198

Installing Ceramic Tile 202

Installing
Wood Strip Flooring 208

Installing
Wall-to-Wall Carpeting 214

FLOORS

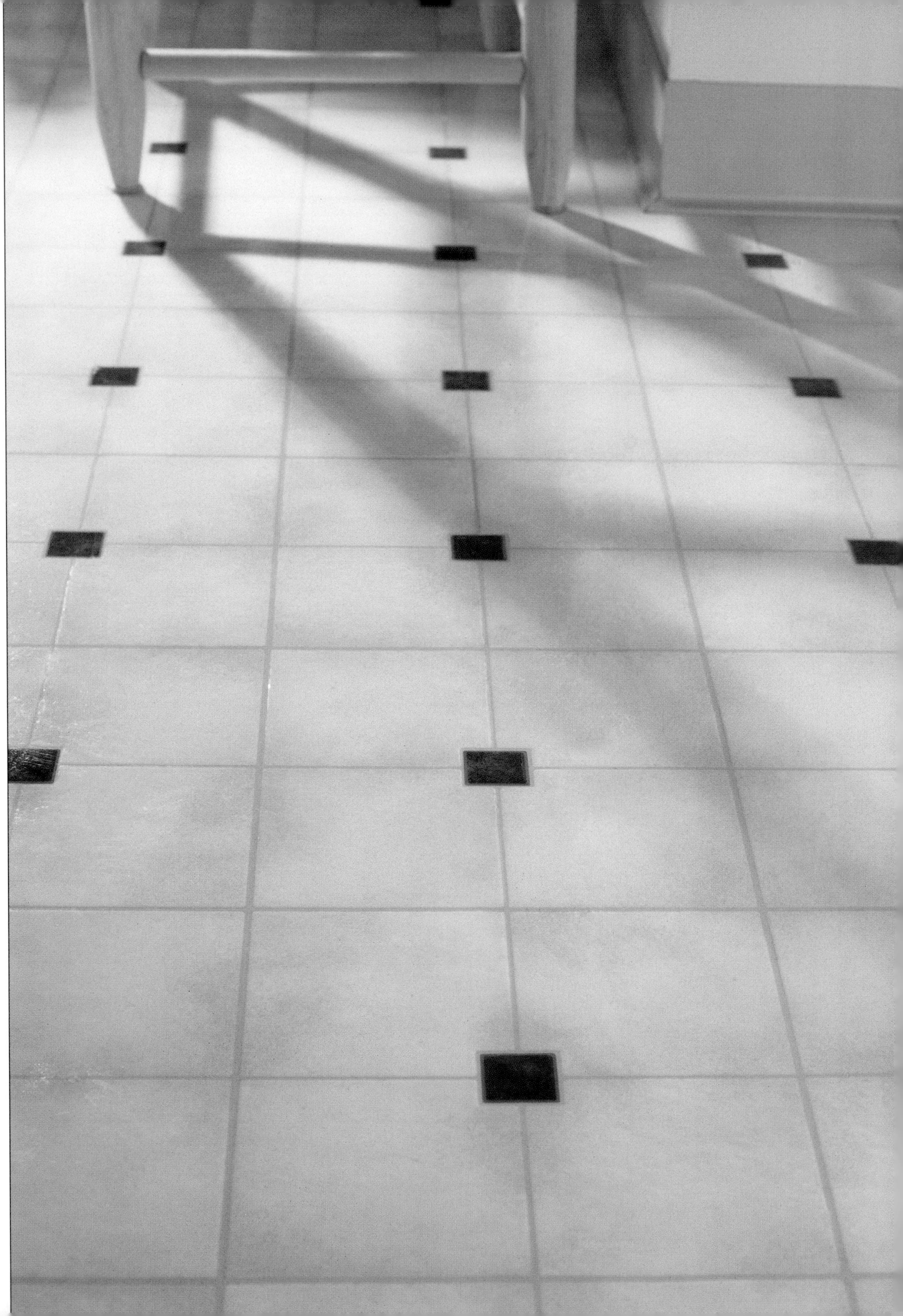

Resilient Sheet Flooring

Resilient sheet flooring is easy to clean and durable: the perfect choice for high-traffic areas.

Most resilient flooring is made of vinyl. Compared to ceramic tile and even wood, vinyl floors are a little softer underfoot. On the down side, this feature makes some grades of vinyl flooring susceptible to denting from sharp impacts, like a dropped can, or even from high-heeled shoes.

Resilient flooring comes in 6' and 12' widths, so you can often do a whole room without any seams. But working with 12' rolls of vinyl requires two people, so don't plan on tackling a large room installation by yourself. Even the pros sometimes choose to work with the smaller 6' rolls and make a center seam, because it's easier to fit the pieces at the walls.

More important than 6' versus 12' is the distinction between perimeter-glued and overall-glued floors. I recommend only a perimeter-glued vinyl floor for the do-it-yourselfer and would leave the completely glued floors to a professional installer.

Tools

Claw hammer or pry bar
Nail set
Tape measure
Chalk line
Wide putty knife
Utility knife
Framing square or straightedge
Compass
Heavy-duty stapler
Notched trowel
Mason's trowel
Laminate roller or wide chisel
Rolling pin or seam roller

Materials

Leveling compound
Kraft paper or building paper
Masking tape
Resilient flooring
Adhesive (the type depends on if the floor being covering is porous [wood subfloor] or nonporous [existing vinyl or linoleum floor])
3/8" staples
Vinyl cove base or wood trim
Cove base adhesive
1¼" finish nails

Preparation

Resilient flooring can be laid over most subfloors, including vinyl and concrete, but the surface must be structurally sound and smooth.

If the floor squeaks in areas, now is a good time to screw through the subfloor into the joists. Just be sure to drive the screws in far enough so they don't protrude above the surface of the existing floor.

LEVEL OF DIFFICULTY
Moderate to Challenging

TIME REQUIREMENT
2 to 3 days

COST ESTIMATE
$4 per square yard and up

1 REMOVE THE FLOOR TRIM

- For vinyl trim, wedge a wide putty knife behind the top edge of the trim and slide it along as you pull the trim away from the wall. This will prevent the paint from pulling away behind the trim.
- On wood trim, use the claw on a hammer or a pry bar to coax the trim from the wall, but place a piece of protective wood against the wall where you pry.

2 APPLY LEVELING COMPOUND

Leveling compound should be applied anywhere there is a break in the existing floor surface. Choose a cement-based leveling compound. It's available premixed or in a powder-and-liquid combination that you mix yourself. If you're laying new flooring over existing flooring, examine it carefully for areas that are lifting or cracked.

- Cut old loose flooring away with a utility knife. Then fill these gaps with leveling compound. Also fill any dents caused by the feet of appliances.
- If it's a new subfloor, apply a thin layer of leveling compound at the seams.

3 APPLY LEVELING TO SEAM AREA

Some manufacturers suggest a thin coat of leveling compound be applied under the seam area to ensure a strong bond.

- Determine where the seam will fall, and strike a chalk line.
- Cover a 9" to 12" area centered on the chalk line with leveling compound.
- If your existing flooring is highly embossed, you may need to cover the entire floor with leveling or embossing compound to prevent the existing pattern from telegraphing through to the new floor—check your installation instructions.

4 MAKE TEMPLATE OF FIRST WALL

Select the wall with the most irregularities, and make a template of that edge on kraft paper. Tape smaller pieces together to get a continuous piece the length of the wall.

- Lay the paper on the floor as close to the wall as possible, and tape the template paper to the floor.

- Use a square to transfer the straight sections of the wall to the template. The outside edge of the square represents the wall, while the inside edge represents the offset. By working in relatively short sections, the framing square registers the small irregularities found in most walls.

- Use a compass to transfer obstacles, like a pipe; open the compass to equal the offset of the framing square (*inset*).

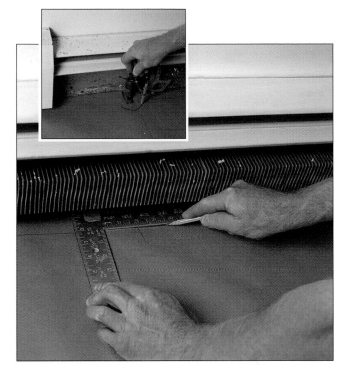

5 CUT THE FIRST EDGE

The floor shown is made up of two 6'-wide sections with a seam down the middle. If you're working with a single, wider piece, mark and cut the opposite wall only after you've cut and test the fit of the first wall.

- Lay out the flooring; tape the template to it so the cut you'll make will fall where you want it on the flooring pattern.

- With the inside edge of the straightedge on the pattern line, cut along the outside edge of the straightedge.

- Transfer the shapes you made with a compass to the flooring, and cut these with a utility knife (*inset*).

- Check the fit of the edge to the wall.

- Cut the seam edge on the first piece. With a straightedge, cut along a grout line (if applicable).

FLOORS

6 APPLY ADHESIVE TO SELECT AREAS

When installing perimeter flooring (as shown here), adhesive is applied only at the perimeter where staples would show, at high-traffic areas (such as door thresholds), at areas cut out around pipes, and at the seam (this is done later; see Step 12).

- Apply a 3" band of adhesive with the recommended trowel.

- Leave at least 6" unglued near the seam so the flooring can be pulled back later when gluing the seam.

7 SECURE FLOORING WITH DIRECT PRESSURE

In perimeter areas where the floor will not be covered by trim of some kind (like doorways), and on concrete floors, you'll need to apply pressure to help the adhesive bond.

- Use a wide chisel or a laminate roller (*see page 31*) to press the flooring down. Note: Make sure the edges of the chisel are smooth, or place a rag under it.

8 SECURE FLOORING WITH STAPLES

Along perimeter areas that will be covered by floor trim, cabinetry, etc., you can secure the flooring with staples.

- Use a heavy-duty stapler with ³⁄₈"-long staples

- Fasten the flooring in place with a staple every 3".

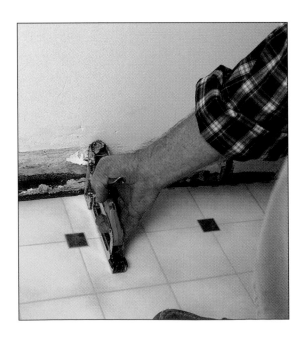

9 MAKE TEMPLATE TO MATCH DESIGN PATTERN

The purpose of making a template for the second piece is to ensure that the pattern matches perfectly along the seamed edge.

- Lay down a strip of kraft paper adjacent to and running the exact length of the first piece.

- Transfer two or three of the grout lines and pattern marks (on this floor, the dark squares) from the first piece onto the paper template.

10 MATCH DESIGN ON SECOND PIECE

- Position the template on the second piece so the pattern marks line up with the pattern on the flooring. On patterns with light grout lines, it's helpful to mark the lines as shown to make it easier to position the template.

- Tape the template in place and then cut the second piece to length to match the first piece.

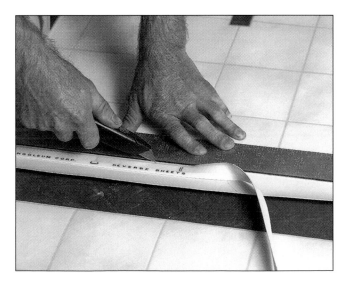

11 CUT SEAM EDGE ON SECOND PIECE

Before you cut the seam on the second piece, it's important to choose the grout line (if applicable) that will ensure a consistent pattern on both sides of the seam.

- Remove the template and then cut the seam edge on the second piece as you did on the first piece.

FLOORS

12 APPLY ADHESIVE TO SEAM AREA

- Fold back at least 6" of each piece of flooring at the seam.
- Make sure there is no dirt or debris on the subfloor in the seam area.
- Apply a 6" swath of adhesive.

TOOL
KNOW-HOW

Vinyl Flooring Seam Rollers

Flooring contractors use a special roller to press down the seams in a vinyl floor. It's not something you'll most likely find at the local hardware store.

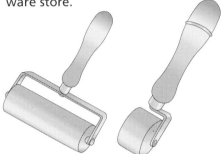

A good substitute is a wallpaper seam roller (*right*). It has a wooden wheel that's sure to make good contact with the whole seam. You can find one at better paint and wallpaper stores. A similar roller used for pressing wood veneer seams can be found in woodworking supply catalogs or stores. A slightly wider roller used for applying ink (*left*) has a hard rubber wheel that also works well. You can find them at art supply stores.

Whichever roller you use, be sure to apply hard, consistent pressure along the seam.

13 ROLL THE SEAM

- Press the seam area down by hand and examine the seam.
- Where there are gaps in the seam, coax the flooring pieces together with finger pressure, then apply a piece of masking tape. The tape will hold the seam closed while the adhesive grabs.
- Apply pressure to the entire seam area with a roller—wooden rolling pins work, but seam rollers are best (*see above*).

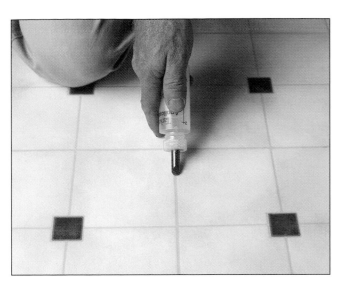

14 APPLY SEAM SEALER

Seams in vinyl flooring need to be sealed to prevent water and dirt from sneaking in and breaking the adhesive bond.

- Follow the instructions on the sealer—you usually need to wait a specific time after you've glued the floor down before applying the seam sealer.

- Run the seam sealer applicator carefully along the seam, applying a consistent amount of the sealer as you go.

- Allow the sealer to dry (typically 24 hours) before walking on the seam.

Ron's PRO TIPS

Appliance Movers

Kitchens present a special problem when you're installing a new vinyl floor: How do you move the appliances over the new floor without damaging it? Whatever you do—DON'T attempt to slide appliances over a new vinyl floor! Especially if the floor is glued only at the perimeter, the material will buckle and most certainly tear.

Appliance companies have solved this problem with flat sheets of ultra-smooth plastic, called appliance movers, on which appliances can be easily and safely slid into position. You should be able to rent or borrow them from an appliance

dealer or moving company for a couple of hours. You'll also need two or more strips of 1/8" or 1/4" smooth plywood.

Here's how to use them: Lift each side of the appliance enough to slip one of the movers under. Next, lay down the strips of plywood in the path of travel on the new floor. Pull the ends of the movers, and have a helper push the appliance. Once it's in place, remove the plywood strips and the plastic movers, one side at a time.

15 REAPPLY THE TRIM

Vinyl cove base and wood trim are two good ways to hide the staples around the perimeter.

- Use cove base adhesive to apply vinyl cove base.

- Nail wood trim in place with 1¼" finish nails, and countersink the nail heads.

Installing a "Floating" Laminate Floor

Laminate flooring is as easy to install as it is great looking.

Flooring made with a plastic laminate face marks a revolution in the flooring industry, especially for the do-it-yourself homeowner. It's easy to install compared with other flooring materials and can be laid on top of any existing floor, even on a concrete slab. I readily suggest it to those who want to do the job themselves.

Laminate flooring needs no finish and virtually no upkeep. And because the surface you walk on is made the same way that plastic laminate countertops are made, the available designs go far beyond wood grains to include simulated marble, tile, and stone, as well as colorful "artificial" surfaces that can brighten any room.

Laminate floor systems are called "floating" floors because the material is not attached to the subfloor or slab underneath in any way. No nails or screws, and no adhesive holds the floor down to the subfloor or slab. Instead, the laminate panels have tongue-and-groove edges that are glued together. You end up with a single panel the size of the entire floor, which rests on a thin layer of foam.

Finally, each of the flooring manufacturers provides an installation kit that includes all the necessary tools and accessories for a successful installation. Installing a new floor could hardly be easier.

Tools

Tape measure
Combination or quick square
Utility knife
Claw hammer
Nail set
Hand or trim saw
Plastic putty knife
Installation kit tools for tightening joints (purchase with flooring material)
Floor clamps (can be rented)

Materials

Foam underlayment
Packing tape
Shims (scraps of ¼"-thick wood)
Laminate flooring
Clean rags
Glue (specific to flooring)
Wood trim
1¼" finish nails
Leveling compound (optional)

Preparation

Make sure the existing floor or subfloor is clean and relatively level. Fill low spots with leveling compound (*see page 180*). Set any protruding nail heads with a nail set, and sand or scrape away any high spots.

LEVEL OF DIFFICULTY
Moderate

TIME REQUIREMENT
2 to 3 days for an average-sized room

COST ESTIMATE
$2 to $5 per square foot

FLOORS

1 LAY OUT STARTER COURSES

Before gluing anything, dry assemble the first three rows. Repeat the pattern you establish here for the remainder of the floor.

- Arrange the end pieces so all the joints are staggered at least 12" apart
- After laying out all the pieces in the first three rows, number the pieces (on masking tape) so you can reassemble them in the same sequence when you apply glue.

2 CUT THE END PANELS

Laminate flooring can be cut with just about any hand or power saw.

- Measure each piece and mark the cut right on the flooring using a combination or quick square.
- Subtract ¼" from the length of any piece that butts up against a wall. This will create a gap that will allow the flooring to expand with seasonal changes.
- When using a hand saw or table saw, cut with the face up. If you're using a circular or saber saw, cut with the face down.

CHOOSING
Materials

Laminate Flooring

Laminate flooring is made by sandwiching a ¼" or ⅜" core of medium-density fiberboard (MDF) between two thin layers of plastic laminate. This forms an extremely stable product that will stay perfectly flat.

I've discovered that most manufacturers produce more than one grade of flooring, and the packages sold in many home centers may not be their best grade. A specialty flooring supplier will be better able to show you the range of products available and also provide comprehensive installation instructions. The primary difference between grades is in the thickness of the top surface laminate; thicker laminates wear longer and resist damage better.

Taking laminate systems to their logical extreme, one manufacturer has developed a product with an edge pro- file that snaps together without glue. This simplifies installation and allows you to unsnap the panels if you make a mistake during installation, or if you need to replace a damaged panel several years later.

FLOORS

3 ROLL OUT THE FOAM UNDERLAYMENT

Cut one strip of foam underlayment for the first three rows. Lay down a second strip only after the first strip of foam is covered.

- On concrete floors, tape the seams of the foam together with polyethylene packing tape.
- On other floors, just butt the strips of foam together, making sure there isn't any overlap.

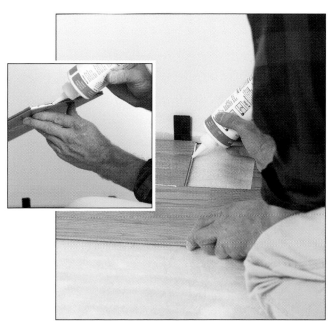

4 APPLY THE GLUE

A good glue bond at every seam makes a laminate floor job successful and long lasting. The best evidence of a good glue joint is a thin bead of glue "squeeze-out" at each joint when the panels are forced together.

- Apply a bead of glue on the top of each tongue.
- Apply glue to the bottom edge of each groove (*inset*).
- Lay panels in the first row so the groove is facing the wall.
- To maintain a consistent gap around the perimeter of the flooring, insert $1/4$"-thick shims between the wall and the flooring.

5 TIGHTEN THE JOINTS

Each installation kit includes a block designed to fit over the edge of the panels so you can tap the panels together, as well as a device to tighten the short cross seams.

- After gluing and assembling each panel, slide the block over the tongue edge and tap the edge of the block with a hammer.
- Tap until you see good glue squeeze-out.
- Go back and check the panels periodically because the joints may open slightly after installing additional panels in a row.
- At the end of each row, use the supplied tool to tighten the cross seams.

FLOORS

6 CLAMP TOGETHER THE FIRST THREE ROWS

The seams between the first few rows are more likely to open up as you assemble one panel to the next. Clamping the first rows provides a solid base so subsequent rows can be glued on without clamps.

- Work quickly to apply glue to all the panels in the first three rows, butting the seams as you go.

- Apply the floor clamps. To prevent the edges of the assembly from lifting, weigh down the clamped assembly with boxes of flooring.

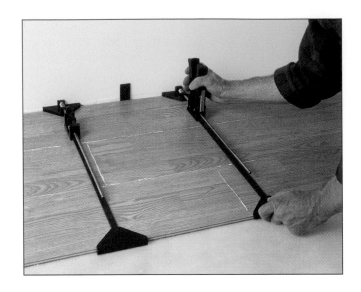

Clamping with Wedges

Ron's PRO TIPS

Theoretically, you won't need any significant pressure to close the seams in a laminate floor after the first three rows are glued and clamped together. But even the smallest gaps can accumulate and magnify until you do have trouble closing a seam. Here's an easy solution: Cut two tapered wedges from scrap wood. Position the wedges opposite one another and lay them against the seam-tightening block, as shown. Screw a scrap of 1 by 2 to the subfloor, trapping the wedges between the scrap and the seam block. Tapping one (or both) of the wedges will force the adjacent seams to close. Leave the wedges in place for a half hour or so while the glue sets up. Then remove the pieces and start the next row.

7 REMOVE EXCESS GLUE

It's important to remove the excess glue as you work. Any residue left will be much harder to remove after it's dry.

- Let the glue squeeze-out set up for about 15 minutes, and then scrape the glue beads off with a plastic putty knife.

- Wipe off any remaining residue with a cloth slightly dampened with warm water, then immediately dry the floor.

- Let the first three rows set in the clamps for a few hours before continuing.

8 FIT PIECES AROUND OBSTACLES

At doorways and other obstacles, cut the flooring to fit. Remember to allow a ¼" gap for expansion where the flooring will be covered by base molding.

- Lay the panel to be cut up against the obstacle, and mark the panel.
- Make the cuts with your choice of saws.
- If you use a saber saw, transfer the cut marks to the underside to avoid chipping the face laminate.

9 UNDERCUT DOOR TRIM

It's easier to cut door trim where it meets the floor, and slide the flooring under it, than it is to notch the flooring around the casing.

- Use a cut-off piece of the flooring as a height guide to make a flush cut with a hand saw.

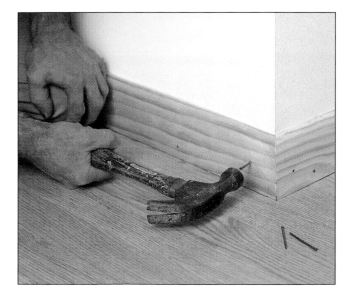

10 APPLY BASE MOLDING

Base molding conceals the expansion gap left at all the walls. Don't press the base molding too hard against the floor.

- Cut the molding to fit, mitering the corners.
- Nail the molding to the sole plate (no more than 1½" from the floor).
- If there are gaps between the base molding and the floor, add a shoe molding; but nail it to the base molding, not to the floor.

Installing Floor Tiles

Tiling is the simplest way to upgrade your kitchen or bathroom floor.

In spite of the innovations in floor coverings, homeowners continue to rely on vinyl floor tiles. These squares are easy to put down—especially the peel-and-stick variety—and a cinch to cut to size. A few years from now, when an area becomes damaged or shows wear, you can replace that spot rather than the entire floor. Just soften the adhesive with a heat gun, then lift the tile with a putty knife. It's a good idea to keep an extra box of tiles on hand for replacements, even if that color or style hasn't been discontinued: New tiles might not quite match your floor.

If the mention of vinyl tiles brings up childhood memories of tacky-looking kitchen floors, it's time to visit a flooring supplier or home center to see what's on the market today. I think you'll be pleased by the selection. You can still find old-fashioned tiles if you want a retro linoleum look to go with your breakfast nook and Fiestaware. But I prefer the subtler shades and patterns that are a break with tradition.

Tools

Tape measure
Framing square
Chalk line
Hand saw (if required)
Electric drill
Vacuum cleaner
Utility knife or tile knife (for cutting vinyl tiles)
Saber saw (for wood tiles)
Notched trowel (for non-adhesive tiles)
Laminate roller or rolling pin

Materials

Plywood underlayment (if required)
1⅝" drywall screws (for underlayment)
Floor tiles
Tile adhesive and masking tape (for nonadhesive tiles)
Adhesive remover
Waterproof caulk
Floor-patching compound

Preparation

To ensure consistency, check that tile boxes have the same pattern and dye lot numbers.

Temporarily remove appliances and baseboards so you can run flooring under them.

Plan on using underlayment if tiles are embossed or coming loose, if the floor is uneven or damaged, or if the subfloor is particleboard or flakeboard.

Fill voids and gaps with floor-patching compound.

LEVEL OF DIFFICULTY
Easy to Moderate

TIME REQUIREMENT
1 day

COST ESTIMATE
$.50 to $1.25 per square foot for self-adhesive tiles, not including underlayment

1 INSTALL UNDERLAYMENT

Optional underlayment is thin (¼" to ⅜") plywood attached to a subfloor to provide a solid surface for finish flooring.

- If adding tiles and/or underlayment to existing flooring, you can saw through the base of door trim so the new flooring will fit under it; use a hand saw elevated to the correct height on scraps of the new materials. For an alternate method, see Ron's Pro Tips on page 197.

- Cut and fit underlayment so that joints will not align with those of the existing subfloor; attach with 1⅝" drywall screws, making sure to countersink the heads.

2 SNAP LAYOUT LINES

- Measure each wall to find its center-point, and make a mark.

- Stretch a chalk line between one pair of opposing center marks; if you don't have a helper, tack a nail into the floor at a mark and attach the string to it.

- Snap the line, then repeat between the other two marks to make a cross in the center of the room.

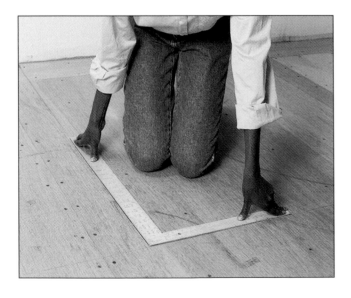

3 CHECK LINES FOR SQUARE

- Use a framing square to check that the chalk lines meet at 90-degree angles.

- Or, mark one line 3' out from the lines' intersection, and mark either adjacent line 4' out. Measure the distance between the two marks; it will be exactly 5' if the lines are perpendicular.

- If the lines are not perpendicular to each other, reposition one of them.

4 DRY-FIT TILES

- Temporarily lay rows of tiles along chalk lines, starting from the center of the room.
- To allow for subfloor expansion, leave a gap of ⅛" to ¼" at walls where it will be concealed by appliances or baseboards.
- Where border tiles along a wall will be subjected to foot traffic or will be highly visible, they should be at least half their original width. If necessary, snap a new chalk line to change the layout of the tiles.

5 VACUUM THE FLOOR

- Go over the floor with a vacuum cleaner to ensure that the tiles will adhere well.
- Make a last check for nail or screw heads that protrude above the surface, and countersink them.
- If you will be using adhesive (for wood or vinyl tiles), protect trim and kickboards with painter's masking tape.

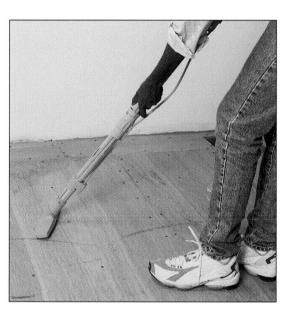

CHOOSING
Materials

Resilient and Prefinished-Wood Tiles

Resilient vinyl tiles are a snap to install, and they make cleanup easy. But some homeowners prefer the warm, traditional look of wood tile (or parquet) floors. These tiles usually require you to lay down adhesive, rather than simply peel off a backing. But they are easier to apply than traditional strip wood flooring. The wood tile shown here incorporates four glued-up squares for quicker installation. Tongue-and-groove edges help lock the tiles together for firmness underfoot. A liability of wood floors is that they will be more vulnerable to damage from water; in the kitchen project on these pages, vinyl tile is being used to replace the room's stained parquet floor.

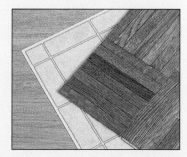

FLOORS

6 BEGIN LAYING TILES

Note that some tiles have directional arrows on the back, indicating how to position them so their patterns will be aligned.

- To lay self-sticking tiles, peel off the paper backing and lightly set the tile in place; don't apply pressure until its position is correct.

- Or, for nonadhesive tiles, use a notched trowel to apply an adhesive recommended by the manufacturer.

- Install a first row of tiles along a chalk line, beginning at the center of the room.

- In the same way, install a second row along a chalk line perpendicular to the first.

7 ROLL THE TILES

- Complete one-fourth of the room, filling in the tiles between the two initial rows.

- For nonadhesive tiles, work from a piece of plywood placed over the tiles you've installed to avoid moving them out of alignment.

- To help the tiles adhere, go over them with either a laminate roller *(see Tool Know-How on page 31)* or an ordinary kitchen rolling pin.

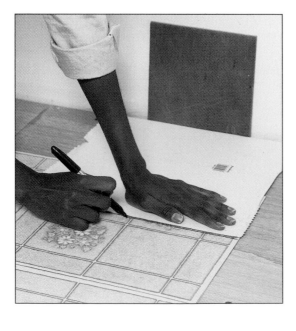

8 CUT BORDER TILES

- Place a ¼"-thick spacer along the wall so the border tile will leave a gap.

- Position the border tile, right side up, on top of the installed tile closest to the wall.

- Place a guide tile (shown wrong side up) on the border tile, and press it flush against the plywood spacer.

- Trace along the guide tile to mark a cut line on the border tile.

- For vinyl tiles, use a utility or tile knife to cut along the line, working where the blade won't harm the flooring. For wood tiles, use a saber saw.

9 CUT TILES AT OUTSIDE CORNERS

- Use thin cardboard to cut a pattern for an L-shaped tile at an outside corner.
- Allow a gap of ⅛" to ¼" along walls if it will be concealed.
- After cutting the pattern to fit the space, trace it onto a tile and cut with a utility or tile knife.

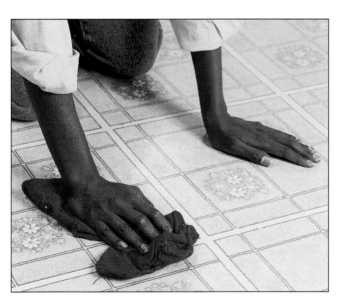

10 FINISH INSTALLATION

- Remove any adhesive from the tiles with a rag that has been dampened with a solvent specified by the manufacturer.
- Use an appropriately colored waterproof caulk to seal around bathroom fixtures and molding.
- To make sure the tiles adhere well, do not subject the floor to traffic or heavy objects for at least a day, or as directed by the adhesive or tile manufacturer.
- Reinstall appliances and baseboards.

Ron's PRO TIPS

Scribing Tiles

Vinyl floor tiles go down fast—until you reach the edges of the room, where border tiles have to be cut to fit irregular outlines. Every tradesperson I know favors a certain way to transfer the outline of trim to the tiles. A contour gauge is a handy gadget with metal fingers that slide to copy the shape; you then trace along the fingers onto a tile. Another solution is to trace around the trim with a compass holding a fine-tip permanent marker; as  the metal point follows the outline, the pen marks the tile. Simpler still, bend a length of solder to conform to the outline, then transfer this shape onto the tile as shown. Cut vinyl tile with a utility or tile knife; to cut wood tiles, use a saber saw.

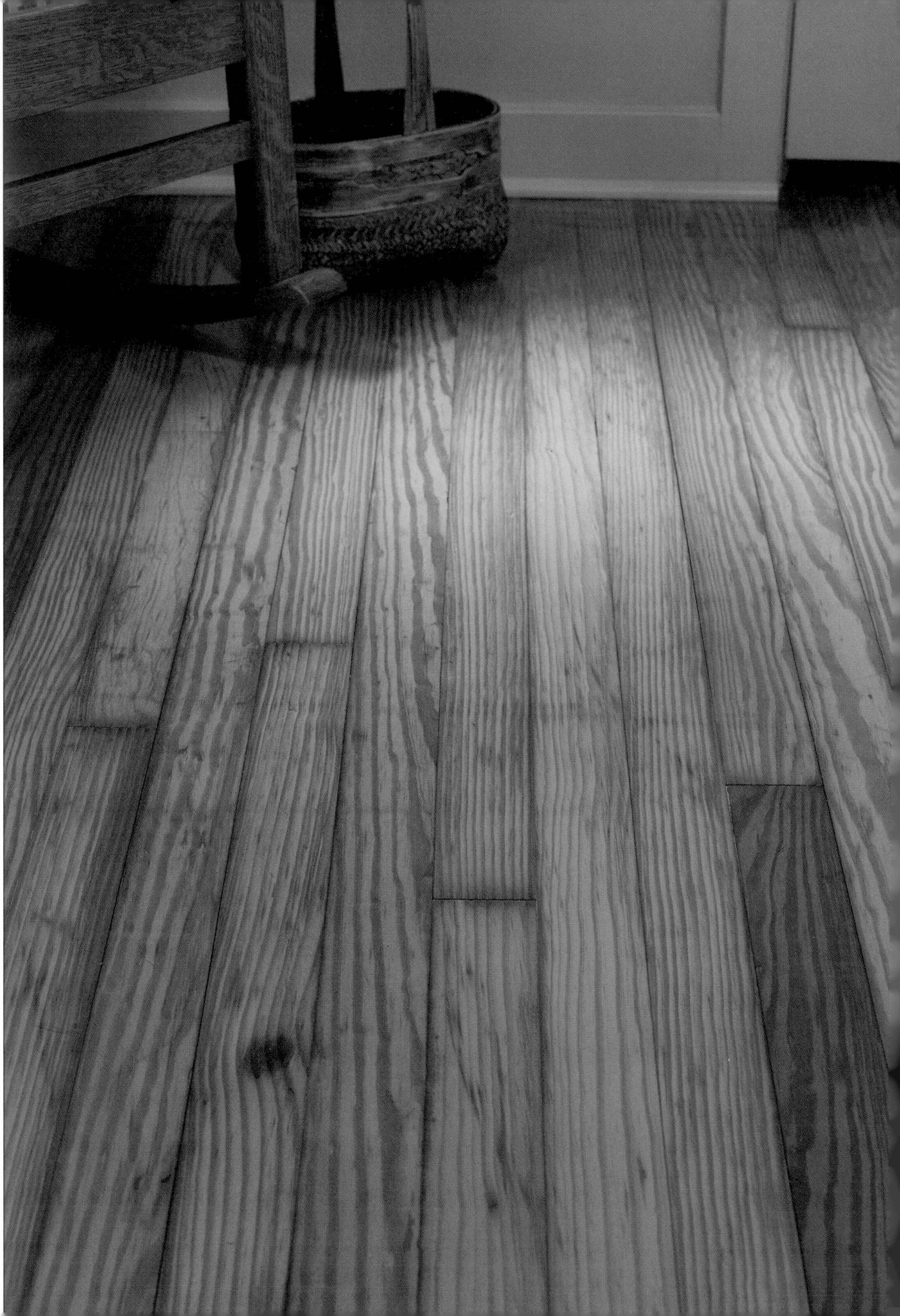

Refinishing a Wood Floor

It's easy to refinish wood floors with an oscillating floor sander and polyurethane varnish.

Years ago, refinishing a wood floor meant renting an industrial drum sander to take off the old finish and smooth the bare wood. I always found these machines hard to handle, and they could all too easily gouge a floor. They also kicked up a tornado of sanding dust that invariably sifted through the entire house.

But now a new type of sander is available at many tool rental companies and even some home centers that makes the job a lot more practical. It's an oscillating pad sander, much like the hand-held variety you might use for sanding woodwork or furniture.

Oscillating sanders are far easier to operate than drum sanders, and most of the dust stays right on the floor, so there's less mess. The only drawback to this type of sander is that they are less aggressive than drum sanders and won't level floors with serious gouges or bumps. But if your floor is in decent shape and just needs a light or moderate sanding before applying the new finish, an oscillating sander is just the ticket.

Applying the finish is the easy part of a floor refinishing job. Polyurethane varnish is a good choice. Each coat dries in four to six hours and can be swabbed on with a lamb's-wool applicator. Three coats make for a durable and beautiful wood floor.

Tools

Claw hammer
Pry bar
Putty knife
Nail set
Oscillating floor sander (can be rented)
Portable random-orbit sander (can be rented)
Shop vac

Materials

Wood filler
Plastic sheeting
Window fan
Sandpaper (60- to 120-grit)
Polyurethane varnish
Lamb's-wool applicator
Paint tray

Preparation

Remove all furniture and window treatments. Wrap ceiling fan or hanging light fixture in a plastic bag and tape the bag shut. Tape over wall outlets with masking tape. If the floor has a waxy buildup, clean it with water and trisodium phosphate (TSP). Otherwise the wax will quickly clog the sandpaper.

Safety

Wear a dust mask when sanding. Before applying a finish, turn off any gas pilot lights in the area and make sure to provide adequate ventilation.

LEVEL OF DIFFICULTY
Easy to Moderate

TIME REQUIREMENT
2 days

COST ESTIMATE
$75 to $100 for one day's sander rental and sandpaper. $40 to $60 for 2 gallons polyurethane, applicator, misc. supplies.

FLOORS

1 PREPARE THE FLOOR

- Check the floor for squeaks and nail any loose floorboards.
- Remove the shoe molding. Use a small pry bar to coax the shoe molding away from the wall. To prevent damage to the wall, insert a scrap of wood between the pry bar and the wall.
- Look the floor over carefully for protruding nail heads, and countersink them.
- Fill any holes with wood filler.

2 ISOLATE AND VENTILATE THE SPACE

Even though the oscillating sander kicks up minimal dust, you'll still want to seal off the rooms being worked on from the rest of the house.

- Drape plastic sheeting across openings to adjacent rooms to create a dust barrier.
- Place a box fan in a window to draw air-borne dust outside.

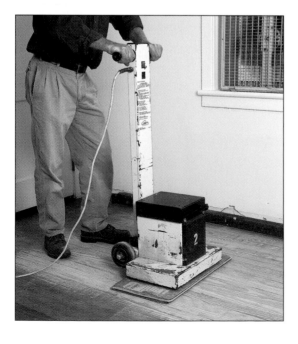

3 SAND THE FLOOR

- Place the sandpaper on the floor (start with 60-grit and work up to 120-grit); then set the cushioning pad supplied with the sanding machine on the sandpaper, pivot the sander back, and rest the plate squarely on the pad.
- Start sanding by moving the machine briskly over an area 2 feet by 4 feet. Note: If you keep the sander in one spot too long, it will heat the remaining finish and clog the sandpaper.
- Stop periodically and check the paper for wear. Clean off any debris that clings to the paper and change the paper when it becomes worn.

FLOORS

4 SAND THE CORNERS

Use a portable electric hand sander to sand more completely into the corners and under obstacles like baseboard heaters. A random-orbit sander is the best tool for the job.

• Sand the corners and under obstacles with the same grits of sandpaper you used on the large sander, vacuuming the entire floor before starting with the next finer grit of paper.

5 APPLY THE FINISH

• Check the floor carefully for areas that need additional sanding. Re-sand as necessary and vacuum again.

• Pour the finish into a wide paint tray.

• Apply the finish with a lamb's-wool applicator, wetting the floor as evenly as possible, swabbing it on with the grain direction of the boards.

• Check the floor for dry spots as you work, and go back over them.

• Let the floor dry (check for required time), then recoat.

Ron's
PRO TIPS

Restoring the Applicator Pad

There's no good way to clean a lamb's-wool applicator loaded with polyurethane or varnish. The material is just too soft and dense—that's what makes it a great applicator for finishing floors. But you don't need to use a different applicator for each coat of finish. Instead, leave the applicator on the pole and wrap the applicator in a plastic bag when you're finished with each coat. Se-cure the bag with masking tape and also wrap the tape around the pole for a good seal. Set the whole thing in a cool place with the applicator on the floor. This will prevent the lamb's wool from drying out; when you go to apply the next coat, the applicator will still be fresh and ready for use.

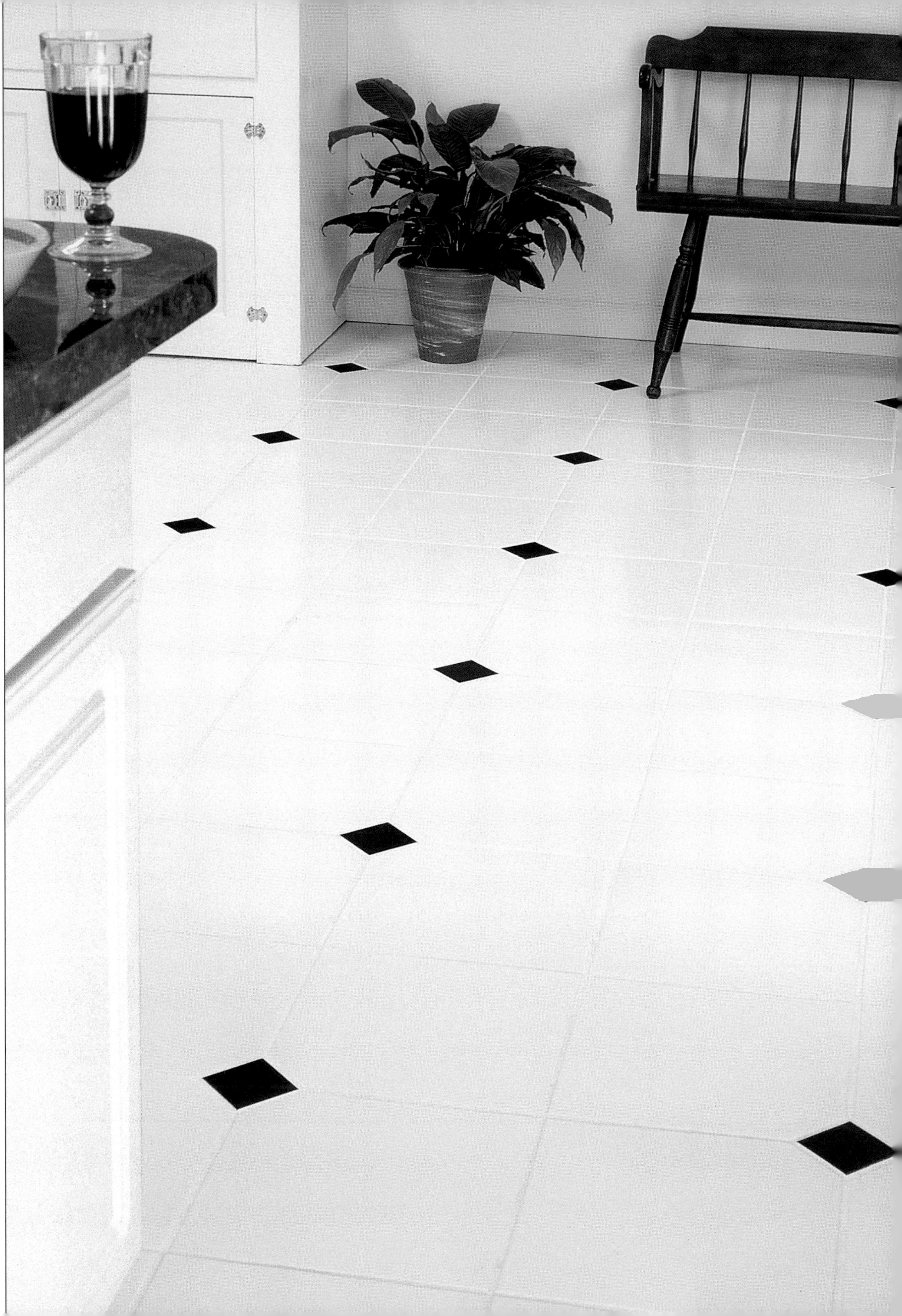

Installing Ceramic Tile

A ceramic tile floor can be a colorful, unique, and long-lasting feature of any room in the house.

To most homeowners I talk with, installing ceramic tile floors seems like one of those jobs better left to the professional. There may be some truth to that, if the job is large or complicated. And tile work does it have its own unique requirements in terms of tools and techniques. But it's also expensive work to get done by an experienced pro.

Installing ceramic tile seems more daunting than it really is. Planning the layout and where to start can be tricky, but you can take your time and do that in advance—before mixing any adhesive. You can even lay out the whole floor in advance. Laying the tiles is the easy part. Cutting them is simple when you rent a saw or have a tile supplier cut them for you. Then there's the grouting, which seems a little mysterious, but it requires more elbow grease than skill or savvy.

Ceramic tile is more work to install than some other flooring materials, but it's likely to last a lot longer, too. So if your budget is tight, and you're up for a challenging but rewarding project, consider doing it yourself.

Tools

Chalk line
Claw hammer
Notched trowel
Soft rubber mallet
Padded length of 2 by 4
Rubber tile float
Electric drill and mixing attachment (optional)
Tile saw or manual tile cutter (either can be rented)
Bucket and grout sponge
Small brush (for grout sealer)

Materials

Ceramic tile
Thin-set adhesive
6"-wide strips of ¼"-thick plywood (for starter strips)
2" box nails
Tile spacers
Latex-modified tile grout
Clean rags
Silicone grout sealer

Preparation

Ceramic tile can be installed over other flooring material that is well bonded. If installing new subfloor material, use plywood, not particleboard.

Fill cracks and seams with leveling compound. Scrape away any debris.

LEVEL OF DIFFICULTY
Challenging

TIME REQUIREMENT
2 to 4 days for an average-sized room

COST ESTIMATE
$1 to $3 per square foot

FLOORS

1 STRIKE LAYOUT LINES

Before laying tile, you'll need to determine how the tile falls at the perimeter of the room. Ideally, perimeter tiles will be of equal width, which is easy to accomplish by starting the tile on centerlines. But you can shift the starting line off center. This will give you a full tile along one wall and a slightly smaller tile on the opposite wall.

• Measure out from each wall at the ends of the room and snap two perpendicular chalk lines.

2 ATTACH STARTER STRIP

Instead of relying on a chalk line alone, pros often use a straightedge guide to start the first row of tile. A dead straight starter row makes the rest of the job go much more smoothly.

• Cut (or have a home center cut) a 6"-wide strip of ¼"-thick plywood. Make sure the plywood edge is straight.

• Nail down the plywood strip along the longest layout line.

CHOOSING
Materials

Ceramic Tiles

Ceramic tile, made from clay fired in a kiln, is one of the most durable and maintenance-free flooring materials. It's available in a wider range of textures and natural colors than other flooring materials, and it lends itself better to unique designs at the hands of the installer. You can combine two or more tile colors, or add small detail tiles at corners or around the perimeter. And you can choose colored grout as a design element. In short, every ceramic tile floor can be unique.

Though the choices seem infinite, start by selecting either glazed or unglazed tile. Generally, glazed tile should be used wherever it is likely to get wet routinely, like in a bathroom. With that decision made, the choices of color and size get easier to navigate.

FLOORS

3 MIX THIN-SET

The adhesive mortar for laying ceramic tile is known generically as thin-set. It's a two-part mix. Mix only as much thin-set as you can use in the specified "working time."

- In a clean bucket, pour the powder portion; then mix in the liquid additive.
- For larger jobs, use a drill and a mixing attachment to mix the thin-set.

4 TROWEL ON THIN-SET

The type of tile you use will call for a specific notch in the trowel used for spreading the thin-set. The notch size determines the thickness of the mortar bed the tile lays in.

- Trowel on the thin-set with a mason's trowel.
- Spread the thin-set onto the floor using the notched trowel held at an angle to the floor. Keep the overall thickness of the thin-set as even as possible and comb in one direction to prevent trapping air under the tile.

5 LAY FIRST TILES

Tiles with uneven backs may need to be "back-buttered" to achieve a strong bond. As the name implies, this amounts to buttering the back of the tile with some thin-set, just like you'd butter a biscuit.

- Place the edge of the first tiles against the starter strip and drop them into the thin-set.
- After several tiles are laid in each direction, insert grout spacers to maintain even spacing between the tiles.
- Add detail tiles as you go (*inset*); don't leave the thin-set exposed.

6 SET TILES

Each tile needs to be pressed into the mortar to guarantee a good bond.

- Lightly tap each tile a couple inches in from each corner with a rubber mallet.
- Tap with the edge of the mallet face; do not hit the tiles with the full face of the mallet, or they may crack.

7 LEVEL TILES

The thin-set mortar for floor tiles can be as thick as ⅜". That leaves a lot of room for the tiles to set unevenly into the mortar.

- After setting several tiles in an area as described in Step 6, go back and level the tiles one to the other with a padded leveling board and a rubber mallet. A straight length of 2 by 4 wrapped with carpet or a towel works well.
- Lay the leveling board across the tiles and tap the board firmly.

8 MARK AND CUT PERIMETER TILES

- Mark the width for each perimeter tile. To do this, place the perimeter tile to be marked squarely on top of the adjacent full tile. Then place another full tile on top of that one so it butts against the wall, but with a third tile against the wall as a grout spacer.
- Cut the tiles with a tile cutter, as described in Tool Know-How on the opposite page.

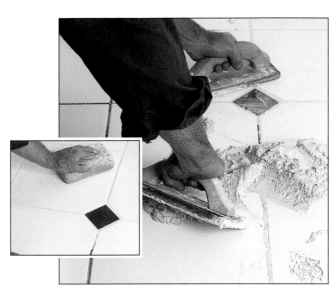

9 GROUT THE TILES

Grouting tile is a physical task. You have to work the grout well into the joints, and you should try to do the entire floor in one continuous session.

- Thoroughly mix the grout as instructed on the package.
- Spread the grout vigorously across the tile with a rubber tile float, working diagonally to the grout lines. Then hold the float at a 45-degree angle and scrape off any excess grout.
- To remove the remaining grout, use a tiling sponge (*inset*). Move the sponge in a circular motion, rinsing frequently.
- Allow the surface to dry, then wipe off the haze with a clean, dry cloth.

TOOL
KNOW-HOW

Tile Cutters

The pros use an electric wet saw to cut ceramic tile. But these cost hundreds of dollars, and even renting one can be expensive (for large floors, it may be worth it). A cheaper alternative is to buy (or rent) a manual tile cutter.

To use a manual tile cutter, you simply lay the tile on the base of the tool, position it so the scoring cutter is on the cut line you've marked, and drag the cutter across the face of the tile. Make sure the score line is complete, or the corners of the tile may chip. Raising the handle of the cutter applies pressure that snaps the tile along the scored line.

Thicker tiles are harder to cut with manual cutters, and breakage is possible. Regardless of what type of tile you use, be sure to buy extra tiles in case some break.

10 APPLY GROUT SEALER

Grout is porous and must be sealed to prevent liquids from penetrating and staining the grout. But sealer can't be applied until the grout is absolutely dry—typically 30 days after the tile is laid.

- Pour the sealer into a jar, then brush it liberally onto the grout lines. Cover a square yard or so of tile at a time.
- Wipe the excess from the tile surface with a clean cloth.

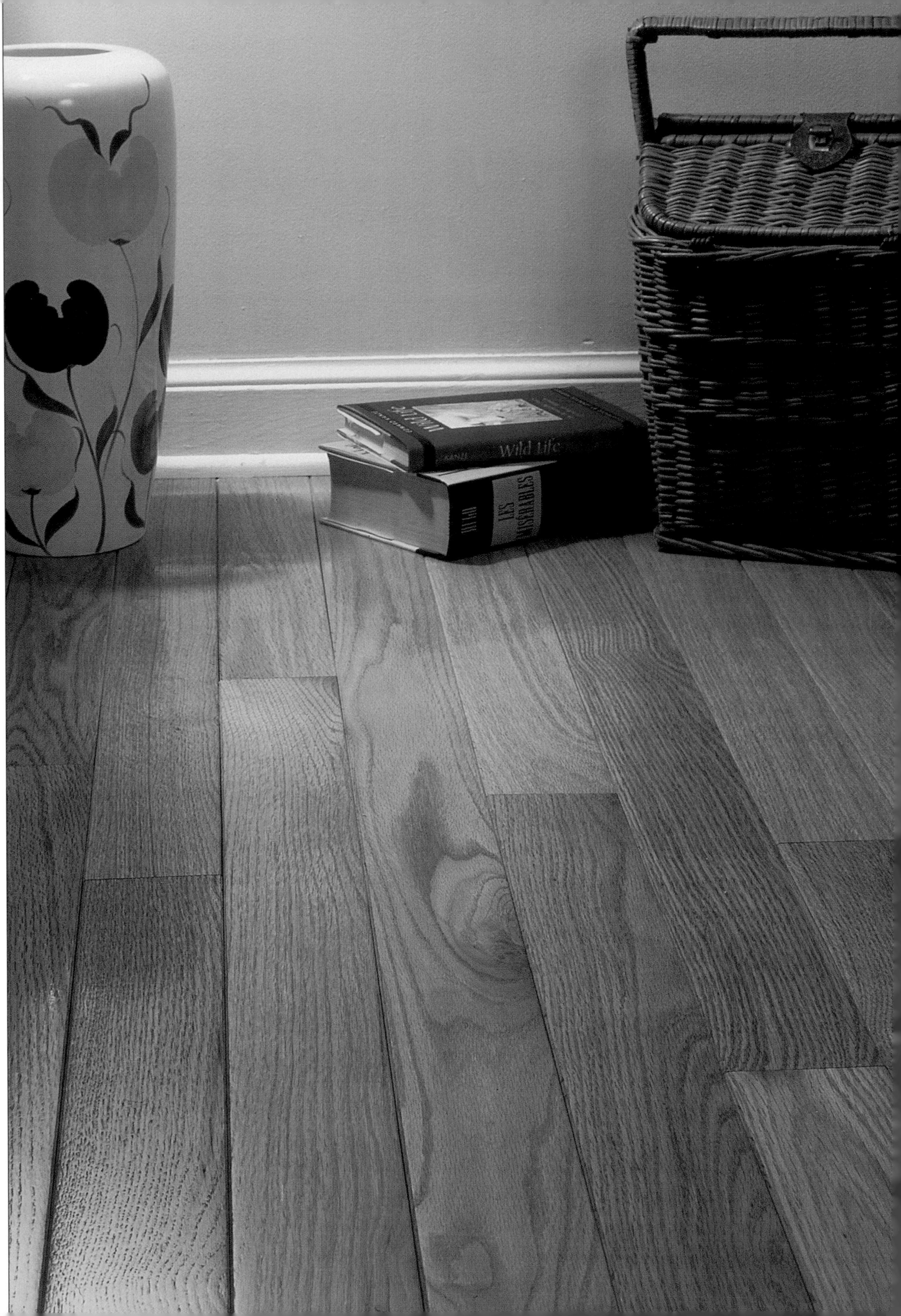
Wild Life
LES MISÉRABLES

Installing Wood Strip Flooring

Nothing beats the beauty and warmth of a real wood floor.

Many of the new houses built today feature wall-to-wall carpeting in all the rooms except the kitchen and bath. When the carpeting wears out (usually far too soon), owners of newer homes often complain that they're stuck with carpeting forever.

Of course, they're not stuck with it. There are no real obstacles to laying new hardwood flooring over an existing subfloor. Solid-wood strip floors usually last for the life of a home. If they do suffer serious wear over the years, they can be refinished to look brand new once again *(see page 198)*.

Strip flooring is milled with an interlocking tongue-and-groove profile along the edges and ends, which keeps the surface of all the strips level. Installing it involves nailing through the tongue edge on each strip with a special flooring nailer available at most tool-rental stores.

A recent boon to the do-it-yourself homeowner is prefinished strip flooring. This eliminates a messy part of the job—sanding and finishing. Most strip flooring comes in bundles of about 20 square feet made up of random lengths. Home centers typically stock 2¼" widths, but they can order 3¼" widths (be prepared for a cost increase of around 20 percent more per square foot for this).

Tools

Tape measure
Claw hammer and nail set
Heavy-duty staple gun
Chalk line
Utility knife and putty knife
Electric drill and twist bits
1½"- to 2"-wide chisel
Pry bar
Flooring nailer (can be rented)
Hand saw and miter box, or power miter saw (can be rented)
Coping saw or saber saw

Materials

Strip flooring (add about 10 percent to the actual room square footage for waste)
15-pound building paper
2" finish nails
⅜" staples
½"-thick strips of plywood (for perimeter spacers)
Wood putty to match flooring
Base or quarter-round molding

Preparation

Allow the wood strip flooring to acclimate to the room for two or more days before you install it. Unwrap and lay the bundles on the floor.

Before you begin, seek out and eliminate squeaks by driving screws through the existing flooring into the joists.

LEVEL OF DIFFICULTY
Moderate to Challenging

TIME REQUIREMENT
2 to 3 days for an average-sized room

COST ESTIMATE
$3 to $6 per square foot for strip flooring; $25 to $50 per day for rental of flooring nailer

FLOORS

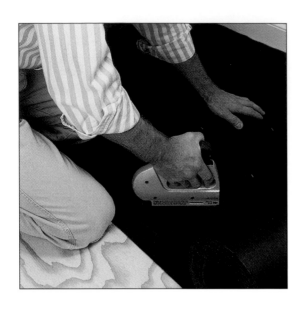

1 STAPLE DOWN BUILDING PAPER

I recommend laying down a layer of 15-pound building paper under the flooring; it serves as a vapor barrier and also may reduce squeaking that might develop.

- Unroll one strip of building paper and staple it to the floor.
- Wait until most of the first strip is covered by the new flooring before laying down the second strip.
- Overlap subsequent strips of building paper 3" or 4".

2 SNAP CHALK LINE FOR FIRST ROW

It's very important that the first course of strips be dead straight. If the wall or baseboard is straight, you can use it as a reference and insert pieces of ½" plywood as spacers. But walls are rarely perfectly straight, so a chalk line is more reliable.

- Snap a chalk line the width of one strip plus ½" away from the wall. The ½" gap allows the wood to expand as the weather changes.

3 FACE-NAIL FIRST ROW

The first and possibly second row of strips must be face-nailed; most flooring nailers can't be positioned on the edge of the strips, since they're too close to the wall.

- Drill pairs of holes, each about ½" in from the edge, every foot or so along the first strip.
- Nail the first strip down with 2" finish nails.
- Set the nails beneath the surface of the wood and fill with wood putty.

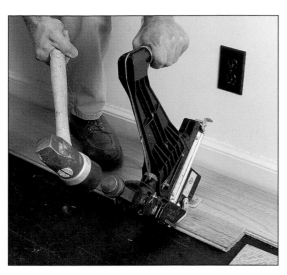

4 NAIL WITH FLOORING NAILER

After the first row or so is face-nailed, you can switch to using the flooring nailer. Don't be surprised if it takes a few misfired nails to get the hang of it.

- Position the nailer along the edge of the wood strip.
- Holding the nailer steady with one hand, strike the activator head sharply, using the mallet supplied with the gun.

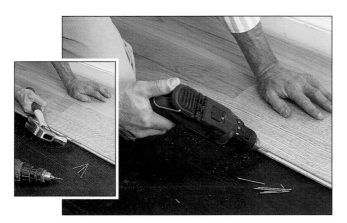

5 FASTENING WITHOUT A FLOORING NAILER

If you've got a lot of patience or are covering a small room, you can get by without a flooring nailer.

- First, drill through the tongue every foot or so at roughly a 45-degree angle.
- Then drive a nail into the hole *(inset)* and set each nail with a nail set.

TOOL
KNOW-HOW

Flooring Nailers

A flooring nailer is a specialized nail gun designed for tongue-and-groove strip flooring. It drives $1\frac{1}{2}$" or 2" nails at an angle through the tongue edge of the wood strip. The manually operated version of this tool requires a heavy rubber-headed mallet to drive the nails. The gun and mallet come together as a set from most tool-rental companies. Typical rental fees are between $25 and $50 per day. There are also pneumatic nailers, which require a compressor. Though easier to use, they are less likely to be available at rental stores.

Using a flooring nailer is physically demanding and can be especially hard on your back. But once you get the hang of it, it's no more difficult than driving nails with a regular hammer.

FLOORS

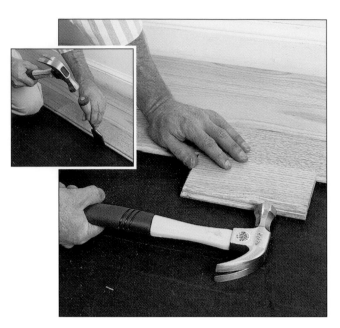

6 TIGHTEN SEAMS

Even though the flooring may be top-quality, it often requires persuasion to get the seams tight.

- Cut a small scrap from the end of a strip, position it over the edge of the new piece, and tap it with a hammer.

- When a gap won't close, use a wide chisel as a pry bar *(inset)*. Hold the chisel against the edge of the strip at a slight angle away from it, and tap it into the subfloor. Then lever the chisel toward the strip to close the gap.

Make Your Own Miter Box

Ron's **PRO TIPS**

A miter box is a simple device used to guide a hand saw when making 90-degree crosscuts or 45-degree miter cuts. For a flooring job you only need to make the straight crosscuts. Rather than buying a miter box for the job, make a simple crosscut box from scrap wood. Use 1 by 3 pine or ¾"-thick plywood. The bottom of the U-shaped box should be just slightly wider than the strips you need to cut. Make the vertical walls about 2" to 3" tall. Drill pilot holes through the walls, and screw the walls to the bottom. Then mark across both walls about 2" in from one end, and make a square cut down through the walls all the way to the bottom. To use the crosscut box, just hold the stock firmly against one of the walls, slide your saw into the slots, and make the cut. Your crosscuts will be square every time.

7 CROSSCUT END PIECES

When you reach the end of each row, you'll need to measure and cut a piece to fit. Since the ends of the strips have either a tongue or a groove, only one end of any given piece be can be used.

- Mark the strip to be cut by holding it in place on the floor; remember to leave the ½" gap at the ends for expansion.

- Cut the strips with a power miter saw or a hand saw and miter box *(see Ron's Pro Tips, above)*.

8 FIT PIECES AROUND OBSTACLES

You'll most likely need to fit some pieces of flooring around obstacles.

- Lay the piece to be cut as close to its final destination as possible, and mark it directly from the obstacle.
- Maintain the ½" gap between the flooring and the walls.
- Cut the strips with a coping saw or an electric saber saw.
- Don't cut the flooring around door trim. Instead, undercut the door trim (see Step 9 on page 191).

9 TIGHTEN LAST ROW

The last row may not come out even, and you'll have to rip the strips to fit. A table saw is the best tool for the job, but you if your hand is steady, a hand saw will do.

- Once you've cut the strips to width (allowing for a ½" gap), set them in place and tighten the seam with a pry bar; use a wood shim to protect the molding.
- Drill pilot holes and face-nail these strips as you did the first row of strips.

10 APPLY BASE OR SHOE MOLDING

To cover the expansion gap around the perimeter of the room, apply a base molding, or a quarter-round shoe molding if the base is in place.

- Nail a base molding to the wall studs.
- Nail a shoe molding to the base molding, not to the floor. The flooring needs to be free to expand and contract under the shoe molding.

FLOORS

Installing Wall-to-Wall Carpeting

Wall-to-wall carpeting is soft yet long lasting and imparts real warmth and serenity to any room.

Installing wall-to-wall carpeting is a job that many homeowners avoid. But some carpeting jobs can be tackled by the do-it-your-selfer—it all depends on the type of room to be carpeted. Large or complex rooms can require long, heavy rolls that need to be seamed. These jobs are best left to a professional. But if you're planning to carpet a small and simple room, like the bedroom shown here, there's no reason not to do it yourself.

The only real challenge to laying carpet successfully—even in a small room—is to get the carpet to lie perfectly flat. The trick is to stretch the carpet and tack it around the perimeter. Stretching a carpet requires one or two simple tools that you can rent for the day at most tool-rental companies. At a minimum, you'll want a knee-kicker *(see Tool Know-How on page 218)*, which relies on a strong knee and leg. But I've had best luck when I've used both a knee-kicker and a power stretcher, which requires less brute strength.

Tools

Tape measure
Claw hammer
Nail set
Pry bar
Utility knife
Heavy-duty staple gun
Leather gloves
Tin snips
Chalk line
Straightedge
Carpet knee-kicker and power stretcher (can be rented)
Wide-blade putty knife

Materials

Carpeting
Padding
3/8" staples
Tack strips
Duct tape
Transition strips (if needed)

Preparation

To get a good carpet installation, it's important to start with a solid underlayment.

Set any nails that show, and add nails or screws at joists if the floor squeaks.

Also, remove the shoe molding with a small pry bar.

LEVEL OF DIFFICULTY
Moderate

TIME REQUIREMENT
1 day for a small room

COST ESTIMATE
$200 to $400, depending on the size of the room and the quality of the carpet

FLOORS

1 INSTALL TACK STRIPS

Tack strips hold the carpet to the floor around the perimeter of the room.

- Position the tack strips about ½" away from the wall. The carpet gets tucked into this gap after it's trimmed.
- Make sure the spikes on the strips are facing the wall, not into the room.
- Nail the strips securely to the floor.

Cutting Tack Strips

Ron's
PRO TIPS

No matter how carefully you try to handle tack strips, you'll inevitably get stuck by the sharp barbs sticking out one side or the tack nails sticking out the other side. The trick is to wear gloves and hold the strips gently.

But that doesn't work when you have to trim one to length, because you have to hold the strip firmly as you make the cut. Instead of attempting to cut a tack strip with a saw, hold it with a pair of leather work

gloves and snip it to length with a pair of tin snips; be sure to discard any scraps where they can't get walked on.

2 ATTACH PADDING

Padding prolongs the life of the carpet and makes it feel thicker. Choose a padding type recommended by the manufacturer of the carpet.

- Unroll the padding so it overlaps the tack strips.
- Staple the padding to the floor every 10" or 12". Check that the staples are fully inserted, and tap them down with a hammer if they are not.

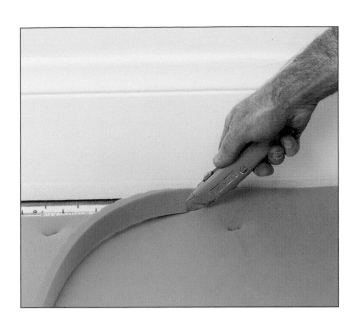

3 TRIM THE PADDING

The padding should not cover any of the tack strips, and it needs to lie just inside the strips.

- Trim the padding against the inside edge of the tack strips with a utility knife.
- To prevent tearing the padding as you cut, replace the blade in the utility knife frequently.

4 SEAM THE PADDING

Padding comes in a variety of widths. For rooms that are wider than the padding, you'll need to seam pieces together.

- Where possible, use the factory edges of the padding for seams.
- Keep the staples an inch or so away from the seam; otherwise the padding may pucker.
- Lay a piece of duct tape carefully along the seam to hold the padding together.

5 ROUGH-CUT THE CARPET

Plan to cut the carpet about 6" oversized in each direction so there will be 3 inches extra along each edge.

- Be sure to measure at the widest parts of of the room.
- Lay out and cut the carpet face down in a larger room, or outdoors on a clean, flat area.
- Snap chalk lines at the measured marks, then cut along the chalk lines with a straightedge and a utility knife.

6 RELIEVE CORNERS

With the carpet positioned in the room, you'll need to make a cut down into the corner through the excess so the carpet can lie flat against the walls.

- Press the carpet as close as possible into the corner.
- Begin the cut with a utility knife from the outside edge and work it down toward the corner, checking as you go.

TOOL
KNOW-HOW

Carpet "Knee-Kicker"

Wall-to-wall carpeting needs to be stretched before attaching it to the floor, or it will bunch up as it relaxes. A knee-kicker is a simple but effective tool for the job, available at tool-rental stores and some carpet retailers. The working end has a dozen or so rows of adjustable teeth that reach through the carpet and grip the backing.

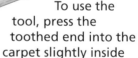

To use the tool, press the toothed end into the carpet slightly inside the tack strip, holding it down firmly; then give the padded end a good whack with your knee. The carpet gets stretched and hooked to the tack strip at the same time.

7 STRETCH AND ATTACH CARPET

The best way to lay a flat carpet is to use two stretching tools in tandem: a knee-kicker and a power stretcher. If necessary, you can get by using a knee-kicker alone.

- Secure the carpet along one wall by latching it onto the tack strips with a knee-kicker *(inset)*.
- Assemble the power stretcher and adjust it to fit the room.
- With the fixed end of the stretcher against the first wall, press the end with the lever into the carpet about 1 inch from the wall to stretch the carpet. Then press it firmly onto the tack strips.
- Repeat the sequence on the other walls.

8 TRIM EXCESS CARPETING

Use only a utility knife with a new sharp blade to trim the carpet.

- Hold the utility knife almost flat against the carpet, and make several passes to cut all the way through.
- Pull the excess slightly away from the wall so you don't cut into the baseboard.

9 TUCK CARPET EDGES

Most carpet will fray a little when cut from the face side with a utility knife.

- Cut any loose strands of fiber—don't pull them, or they may run.
- Tuck the cut edge of the carpet down into the gap behind the tack strip with a wide-blade putty knife.

10 APPLY TRANSITION STRIPS

Transition strips are used where the new carpet meets a different material at a doorway or closet.

- Measure the transition strips to fit and cut them with tin snips.
- Nail the strips into the floor so they hold the carpet securely.

Wallpapering a Ceiling 222

Installing
Crown Molding 226

Installing
a Suspended Ceiling 234

Soundproofing
a Ceiling. 240

Installing
Acoustical Ceiling Tile. 244

Adding Track Lighting. 250

Installing
a Thin-Line Skylight 254

Hanging a Ceiling Fan. 260

CEILINGS

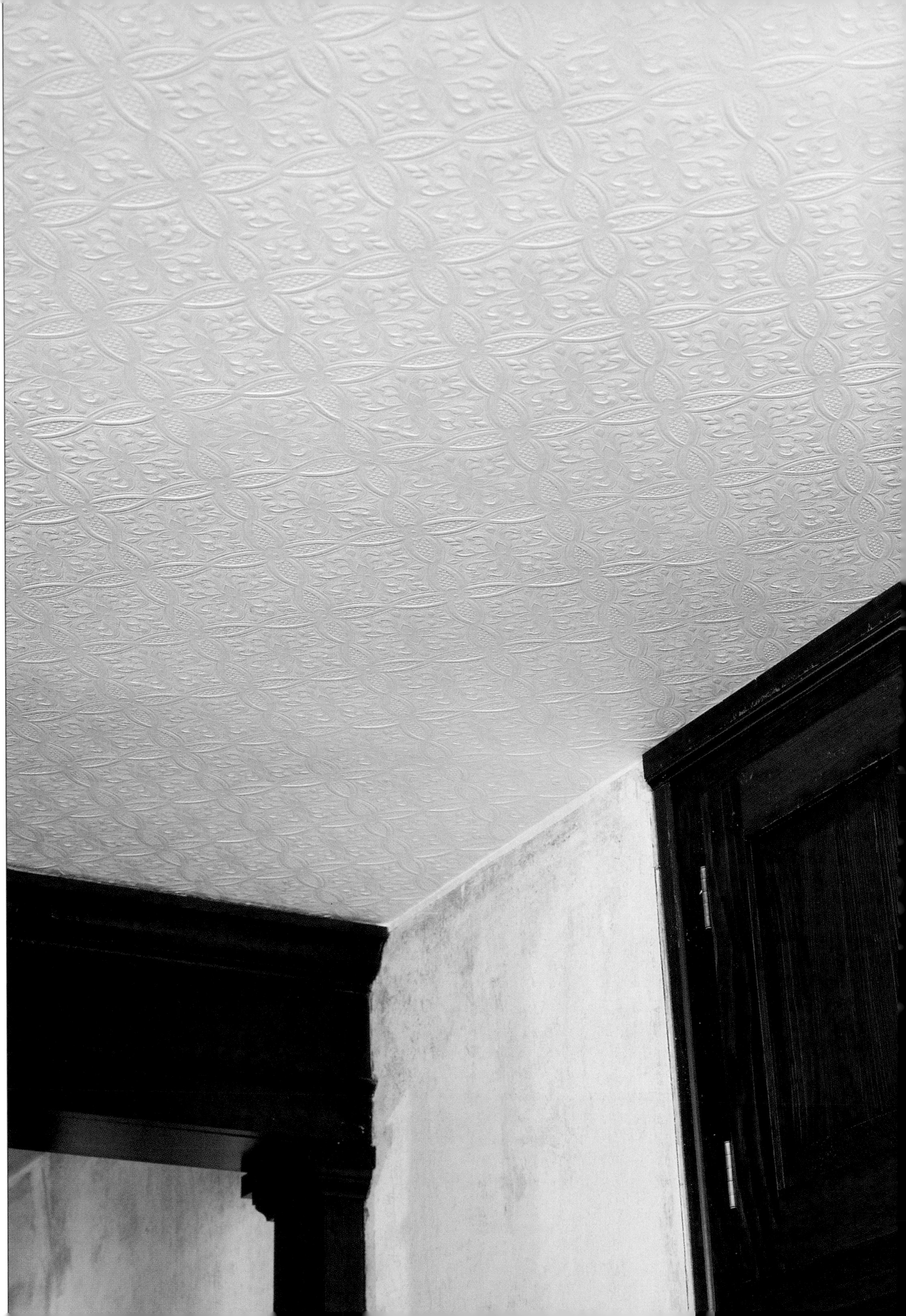

Wallpapering a Ceiling

Papering a ceiling needn't be a pain in the neck.

This is one wallpaper job that sends homeowners running to the phone book for the number of a professional hanger. The strips are longer than those used on walls; they are being applied against the pull of gravity; and you've got to have the strength and balance to hold your arms above your head while standing on scaffolding. But think a moment before making that call. The pros I've talked to love papering ceilings because the work goes so blessedly quick. There are few, if any, of the time-consuming cutouts and trimming tasks involved with papering a wall. So if you consider yourself in reasonably good shape, this is a good candidate for a weekend project.

There are two basic types of ceiling paper. One has a plastic finish and printed pattern; the other is embossed and is intended to be painted. I like paintable papers for a couple of reasons: The paint helps conceal joints between strips, and the appearance of the ceiling can be refreshed simply by rolling on a new coat of paint.

Tools

Scaffolding (can be rented)
Tape measure or folding rule
Chalk line
Water tray (if pre-pasted paper)
Paint roller or brush (if unpasted paper)
Wallpaper brush and sponge
Scissors and utility knife
Wide-blade putty knife
Seam roller

Materials

Wallpaper
Wallpaper paste (if unpasted paper)
Spackling compound
Mesh tape (for wide cracks)
150-grit sandpaper

Preparation

Plan on papering the ceiling before papering the walls.

Either rent scaffolding or improvise a sturdy, movable platform that will allow you to work from one end of the room to the other.

Strip old paper for best results. *(See Stripping Wallpaper on page 114.)*

Patch cracks with spackling compound; to span larger cracks, use mesh tape.

Lightly sand a painted ceiling with 150-grit paper to remove any small bumps and to smooth patching. A glossy ceiling should be sanded to lessen its sheen.

LEVEL OF DIFFICULTY
Moderate; you may want a helper when applying the paper

TIME REQUIREMENT
½ day

COST ESTIMATE
$60 to $150 for a 12' by 12' room

CEILINGS

1 MARK OFF THE CEILING

Plan on running strips across the shorter dimension. An exception would be if the dimensions are roughly equal and people entering the room would be looking along the seams rather than across them.

- At one short wall, mark the ceiling to determine where the first strip will go. Measure out from the wall a distance equal to the width of the wallpaper minus ½"; this will create an overlap where the first strip meets the wall. Make marks at both ends of where the strip will go.

2 CONNECT MARKS

- Use a chalk line to connect the end marks.
- Take several measurements along this line to be sure a bow in the wall won't create a gap where the first strip fails to reach.
- If necessary, make a second line closer to the wall.

Ron's
PRO TIPS

Booking Wallpaper

How do you get those long, gloppy strips onto the ceiling without papering yourself in the process? You can "book" each strip—pile it in loose folds with the pasted sides touching. This is done for hanging walls, too. But for long ceiling strips, you can make extra folds to form a tidy stack something like an accordion. Balance this stack on one fore-arm, get up on the scaffolding, and use your free hand to unfold the paper and in-stall it. This may feel awkward at first, and I sug-gest a practice

booking session with dry paper. If you find you aren't comfortable with this high-wire act, have a helper hold the stack as you in-stall the strip. Booking has another purpose: The manufacturer may instruct you to allow the paper to rest at this stage for several min-utes so the paste can become fully activated without drying out.

3 POSITION FIRST STRIP

- Cut the first strip to length, allowing 4" extra for an overlap at both ends.
- Soak or paste the strip.
- "Book" the strip *(see Ron's Pro Tips on the opposite page)*.
- Starting at one end, press the paper into place, allowing a 2" overlap at the wall.
- Use a wallpaper brush to smooth the paper along the ceiling.

4 TUCK CORNERS

- With a wallpaper brush or a wide-blade putty knife, press the paper into the corners where the ceiling meets the wall.
- If you're using a wide-blade putty knife, be careful not to puncture the paper with the edge of the blade. Although the blade isn't that sharp, the paper is wet and under tension.

5 TRIM OFF EXCESS

- If the walls are to be papered, pull the ends of the strip from the wall and cut parallel to the crease with scissors, allowing ½" overlap. For a room that has crown molding, you may be able to use a wide-blade putty knife to slip the ends in the gap between molding and ceiling.
- Or, if walls will be painted, not papered, use a utility knife guided by a putty knife to cut the paper along the corner between ceiling and wall.
- Sponge each strip with clean water to rinse away excess adhesive.

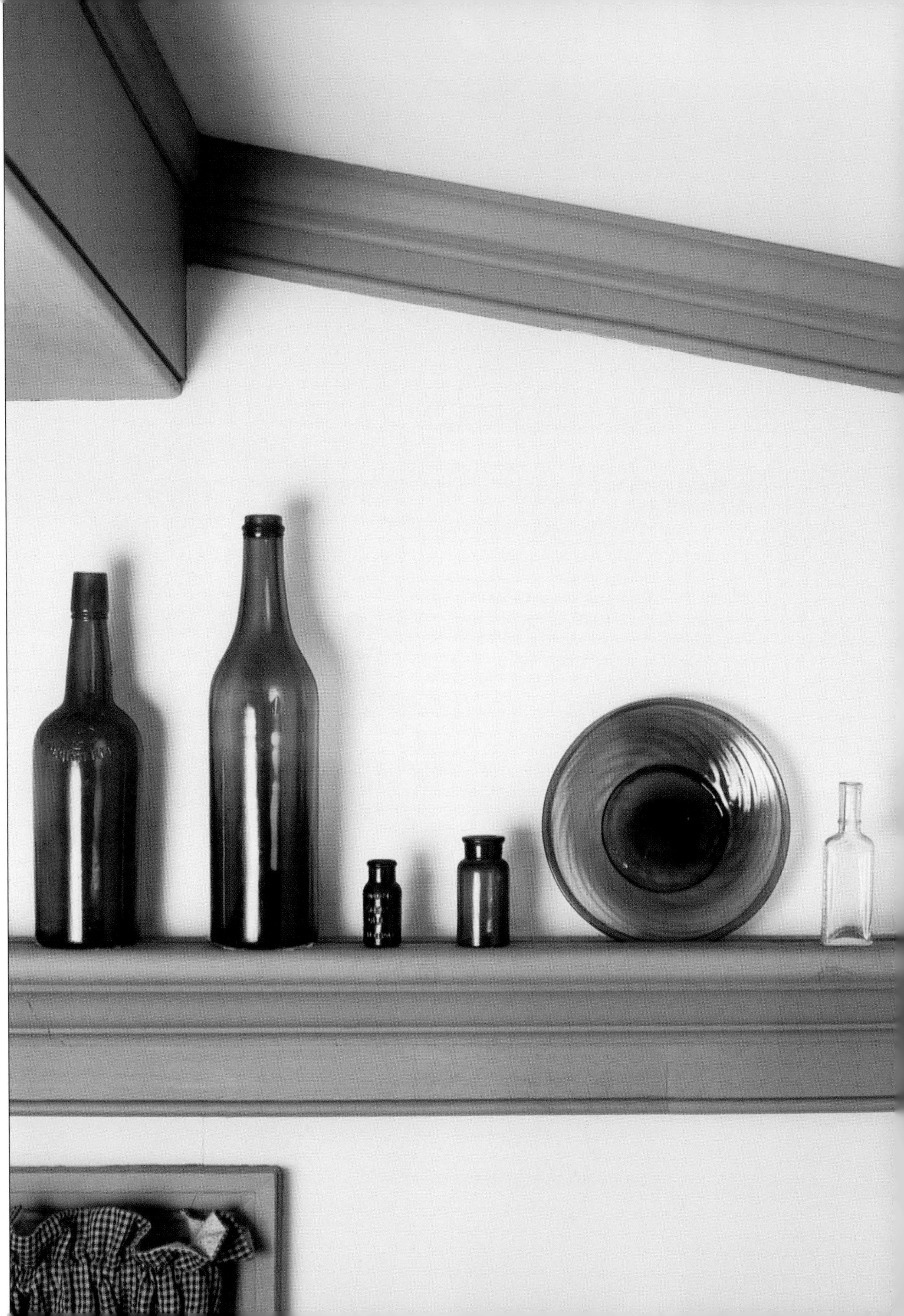

Installing Crown Molding

This finishing touch gives rooms a traditional look.

Not every home cries out for crown molding. Low rooms and modern decor may look better without it. But this traditional way of making the transition from wall to ceiling can add visual interest when other architectural details are lacking; it gives a finished appearance to rooms with period furniture; and it can have the effect of bringing in the walls to make a room seem more intimate.

As a rule, I suggest fairly simple molding for smaller or lower rooms; I like to reserve beefier molding for larger spaces that can handle heavy trim. (If you put up crown molding and find that it looks a little too prominent, you can play it down by using a trim color similar to the wall paint.) I often recommend built-up, two-piece moldings, like the one in this project, because they look more substantial than typical off-the-shelf stock from home centers. And they don't require greater expertise or a lot of additional work. If you don't find profiles you like, consult the yellow pages under "millwork" for local companies that can come up with custom molding in the wood of your choice.

Tools

Claw hammer and nail set
Stepladder
Stud finder (optional)
Tape measure
Electric drill and twist bits
Framing square
Power miter saw (can be rented)
Coping saw
Small round rasp or file
Putty knife
Caulking gun
2" trim brush

Materials

Primer and paint or varnish
2" finish nails
150-grit sandpaper
Paintable acrylic latex caulk or caulk color-matched to the finished trim
Wood putty to match trim

Preparation

Use a carpenter's level or another long straightedge to see if the joint between walls and ceiling is excessively uneven; crown molding can make a wavy joint more obvious.

If you will be using custom-milled molding, order it well in advance.

Consider applying paint or a clear finish to the molding before nailing it up, to avoid taping off walls and ceiling and working from a ladder.

LEVEL OF DIFFICULTY
Moderate to Challenging

TIME REQUIREMENT
1 day, with a helper to hold long stock for marking and nailing

COST ESTIMATE
$75 (pine) to $150 (oak) for 1-piece molding in a 12' by 12' room

CEILINGS

1 PRIME THE MOLDING

- Even if you don't choose to prefinish the molding, it's best to brush a coat of primer on the backs now to reduce the chance of warping.

2 MEASURE WALL FOR FIRST CUT

- Measure the wall near the ceiling—not at a more convenient height—to get an accurate reading.

- For a two-piece molding like the style shown here, install all of the flat base stock before applying the crown molding on top of it; the base stock meets at each of the corners with simple 45-degree miter cuts.

- If the stock isn't long enough to span a wall, scarf two or more pieces as described in Step 4.

- Along the first wall, the crown molding is cut square on both ends to butt into the corners.

CHOOSING
Materials

Crown Molding Profiles

Today, most homes are built without crown molding. But judging by the profiles available at home centers, many homeowners feel a need to grace the junction of walls and ceilings with molding. In smaller

rooms, especially with low ceilings, a one-piece molding (like those shown here) is usually sufficient. The styles include cove with a simple

concave curve and a crown-and-bed with an irregular profile that includes a convex curve.

3 LOCATE THE STUDS

To firmly anchor molding, nail it into the studs behind the walls.

• Use a stud finder to locate the studs.

• Or, use a nail as a probe, as shown, tapping it through the wall where the holes will be concealed by the molding.

• Make erasable marks on the wall just below where the molding will go.

Backing Blocks

Ron's
PRO TIPS

Convex molding is usually nailed at the outermost part of its curve, to avoid dinging the wood with the hammer. But the molding has a lot of air behind it, and you can do a better job of attaching those long strips by nailing into backing blocks. These are nothing more than triangular pieces of 2-by stock, sized to fit snugly behind the molding. To find the correct size for a block, hold a short scrap of molding in place and measure the horizontal and vertical dimensions of the space that's created. Transfer the measurements to a piece of lumber, and saw a test piece. Tuck it behind the scrap of molding and adjust the measurements as necessary. Then cut a block for each stud you've marked, drill pilot holes in them, and nail into place at stud locations. The molding is nailed to the blocks.

4 SCARF LONG RUNS

If the stock isn't long enough to make a run, lap two pieces with 45-degree cuts to make a scarf joint.

• Hold a piece of molding in place and mark it for an angled cut at a stud.

• Hold up another piece to complete the run, and mark it for a cut at the stud. Note that the combined length of the two pieces will be greater than the length of the wall, to allow for the mitered overlap.

• Make the angled cuts with a miter saw.

• To minimize splitting (especially at the ends), and to ease driving nails through hardwood molding, drill pilot holes before installation *(inset)*.

CEILINGS

5 ATTACH MOLDING

To make sure the molding goes up just right, "tack" it in place by driving the finish nails only partway at first.

- For a two-piece molding, begin by installing the base around the room *(inset)*. When the installation appears correct, drive the nails home.

- Apply crown molding in the same way, as shown.

- Smooth the joint between scarfed pieces by sanding lightly.

6 PREPARE FOR COPED CUT

The crown molding for the second wall has a coped end where it meets the molding on the first wall; its other end is cut square. The molding for the third wall is treated the same way. Along the fourth wall, the molding has two coped ends, so it has to be bowed slightly in order to fit snugly in place.

- Measure the length of the wall.

- If you are new to coping, cut molding stock several inches longer than the wall to allow a couple of tries.

- With the molding upside down, as shown, cut a 45-degree miter on the end to be coped; this reveals the molding's profile to guide the coping cut.

7 MARK A LINE AT 90 DEGREES

- To define where you'll cut the molding, draw a line perpendicular to the molding's face, on the top of the molding's mitered end.

8 MAKE COPED CUT

This step is the trickiest part of the job; again, if you haven't done much coping, I suggest you make several practice cuts to get the hang of it.

- Using a coping saw, begin cutting along the line that you drew perpendicular to the molding's face.

- Keeping the saw at 90 degrees to the face of the molding, follow the contour of the cut edge from the top to the bottom, freeing a wedge-shaped piece.

TOOL KNOW-HOW

Coping Saws

A coping saw is used to cut irregular shapes—anything from puzzle pieces and scrollwork to the curves of a coped molding. It is suited to this nimble work because of the thin, fine-toothed blade, held within a C-shaped metal frame. Further leading to the saw's flexibility, the blade can be rotated 360 degrees. Because the blade is so thin, it relies on tension for its rigidity; you turn the handle of the saw to stretch it taut within its frame. All in all, a coping saw is one of the simplest and least expensive hand tools, but it has a place in both carpenters' toolboxes and the most modest workshop.

9 TEST THE COPED CUT

- To test-fit the coped end, hold it in place; you can scribe a pencil line along the coped piece to help in fine-tuning the cut, as shown.

- Use a file to further shape the cut; see Ron's Pro Tips on page 232.

- If too much correction is needed, make another miter cut and begin again.

CEILINGS

10 CHECK OUTSIDE CORNERS

At outside corners, the crown molding meets with a mitered joint.

- Check the outside corner with a framing square.
- Make the cuts at 45 degrees with the miter saw; but if the corner is substantially out of square, adjust the saw angle accordingly for a tight joint along the outer edge of both pieces.

Filing Coped Cuts

Ron's PRO TIPS

In a perfect world, coped cuts would mate seamlessly with their companion pieces. Chances are, though, your cuts won't quite be to this standard—not at first, anyway. You can cheat a little by removing wood here and there with a file. Use a coarser rasp to take wood off quickly. But to do a delicate touch-up, you're better off with a rat-tail or round file. For still finer work, use a piece of sandpaper wrapped around a square or round block of wood. Check the fit often to  avoid taking off too much. And take care to keep the file or sandpaper block parallel with the cut, rather than risk rounding the edge that will show. Remember, it's okay to allow a gap along the inside of the joint, where it won't be seen.

11 ATTACH MOLDING AT OUTSIDE CORNERS

- Test the fit of the mitered pieces by holding them in place and pressing them together, as shown. If there are gaps, see Ron's Pro Tips on page 154.
- Tack one piece in place.
- Nail the second piece in position with 2" finish nails and cross-nail at the corner.
- Lightly sand the joint with 150-grit sandpaper to smooth it.

12 DRIVE AND SET THE NAILS

- When all the crown molding is properly in place, drive the nails home.
- Then work around the perimeter of the room and countersink each nail with a nail set.

13 PUTTY NAIL HOLES

- Go around the room puttying nail holes, using a matching putty if the trim will be finished clear.
- You can also putty any gaps that show in the mitered joints; but a niftier solution is to "burnish" the joint *(see Ron's Pro Tips on page 154).*
- After the putty has dried, sand it flush with the surface of the molding with a piece of fine sandpaper.

14 CAULK ALONG WALLS AND CEILING

- If you're planning on painting the molding, run a bead of paintable acrylic latex caulk along the upper and lower edges of the molding to fill in any gaps.
- Touch up with paint as needed to conceal the gaps.
- For molding with a clear finish, apply caulk that matches the finished trim.
- If you didn't pre-paint the trim, mask it off and apply a coat or two of paint.

Installing a Suspended Ceiling

A suspended ceiling hides unsightly pipes and ductwork while still providing instant access to them.

When you're improving an un-finished space like a basement, the ceiling presents a unique challenge due to obstacles like utility ducts, pipes, or wires that hang below the joists. Suspended ceiling systems offer one of the easiest solutions for a clean-looking ceiling, while still allow-ing complete access to the space above it.

In a nutshell, suspended ceilings are made up of inter-locking metal channels that hang on wires from the joists. Precut acoustical panels are then dropped into the grid openings. Suspended ceiling systems can include accessory hardware for lighting fixtures.

The mechanics of installing a suspended ceiling are very simple. The most important step is the first one—establish-ing a level line around the perimeter of the room. Consider renting a laser level for this; see Ron's Pro Tips on page 236. With that done, completing the rest of the job is a lot like playing with Legos: It's just a matter of snapping all of the pieces together.

You can purchase suspended ceiling hardware in prepackaged kits or by selecting the various pieces in the exact quantity needed; see Choosing Materials on page 239 for the pros and cons of each approach.

Tools

Tape measure
4' level
Laser level (optional; can be rented)
Chalk line
Stud finder (optional)
Claw hammer
Tin snips or hacksaw
String or mason's cord
Wire-cutting pliers
Straightedge
Utility knife
Fine-tip permanent marker

Materials

Suspended ceiling hardware
Acoustical panels
1" underlayment nails

Preparation

Draw up a plan of the room to determine the amount of materials needed. Perimeter track runs along the entire room perimeter. The main runners go perpendicular to joists, spaced 4' apart, and 4' cross-tees go every 2' between main runners. If you are using 2' square ceiling panels, add the required number of 2' cross-tees.

LEVEL OF DIFFICULTY
Moderate

TIME REQUIREMENT
2 to 3 days for an average-sized room

COST ESTIMATE
$150 to $250

CEILINGS

1 ESTABLISH LEVEL LINE AROUND PERIMETER

Determine the height of the ceiling based on the lowest obstruction it must clear. Generally, allow at least 4" above the ceiling for clearance to insert the panels.

- Use the floor or the ceiling joists as a reference to mark the ceiling height near the corners of the room.
- Snap level chalk lines to connect the marks.
- Use a level to extend the height lines around short spans of the wall *(inset)*.

2 NAIL UP PERIMETER TRACKS

- If the walls are drywall, locate the studs *(see page 64)*. Mark each stud above the ceiling line.
- Start at one corner and nail up a full-length perimeter track along the ceiling line, using either the nails provided or 1" underlayment nails.
- Working around the room, install as many full-length pieces as you can, then cut track to fill in the gaps; *see Step 3.*

Ron's
PRO TIPS

Using a Laser Level

Establishing a perfectly level line around a room can be quite a challenge. If the room's floor or ceiling joists are level, one or the other can be used as a reference. But it's hard to determine if such a large span is level. And working around a room with a level can lead to a significant cumulative error. But there's a tool available that eliminates the tedium and guesswork of striking a level line.

Revolving laser levels throw a bright beam of light around an entire room, allowing you to mark a line around the perimeter in just minutes. (Use caution and don't stare at the beam.) What's more, you can raise or lower the beam to set the ceiling to clear  the lowest obstacles by the perfect amount. You can rent one for around $75 to $100 a day—a bit steep, but well worth the money. A laser level will save you hours of work and the headache of having to start over when you realize you didn't allow enough clearance for that one pipe in the corner.

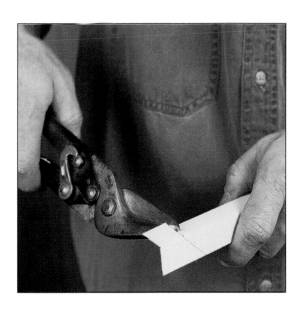

3 CUT PERIMETER TRACK TO LENGTH

You'll need to cut various pieces of track to length, starting with the perimeter track. Tin snips work best, but a hacksaw will also do the job.

- Measure and mark perimeter track pieces to be cut. The ends should butt together, not overlap.
- Cut along the marks with tin snips or a hacksaw.
- At outside corners, let one piece of track extend 1" beyond the corner, to form a butt joint with the adjacent piece. Or miter both pieces.

4 LOCATE MAIN TRACKS

Determine the location of the main tracks, based on your initial layout. Chalk lines across the joists will guide the hanging of the main tracks.

- Drive a nail into the end joists at the marks for the main tracks.
- Stretch a chalk line from end to end, and snap a line across the bottom edge of the joists.

5 LOCATE CROSS-TEES

Before hanging the main tracks, you need to determine where the cross-tees will intersect the main tracks. Again, refer to your initial layout.

- Drive a screw eye or U-shaped hook (provided for hanging the main tracks) into the wall on each side of the room at the location of one of the cross-tees.
- Stretch a string or mason's cord from one hook to the other. The string should be level with the bottom edge of the perimeter track. This string is both a guide to the height of the main tracks and the mark of an intersection for a cross-tee.

6 ATTACH SUPPORT WIRES

- Hammer screw eyes or U-hooks into every other joist along the snapped line for the main tracks.
- Wrap a length of wire around each of the screw eyes/U-hooks, twisting the wire two or three times around itself.
- With wire-cutting pliers, cut the free end of the wires at least 2" below the intended height of the ceiling *(inset)*.

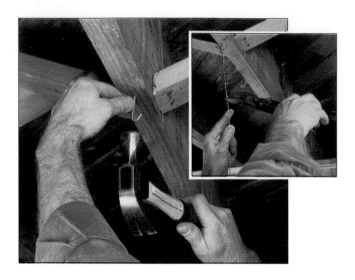

7 HANG MAIN TRACKS

You'll need to cut the first length of main track so the slot for a cross-tee falls exactly over the cross-tee guide string. This is an "offset" cut: The face of the main track butts into the face of the perimeter track, but the vertical part of the main track tee should lap over the perimeter track.

- Guide the wires through the nearest hole in the main track. Rest the main track on the cross-tee guide string, then crimp the wires so the track skims the guide string.
- Twist the excess wire around itself.
- Join lengths of main tracks as needed, using the splice connectors on the ends.

8 CONNECT CROSS-TEES

The 4' cross-tees snap into the main tracks. At the perimeter, the cross-tees rest on the perimeter track; again you use an offset cut as described in Step 7. But they don't lock into the perimeter track. Instead the panels, once installed, will hold these track pieces in place.

- Snap each cross-tee into the slots of the main tracks, and then bend the tabs on the ends 90 degrees against the wall of the main track.
- If you're installing 2' square panels instead of 2' by 4' panels, install the 2' cross-tees now.

9 INSTALL FULL PANELS

Depending on the amount of space above the track grid, installing the panels can be a little tricky. But even in tight quarters you can usually coax a panel into place.

- Slide each panel, one corner first, up into the space above the grid. Once the entire panel is above the grid, let it drop down into place on the tracks.

- In areas where obstructions limit the room above the grid, slide the panel in place from an adjacent space. You can also install a panel first, and then install the second cross-tee to lock it in place.

10 CUT PERIMETER PANELS

Many ceiling panels around the perimeter of the room will need to be cut to size. Measure the opening for each panel at the face of the track grid, and add about 7/8" in each direction.

- Measure, cut, and install each perimeter panel one at a time.

- Mark the face of the panel, then cut with a sharp utility knife riding against a straightedge. Make several passes, keeping the blade perpendicular to the panel.

CHOOSING Materials

Suspended Ceiling Hardware

There are five basic components for a suspended ceiling (from bottom to top): perimeter track is a simple L-shaped piece; T-shaped main track has holes for hanging to the joists, slots for the intersecting cross-tees, and a splicing device at the ends for hooking lengths end-to-end; cross-tees, with tabs on both ends that lock into the main track; and wire and U-hooks to hang the main track on the joists.

You can buy suspended ceiling hardware in kits; for a given square footage of ceiling, you'll need a specific number of kits. The downside to this is you'll likely get more of a certain component than you need. Also the main track and perimeter pieces are only 6' long in kits, which requires more joining of pieces. Sold individually, main track and perimeter track pieces are 10' long. Generally, you'll save money buying individual components.

Soundproofing a Ceiling

How to keep basement noise in the basement

Sometimes you can't shut out noise simply by shutting a door. Take the basement, for example, with its furnace, washer and dryer, shop tools, and Ping-Pong table. The ruckus penetrates to the living area above because floors act as sounding boards. A double-layer drywall ceiling makes a simple, inexpensive barrier, especially when applied over sound-control insulation that's intended for this purpose. And by suspending the lower layer from tracks of special "resilient channel," you can stop even more sound from rising.

Resilient channel was developed for commercial applications. A home center may not stock it, but check with their building materials department about putting in a special order. If that doesn't work, look in the yellow pages under Acoustical Contractors or Drywall Contractors. Home centers are more likely to carry sound-control insulation. And the drywall used in this project is the standard stuff.

Tools

Heavy-duty staple gun
Electric drill with Phillips-head driver
Caulking gun
Chalk line
Tin snips or hacksaw
Utility knife
Work gloves, dust mask, and eye protection

Materials

Sound-control insulation
½" staples
½" drywall sheets
¾" and 1⅝" drywall screws
Silicone caulk
½" resilient channel
Drywall tape, joint compound, and paint (optional)

Preparation

Inspect the ceiling to make sure that you will be able to fit sound-control insulation between the joists and attach drywall to them. Consider rerouting wiring, lighting fixtures, and plumbing if necessary in a particularly noisy area, such as above a furnace.

Arrange for a helper (or two) to assist you in lifting drywall sheets into place.

Safety

Wear gloves, eye protection, and a dust mask when working with insulation.

LEVEL OF DIFFICULTY
Moderate

TIME REQUIREMENT
1 day, with a helper

COST ESTIMATE
$160 for a 12' by 16' ceiling, including batts, channel, and 2 layers of drywall

CEILINGS

1 INSTALL SOUND-CONTROL INSULATION

- Place batts of sound-control insulation between the floor joists.
- Secure the batts by stapling every 8" to 12" through the paper flanges and into the underside of the joists.
- Fill voids around pipes and wires with pieces torn or cut from batts.
- Leave at least 3" of space around lighting fixtures to avoid risk of fire.

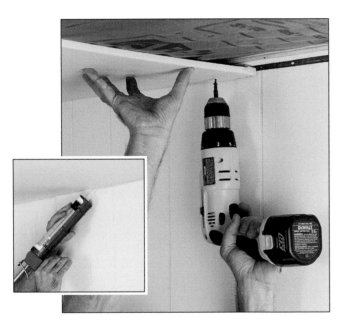

2 ATTACH FIRST LAYER OF DRYWALL

Install panels with their long sides perpendicular to the joists.

- With a helper, raise each panel into place, allowing a ¼" gap on all sides to help isolate vibrations.
- Attach the panels to joists with 1⅝" drywall screws driven every 6" to 12".
- Cut panels to fit as necessary with a utility knife.
- Apply silicone caulk around the perimeter of this layer *(inset)* and between panels; sound, like cold air, finds its way through tiny cracks.

CHOOSING Materials

Resilient Channel

The next time the furnace comes on or your kid's basement rock band plugs in, put your hand on the floor of a room above and notice the vibrations. Some of that energy is converted to sound. Resilient channels work by keeping one layer of the ceiling from bouncing the one next to it. Think of the channels as acoustical shock absorbers, soaking up annoying sounds before they can be broadcast to your living quarters. Resilient channel is commonly available in 12' lengths and comes in ⅜" and ½" thickness (½" is the most common). Although the channel is predrilled for screws, quite often the holes won't match up with your joists. No problem: Drywall screws are self-tapping and will readily pass through the thin metal.

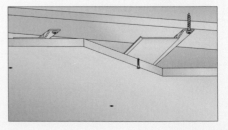

CEILINGS

3 SNAP CHALK LINES FOR CHANNEL

- Snap chalk lines on the drywall to lay out the position of the resilient channels.
- They are 24" apart and should run parallel to the long edges of the panels.

4 INSTALL CHANNEL

- Use 1⅝" drywall screws to install the channel along the chalk lines. The screws go through the shorter flange, through the drywall, and into the ceiling joists; the second layer of drywall will be suspended from the longer flange.
- Cut the channel to length as necessary with tin snips or a hacksaw.

5 ATTACH SECOND LAYER

Use shorter, ¾" drywall screws to attach the second layer. This avoids making contact with the upper sheets and transmitting vibrations.

- With a helper, attach the second layer of drywall perpendicular to the wider, unattached flange of the channel with ¾" drywall screws. Again, leave a ¼" gap between the drywall and the walls.
- Tape the joints and paint the ceiling if you wish.
- Run a bead of caulk around the perimeter as you did in Step 2.

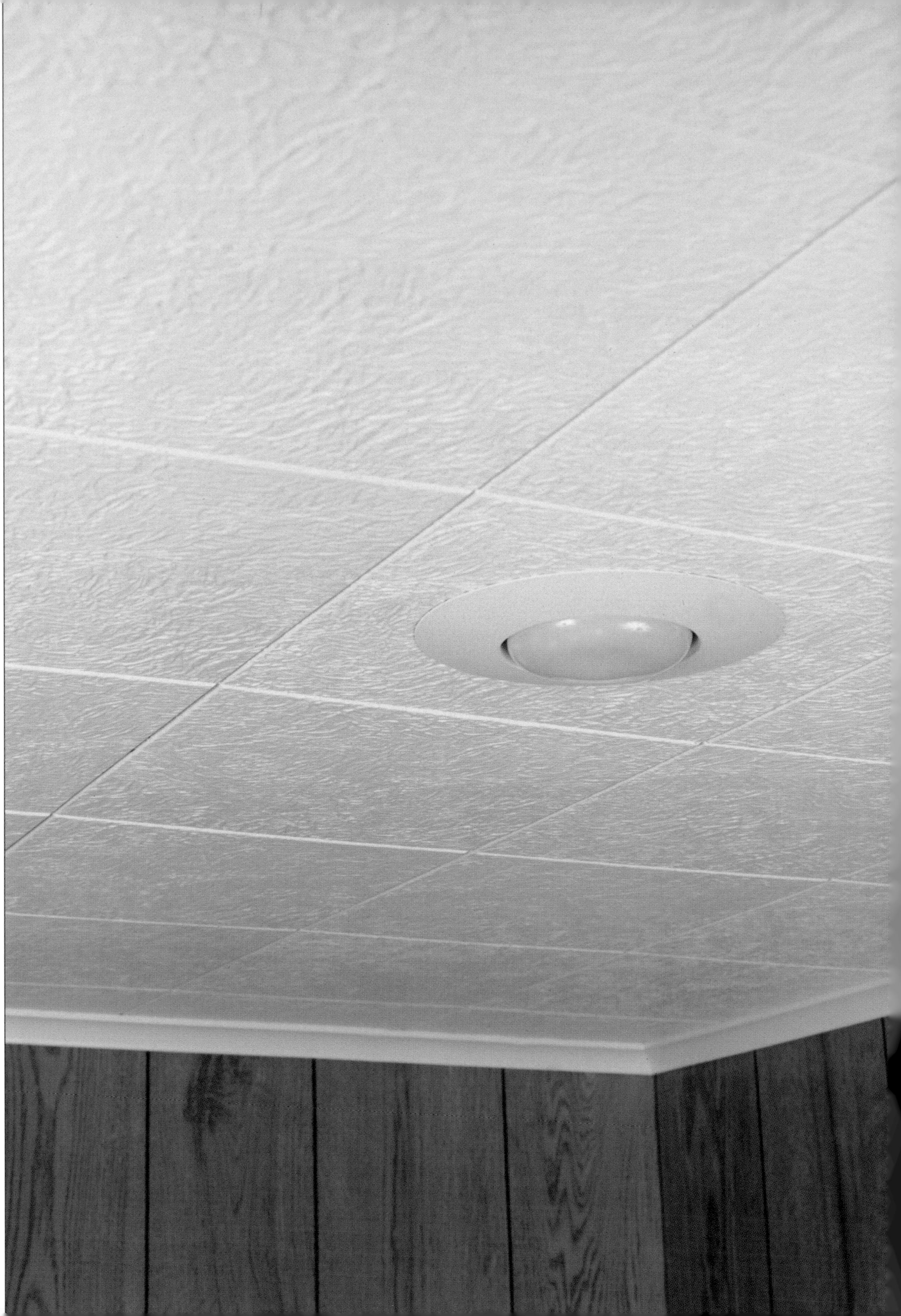

Installing Acoustical Ceiling Tile

Cover an old, cracked ceiling or create a new one with attractive and easy-to-install acoustical tile.

Acoustical ceiling tile offers an easy-to-install remedy to one of the most common cosmetic problems I see in older homes—cracked plaster ceilings. The cracks in the ceiling are usually due to long-term settling of the house. Minor cracks can be patched, if only temporarily; but serious cracks are almost impossible to fix without tearing down the ceiling and starting over. A simpler solution is to cover the problem with acoustical tile. One advantage that ceiling tile has over a suspended ceiling *(see page 234)* is that it takes up less headroom—you'll lose approximately an inch, versus several inches with a suspended ceiling.

In most instances, acoustical tile is stapled to furring strips attached to the existing ceiling. In a pinch, you can even glue acoustical tile directly to drywall or plaster with construction adhesive. Acoustical tile is washable and paintable. It's also perfectly suitable for a newly remodeled space, like the basement fix-up in this project. (The home-owners, both standing 6' tall, didn't want to lose the head-room that a suspended ceiling would have taken.)

Whether for a new ceiling or covering an old one, the procedure is the same—fasten furring strips to the existing ceiling or joists, level the strips, and staple the tile up. Once started, the tongue-and-groove system that joins the edges of the tiles is virtually foolproof.

Tools

Tape measure
Chalk line
3' or 4' level
Electric drill or screw gun
Claw hammer
Nail set
Utility knife
Straightedge or framing square
Staple gun

Materials

Acoustical ceiling tile
1×3 furring strips
½" heavy-duty staples
1⅝" drywall screws
Carpenter's shims
Cove or crown molding
2" finish nails
Nails that match the color of the molding, or wood putty

Preparation

Measure the room and make a plan drawing of the space. Determine the square footage, and purchase the tile all at once to ensure consistency.

Choose 1 by 3 furring strips, which allow a greater margin for error than 1 by 2s.

If new lighting fixtures are part of the plan, run the wiring or hire an electrician for that part of the job.

LEVEL OF DIFFICULTY
  Moderate

TIME REQUIREMENT
  2 to 3 days

COST ESTIMATE
  Starting at as little as $.35 per square foot for the tile, figure anywhere from $.60 to $1.50 per square foot including the other materials needed

1 SNAP CHALK LINES ACROSS JOISTS

Based on a plan drawing of the room, decide on the size of the perimeter tiles, which are typically cut to equal size on opposite sides of the room. This will determine where to start the first furring strip.

- Measure and mark the locations of the furring strips, 12" on center, at opposite ends of the room.
- Stretch a chalk line from one end mark to the other, and snap chalk lines across the joists.

2 SCREW FIRST FURRING STRIP TO JOISTS

Because the tiling procedure starts in a corner, I start the furring strips at a corner as well.

- Place the first furring strip tight against the wall and joists, and screw it to each joist. Use 1⅝" drywall screws, not nails; screws allow you to come back and slide shims in where needed.
- Check the first strip with a level and add carpenter's shims as needed.

3 SCREW ON REMAINING STRIPS

- Center the furring strips on the chalk lines and screw them into each joist.
- After the first four 8' strips are up, check for level both along each strip and across the strips. Wherever necessary, loosen the screws and slide carpenter's shims between the strips and joists to make the strips level.

Staple Guns

You can't put up ceiling tile without a staple gun, but you do have a few options when you go to buy one. The basic mechanical model illustrated here will work fine. Make sure it can shoot staples up to ½" long, the typical length recommended for ceiling tile. Some staple guns have a high and low power setting, but both the tile and the fur-

ring strips are so soft that this feature is not needed. You'll find some models are more er- gonomically designed; one of these will be easier to use if your hands are not particularly strong, and it will reduce fatigue on large ceiling jobs. You can also use an electric staple gun. They're not that much more expensive than a good mechanical one—and they require a lot less muscle—but I find that the cord is a nuisance when I'm working on a ladder.

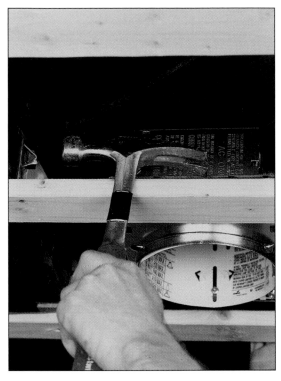

4 INSTALL LIGHTING FIXTURES

In new ceilings, now is the time to install any new recessed lighting fixtures; if you're not comfortable doing this yourself, contact a licensed electrician.

- Position lighting fixtures between joists and between furring strips.

- Set the fixtures at the appropriate level and nail the brackets into the joists. Most fixtures have an internal "can" that can be adjusted to the exact height of the finished ceiling after the ceiling tiles are in place.

5 CUT PERIMETER TILES

- Measure and cut the first couple of perimeter tiles. Always orient the two edges with the long tongue out from the starting corner. *Don't* cut all the perime- ter tiles in advance, because their size is likely to change somewhat along a wall.

- Mark the face of the tiles, then cut through in several passes with a sharp utility knife guided by a flat straight- edge, like a framing square.

CEILINGS

6 STAPLE FIRST TILE IN CORNER

- Position the corner tile out from the wall about ¼". This space allows for adjusting the first courses so that the seams are perfectly straight and tight.
- Staple the corner tile up to the furring strips.
- Since there's no tongue in the corner to staple into, tack a nail or drive a screw up into the very corner of the tile *(inset)*. (The nail or screw will be covered by the trim molding.)

7 STAPLE TILES, WORKING OUT FROM CORNER

The first tiles are the most important for establishing a straight pattern.

- Install three tiles along each wall from the corner, aligning the corners of each tile carefully.
- Proceed to fill in the full tiles, then more perimeter tiles, working in a triangular pattern.

8 FIT TILES AT LIGHTING

- At the light fixtures, align the edges of the tile with the tiles already in place and press the tile against the fixture.
- Apply chalk or lipstick to the edge of the fixture if necessary so it will leave an impression on the back of the tile *(see Ron's Pro Tips on page 142)*; this will show the exact size of the fixture.

CEILINGS

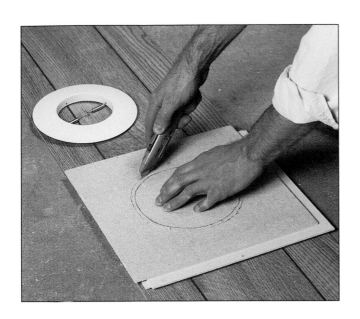

9 CUT TILES TO FIT AROUND LIGHTS

The opening for a light fixture should be slightly larger than the fixture itself. A finished ring or "halo" will conceal the gap in the tile around the fixture.

- On a protected surface, use a sharp utility knife to score a cut line about ¼" outside the mark from the light fixture.
- Then with a sawing motion, work the knife most of the way through the tile. This will leave a score mark on the face of the tile.
- Cut through the last bit of the tile from the face side.

10 ATTACH TILES AT LIGHT

Tiles around lighting fixtures get stapled up just like all the others; but engaging the tongue-and-groove edges and positioning the cutout at the same time is a little tricky, so work carefully.

- Position the inside corner of the tile first, then slip the tile over the fixture while sliding the tongue-and-groove edges together.

11 APPLY MOLDING

- Use a crown or cove corner molding to conceal the gap between the ceiling and the wall. In addition to painted and unpainted wood molding, there are several vinyl molding products available that require no finishing.
- Cope or miter the molding at the corners, and nail the molding to the wall studs with 2" finish nails.
- Countersink the nail heads and fill with matching putty, or use matching colored nails.

Adding Track Lighting

A track fixture is a customizable lighting system.

Once used only for commercial displays, track lighting has caught on in a big way with homeowners. If you have a standard ceiling light, replacing it with a track fixture is a snap. Some fixtures come in a box, ready to install. Others allow you to choose between different light units. And with most models, you have your pick of bulbs—wide-focus "wall washer" bulbs to illuminate a corner, all-purpose bulbs for reading or board games, and tightly focused bulbs to dramatically set off a painting or sculpture. You also have a choice of wattages. And some tracks can be linked together through their "live ends," either in line with each other or at a 90-degree angle.

Tools

Tape measure
4' level or straightedge
Phillips-head and flat-head screwdrivers
Electric drill and twist bits

Materials

Track and lights
Toggle bolts or plastic anchors (if you're mounting the track on drywall)
Wire nuts

Preparation

Make sure the fixture will allow sufficient headroom.

Choose between halogen and incandescent fixtures.

Decide on the track length and the number of lights that you'll attach to it.

Safety

This project involves working with the home's electrical system, and live wires can cause shocks. Make certain the circuit has been turned off at the service panel before you get under way. If you are uncomfortable with doing electrical work, buy the fixture and hire an electrician to install it.

LEVEL OF DIFFICULTY
Easy

TIME REQUIREMENT
Less than ½ day

COST ESTIMATE
With 3 halogen lights, $50 to $250

CEILINGS

1 REMOVE OLD FIXTURE AND ATTACH CROSSBAR

Turn off the power at the service panel. If the existing fixture has a good bulb, you can confirm that the circuit is dead with a flick of the switch.

- Remove the screws holding the fixture in place.
- Untwist the wire nuts in the recessed electrical box, and separate the wires.
- Using the parts that come with the new fixture, attach its mounting bracket to the box *(inset)*.

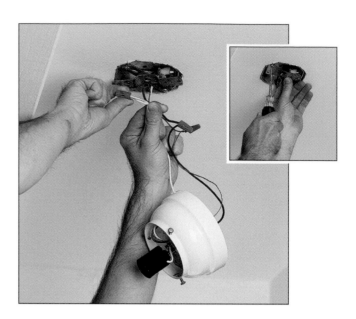

2 LAY OUT CENTERLINE FOR TRACK

Fixtures come with mounting clips that are attached to the ceiling; the track is then snapped into place. This creates a gap above the track that minimizes the unevenness of a ceiling.

- Use a level or straightedge to draw a line parallel to the wall. If the fixture's wiring can be located anywhere along the track, you are free to place the track more to one side of the box than the other.

CHOOSING
Materials

Choosing a Track Fixture

The basic choice in shopping for track lights is between incandescent and halogen fixtures. Both have advantages. Incandescent fixtures *(top of photo)* are less expensive, put off less heat (a factor in summer), and produce a warmer-looking light. Halogens radiate brilliant white light, and some homeowners like the modern, high-tech look of certain models. Either type of fixture may give you the option of plugging directly into an outlet, with a pre-installed cord or one you fit into an end of the track.

3 INSTALL TRACK

Track is attached to drywall ceilings with hollow-wall anchors (*see page 175*). Consult the manufacturer's directions for the exact diameter to drill through the ceiling.

- To use mounting clips, drill holes for them along the centerline and mount with the hardware. Snap the track in place.

- To attach the track directly, hold it in place and make marks through the mounting holes. Remove the track, drill the holes, and then hold the track in place once again and mount with the hardware.

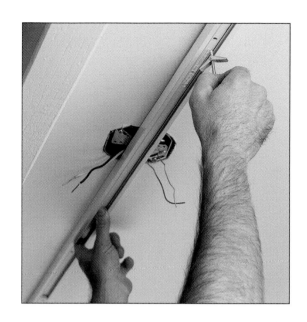

4 CONNECT WIRING

Before continuing, double-check to make sure that the power to the fixture is off.

- Following the manufacturer's directions, attach the fixture's wires to the box wires. Secure the connections with wire nuts, and gently push the wires inside the box.

- Attach the cover plate over the electrical box.

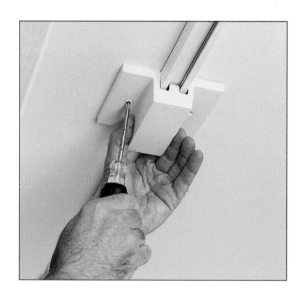

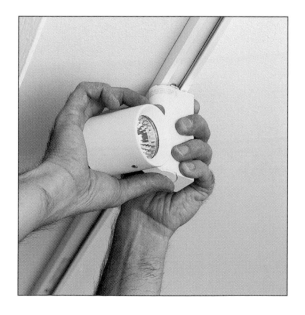

5 ATTACH LIGHTS

- Install bulbs in the light units, and attach the units to the track as indicated in the manufacturer's directions.

- Restore power to the circuit, and adjust the lights as necessary.

Installing a Thin-Line Skylight

A thin-line skylight can dramatically improve the quality of any room by bringing in more natural light.

All skylights require cutting a hole in the roof, and that's a task that will cause even an experienced do-it-yourself homeowner to hesitate. But a thin-line skylight, like the one described here, makes the job easier since you don't have to cut any of the roof joists. Instead, the unit fits between any two joists spaced 16" on center. So there's no breach in the existing roof framing.

Also note that this project was made easier by the fact that the skylight is installed directly in a cathedral ceiling. This means that no tricky light well (basically a framed box) needs to be built connecting a roof frame to a ceiling frame. And most manufacturers offer an optional flashing kit with their skylights to ensure a watertight installation.

Installing a skylight may seem more difficult than some of the other projects in this book. But in fact, it's not much harder; there's just more at stake if the job isn't done right. Talk with a roofing contractor or someone experienced at installing skylights before starting.

Tools

Tape measure and chalk line
Keyhole saw or saber saw
Straightedge and utility knife
Combination square and
   framing square
Electric drill and twist bits
Pry bar
Claw hammer
Circular saw
Drywall knife
Paintbrush
Work gloves and a dust mask

Materials

Thin-line skylight with
   flashing kit
1" galvanized roofing nails
Poster board or foam board
Duct tape
Roofing paper and cement
Drywall supplies: $\frac{1}{2}$" drywall,
   corner bead, joint com-
   pound, and drywall tape
$1\frac{5}{8}$" and 2" drywall screws
Paint

Preparation

Plan to do the exterior part of the job when the forecast calls for dry weather. That way, you won't have to seal the opening against rain overnight.

Safety

Working on a roof, especially a steep one, can be dangerous. Don't try this project if you're not comfortable getting up on and down off a roof. Consider using a safety harness, available at rental companies.

LEVEL OF DIFFICULTY
Challenging

TIME REQUIREMENT
2 to 3 days

COST ESTIMATE
$250 to $400

CEILINGS

1 CUT EXPLORATORY HOLE

The first task is to figure out the best location in the room for the skylight; see Ron's Pro Tips, below. To pinpoint the exact location, you'll need to find the roof joists.

- Use a stud finder *(see page 64)* to locate the joists in the area where you want to install the skylight.
- Rough-cut a 2" or 3" hole in the skylight area to locate the joists exactly, then mark the joist lines on the ceiling. Safety Note: If your house was built prior to 1978, it may have been decorated with lead paint. See page 287 before cutting into the ceiling.
- With a framing square, mark the ends of the opening—see the "rough opening" dimensions supplied with the manufacturer's instructions.

Ron's
PRO
TIPS

Locating the Skylight

You know you want more light in the room. But now that you're ready to cut a hole in the roof, you're not quite sure exactly where to locate the skylight.

To get a preview of how a skylight will look at different locations in the ceiling, cut a piece of white poster board or foam board to the size of the rough opening dimensions and tape it to the ceiling. Stand back and have a look.

Consider the amount of sun different parts of the roof get, and also how the areas in the room

below will be used. You may—or may not—want a skylight directly over an area that gets a lot of use, like a couch or a breakfast table. Keep in mind that most skylights let in light that is more intense, and for a greater part of the day, than windows do.

One more thing: If you cut the poster board to the exact size of the rough opening provided with the installation instructions, you can use it as a template for marking the opening right on the ceiling.

2 CUT OPENING

- Plunge a keyhole saw through the drywall and cut along the lines. When making the long cuts, guide the saw by letting it ride against the joists.
- Use a piece of duct tape to prevent the cut-out drywall from breaking before the cut is complete.
- Wearing gloves and a dust mask, cut through any insulation with a utility knife and remove it.

3 TRANSFER OPENING TO EXTERIOR SHEATHING

The roof opening should be the same dimensions as the ceiling opening.

• Use a combination square to transfer the corner marks of the opening across the joists and onto the roof sheathing. Be sure to hold the square in line with the joists, not perpendicular to them.

• Drill a ¼" hole through the roof sheathing and exterior roofing material at each corner mark *(inset)*. Using an extra-long drill bit will make it easier to drill the holes in a straight line.

4 REMOVE SHINGLES

You'll need to remove enough shingles to expose the entire opening.

• Locate the four corner holes, and place a nail or screw in each.

• Begin removing shingles at or just above the top corners. Once the top course is off, you'll be able to see the roofing nails in the subsequent courses.

• To prevent damaging the shingles, use a stiff drywall knife in combination with a flat pry bar to pry up the roofing nails. Slide the knife under the shingle until it hits the nail. Then slide the pry bar under the knife to pry up the nails.

5 SNAP CHALK LINES

• With a nail or screw in each corner hole, wrap a chalk line around all four corners and snap the lines one at a time.

• Double-check the "rough opening" dimensions against the dimensions of the chalk lines (here again, your poster board or foam board template will come in handy).

CEILINGS

6 CUT ROOF SHEATHING

- Set a circular saw for slightly more than a ¾"-deep cut.
- Make a plunge cut at the start of each of the lines, and cut an inch or so beyond the corners.
- After starting the last cut, nail or screw a scrap 1 by 2 cleat across the cut-out piece to prevent it from falling into the room. When the last cut is complete, lift the waste piece out by the cleat.

7 MOUNT SKYLIGHT TO ROOF

Check the manufacturer's instructions for positioning the skylight in the opening— some come with positioning blocks to center the skylight in the opening.

- Position the skylight in the opening.
- Screw the skylight mounting brackets into the roof sheathing with the screws provided.

8 APPLY FLASHING AND SHINGLES

Installing the step flashing is the most critical component of a skylight installation. If your skylight does not include a flashing kit, purchase step flashing from a roofing-materials supplier.

- Starting at the bottom, nail the step flashing to the side of the skylight, but not into the roof.
- After each course of step flashing, lay the roofing shingles back in place, cutting them as needed with a utility knife. Nail the roofing material close to the edge of the step flashing, but do not nail through the step flashing *(inset)*.

CEILINGS

9 COMPLETE INTERIOR FRAMING

- Cut two pieces of framing material that match the joists—typically 2 by 6s or 2 by 8s—and fit them between the joists at each end of the opening.
- Drill angled holes through these pieces and into the joists.
- Screw them in place with 2" drywall screws.

10 APPLY FINISH MATERIAL

The interior of the opening can be finished with wood or with drywall.

- Cut the finish material to fit the four sides of the opening, and nail or screw it to the framing.

11 FINISH OFF SKYLIGHT OPENING

- In a drywalled opening, nail on metal corner bead around the outside corners of the opening.
- Apply tape and joint compound at interior corners.
- Apply joint compound over all nails or screws, and feather it out from the corner bead. This typically requires two or three applications.
- Sand and paint the drywall, or apply a finish like polyurethane to a wood-framed opening.

Hanging a Ceiling Fan

Ahhhh—
a gentle
cool breeze
on a hot
summer day—
at the flip
of a switch.

During the summer, a ceiling fan can cool any room with a quiet flow of air. In cooler months, in rooms with high ceilings, it can keep the warm air closer to the floor, where you want it. And unlike window fans and air conditioners, you never have to put a ceiling fan away.

Additionally, most ceiling fans are designed to accept a light fixture, which makes a great combination—both functionally and aesthetically. The right ceiling fan can add flair to any room. Fortunately, finding the perfect fan is easy since there is such a wide variety of designs available.

Regardless of the design you choose, hanging a ceiling fan can be challenging; the challenges relate directly to the substantial weight of most ceiling fans. The first challenge is supporting this weight as it hangs from the ceiling. *(See Ron's Pro Tips on page 262.)* The second has to do with assembling the fan. It's difficult enough to juggle a heavy fan while up on a ladder—trying to connect wires at the same time is a Herculean task. I strongly recommend enlisting the aid of a helper to assist with the installation.

Tools

Electric drill with screwdriver bit (optional)
Phillips-head and flat-head screwdrivers

Materials

Ceiling fan
Outlet box
Wire nuts
Sliding or telescoping support bracket (optional)

Preparation

Determine whether the existing ceiling outlet box is attached securely to the joists. If it is not, purchase a suitable box or a support bracket *(see Ron's Pro Tips on page 262).*

Safety

Make sure there is adequate clearance for the fan blades: a minimum of 7' between the blades and the floor, and no less than 18" to the nearest wall.

It's imperative that the outlet box you plan on attaching the ceiling fan to is rated to support the fan—and that it is installed properly. Outlet boxes designed for light-fixture use won't support the considerable weight of the fan and should never be used as such.

Turn off the power at the circuit breaker before disconnecting or connecting electrical wires.

LEVEL OF DIFFICULTY
Easy (with a helper)

TIME REQUIREMENT
½ day

COST ESTIMATE
$30 and up, depending on the quality of the fan

1 REMOVE OLD FIXTURE

- Remove the hardware that holds the fixture canopy up against the ceiling.
- Remove the wire nuts that connect the fixture wires to the supply wires, and disconnect the ground wire.
- Unscrew the threaded nipple and hanging bar typically used on light fixtures.

Ron's PRO TIPS

Mounting an Outlet Box between Ceiling Joists

There are two types of adjustable brackets for mounting a fan between joists: one for when you have access to the joists, the other for when you don't. Each comes with an electrical box and necessary hardware.

If you have access to the space above the ceiling, use a sliding bracket *(top)*. Simply rest the bracket on the drywall or plaster lath, and screw the end flanges into the joists. Then hang the box on the nut that rides in the track, and lock the box in place in the ceiling opening.

If you don't have access to the ceiling joists, use a telescoping support bracket *(bottom)*. After removing the old electrical box, pass the bracket up through the opening and position the bar perpendicular to the joists. Reach through the opening and rotate the bar. As you turn the bar, the ends of the bracket will bite into the joists for a secure grip. Then mount the box on the bar with the U-bolt supplied.

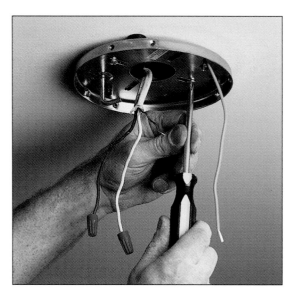

2 ATTACH FAN'S CEILING PLATE

The ceiling plate mounts directly to the outlet box, then the rest of the fan is hung from the ceiling plate.

- Once you have installed an outlet box appropriate for hanging a fan *(see Ron's Pro Tips at left)*, pull the supply wires through the center opening in the ceiling plate, then screw the ceiling plate to the outlet box.

CEILINGS

3 ASSEMBLE FAN

Ceiling fans are mounted either tight to the ceiling for a "low-profile" look or hung from an extension pipe that positions the fan closer to the floor. Most fans allow for both options.

- Thread the fan wires up through the canopy (and extension pipe if used).
- Temporarily hang the fan assembly from the hook on the ceiling plate, or get a helper to assist you.

4 CONNECT THE WIRES

Read the instructions provided with the fan for making the wire connections.

- Connect the white supply wire to the white fan wire with a wire nut.
- Connect the black supply wire to the black fan wire. If there is a second black wire for a light, connect all three black wires with a larger wire nut.
- Connect the ground wires.

5 MOUNT FAN

- Slide the canopy, with the fan motor attached, over the ceiling plate and tighten the mounting screws.
- Assemble the fan blades to the brackets, and then screw the brackets to the motor.
- Attach the light fixture, if included, to the bottom of the fan.

Installing a Replacement
Entry Door 266

Making a Window Box 272

Installing
a Window Greenhouse 276

Painting Exterior Walls...... 280

Painting Exterior Trim 286

Adding Shutters 290

Adding
Low-Voltage Lighting 294

Installing
a Security Light............ 298

Installing a Storm Door 302

Adding a Stone Path 306

A Simple
Brick-and-Sand Patio........ 310

EXTERIORS

Installing a Replacement Entry Door

The main entry door to most homes serves as the visual focal point of the house from the outside.

Because it's one of the first things that guests, visitors, and passers-by notice, most people take special pride in their front door; they want to make a positive, welcoming statement. Unfortunately, many front doors not only look outdated, they often stick in the summer and let in the cold in the winter. It should come as no surprise, then, that replacing the front door is one of the most common projects homeowners seek help with.

One of the first questions I'm asked about doors is whether to choose wood or steel. Steel doors have replaced wood doors as a staple of new home construction. They're more weathertight because, unlike wood, they don't expand and contract with changes in the weather. The same benefits are found in steel replacement door systems. Like new-construction steel doors, replacement steel doors are prehung on a frame with an integral sill. But they are designed for easy installation—you just remove the interior trim and the sill and slide the new unit into place. The weatherstripping stops are installed afterward for a highly weathertight door.

In most home centers, steel replacement doors are a custom-ordered item, and they are more expensive than a similar door made for new construction—but there is a wider selection of these than of standard wood doors.

Tools

Claw hammer
Phillips-head and flat-head screwdrivers
Utility knife
Pry bar
2' or 3' level
Electric drill and twist bits
Caulking gun
Slip-joint pliers
Nail set

Materials

Steel replacement door
Lock set
Wood shims
Acrylic latex caulk (if not included with door)
Silicone caulk
Latex wood filler
1½" and 2" finish nails

Preparation

Carefully measure the existing opening, and take these measurements with you when ordering a replacement door. The height measurement should go to the sill—not to the threshold, which will be removed. Also, make note of which direction the door swings.

LEVEL OF DIFFICULTY
Moderate

TIME REQUIREMENT
1 to 2 days

COST ESTIMATE
$300 to $600 and up

EXTERIORS

1 REMOVE OLD DOOR

It's easiest to remove the door from the hinges, and then remove the old hinges.

- Working from the bottom hinge to the top, use a screwdriver to pry up the hinge pins, then tap the screwdriver with a hammer to remove the pins.
- With the hinge pins removed, lift the door inward and off of its hinges.
- Remove old hinges from the jamb, and remove all weatherstripping.

2 REMOVE INTERIOR TRIM

Replacement doors are installed within the existing frame from the inside—that's what makes the process so easy. But you have to remove the existing trim. Do so carefully, and you should be able to re-use it.

- In order to prevent cracking around the seam between the wall and the trim, especially on painted trim, first score the intersection with a utility knife *(inset)*.
- Pry the trim away from the wall with a pry bar. Place a wood shim between the wall and pry bar to protect the wall.

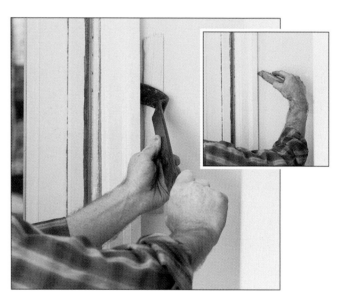

3 REMOVE OLD THRESHOLD

You need a flat surface for the new threshold to sit on. Older doors may have a wood threshold screwed into a separate sill, or a sill/threshold combination. If it can't be removed altogether, you'll need to chisel off the raised portion of the threshold to create a flat surface.

- Remove any visible screws in the threshold. Then pry it up with a pry bar, using a wood shim to protect the floor.

EXTERIORS

4 SHIM OUT FRAME FOR DOOR

Replacement doors are made slightly smaller than the existing opening. Follow the installation instructions to determine the thickness of wood shims needed. If wood shims are not included with your door, purchase a length of ⅛"-thick flat molding stock and cut it into 12" lengths.

- With the door in place, insert shims at four locations: at each of the three hinges and at the strike plate. The shims will butt up against the old door stop.

- Remove the door, and attach the shims to the jamb with 1½" finish nails.

5 APPLY CAULK AND INSTALL DOOR

Once you're sure the new door and frame fit snugly within the new shimmed-out opening, remove the door and frame temporarily.

- Apply a generous zigzag pattern of silicone caulk on the sill area where the new threshold will sit.

- Tilt the door and frame into the opening.

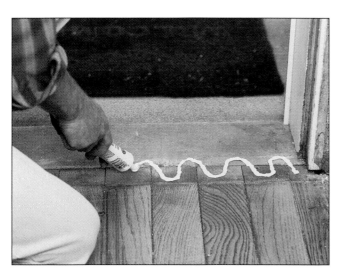

6 LEVEL DOOR FRAME

The door should still be secured in its frame with screws or metal brackets at this time.

- Hold a 2' level on the top edge of the door frame and check it for level. If it's not, slide shims under one side of the sill until it's level. The gap created from shimming will be caulked later.

EXTERIORS

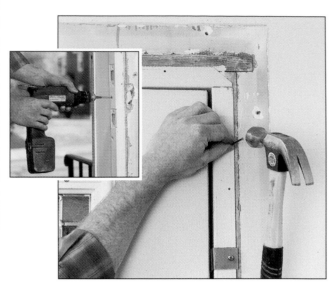

7 NAIL AND SCREW FRAME TO JAMB

- Drive nails (as supplied, or 2" finish nails if not supplied) through the steel flange into the wood frame.
- After the entire frame is nailed in place, open the door by removing the factory-installed screws or retainer bracket that holds it shut in the frame.
- Drive the security screws provided through the designated holes at the hinges and at the lock strike *(inset)*. These screws ensure that the door frame can not be pushed in from the outside.

8 INSTALL LOCK SET

Steel doors come with predrilled holes for a lock set, according to your specifications when ordered. Lock sets are supplied with detailed installation instructions.

- Make sure the lock (or locks, if a dead-bolt is included) works smoothly before nailing the stops in place next.

9 NAIL THE STOPS IN PLACE

Stops create a weather seal for doors. The head jamb and lock jamb typically have a magnetic seal, while the hinge jamb is more likely a compression seal. The door should be locked when you're installing the stops.

- Cut the stop for the head jamb to length and put it in place. Press it snug against the face of the door as you nail the stop in place.
- Repeat for the hinge jamb and lock jamb stops. Note: These two stops are typically angled where they meet the threshold. If they are not precut to the correct angle, make a trial angled cut on a scrap piece of wood first.

10 CAULK THE SILL

- Apply a bead of acrylic latex or silicone caulk where the threshold meets the sill.
- Smooth the caulk with a fingertip moistened with water.

11 INSTALL INTERIOR TRIM

If it's in decent shape, you can reuse the existing interior trim. Pull the nails out through the back side of the wood, using pliers. Otherwise buy similar door trim and cut it to fit. Location of the nails in the trim is important—they have to either miss the new steel door frame altogether or pass through holes in the frame designated for the trim nails.

- Drive 1½" finish nails through the casing and into the wood frame.
- Recess the nails with a nail set, and fill holes with latex wood filler.

Ron's

PRO TIPS

Tight Miters in Door Trim

It's not hard to cut a decent miter joint in door trim; but when you go to nail the pieces in place, the joint always seems to open up a little. Even if you do get it just right, the joint will most likely open up at some time due to seasonal expansion and contraction of the wood.

Here's a technique that will help close a loose miter, and keep it that way. Drive a 2" finish nail through one piece and into the other. Locate the nail in the meatiest part of the trim but not too close to the edge. Place a piece of cardboard between the hammer and the wall to protect the wall from getting scratched as you hammer.

It's best to do this before nailing the trim to the door frame completely. Once the miter is nailed together, drive in the nails nearest the corner.

Making a Window Box

This mini-garden looks great indoors and out.

Window boxes are traditional ways of both ornamenting the exterior of a home and improving the view from the inside. They're a place to put plants where the family will enjoy them the most. The design shown here uses cedar, a wood that doesn't have to be painted or otherwise treated for long life. And the simple mounting bracket, cut from a single board, allows easy removal of the box to work on the plants or to store it in the off-season.

The best plants for window boxes have a long blooming season and aren't finicky about moisture or sunlight. Geraniums are an obvious choice because of their plentiful blossoms and ease of care, but you also can grow herbs and attractive vegetables such as hot peppers. The box shown here includes a blue-flowering rosemary, lavender, verbena, pansies, Alpine asters, and a small fern.

Tools

Tape measure
Sawhorses or other flat work surface
C-clamps
Try square
Circular saw or hand saw
Dust mask and eye protection
Electric drill and twist bits
Phillips-head and flat-head screwdrivers

Materials

1 by 6 cedar or other lumber
$1\frac{1}{2}$" stainless-steel or brass flat-head screws
$2\frac{1}{2}$" stainless-steel or brass flat-head screws
4-mil plastic sheeting
Gravel or pot shards

Preparation

Determine whether the window gets sufficient sunlight for the plants you plan to grow.

Make sure the windowsill is sound enough to anchor a box filled with heavy, moist soil. If in doubt, ask a carpenter to check the sill and suggest alternatives for mounting the box.

Base the length of the box on the width of the window, keeping them roughly equal.

LEVEL OF DIFFICULTY
Easy to Moderate

TIME REQUIREMENT
$\frac{1}{2}$ day

COST ESTIMATE
$20 to $40 for a 3'-wide box, depending on the wood you use

EXTERIORS

1 LAY OUT PARTS

The box shown here is made of 1 by 6 cedar, planed on only one side.

- The front, back, bottom, and mounting bracket are all the same size—the desired length of the box by the full width of the 1 by 6s. The two sides are 8¼" long so they'll cover the ends of the mounting bracket and project slightly at the front of the box.

- Lay the parts out on the stock with a try square, using the clearest wood for the front and sides.

2 CUT PARTS

- Cut the parts to length with a circular saw or a hand saw.

- Cut the mounting bracket stock more or less in half with a 45-degree-angle cut. For help in making a straight cut, use the saw's guide extension, as shown. One half will be attached to the back of the box, and the other to the windowsill.

CHOOSING Materials

Outdoor Woods

All lumber grows outdoors, of course, but some woods hold up to weathering better than others. Several species distinguish themselves, even without paint, stain, or varnish. Their availability may vary by region. From top to bottom, they are Western red cedar, Spanish cedar, cypress, and white oak. Although these woods will hold up well without a topcoat, they'll last even longer if you protect them with either a high-quality outdoor spar varnish or a waterproofing agent.

EXTERIORS

3 ASSEMBLE BOX

The box is assembled with brass or stainless-steel screws, driven into pilot holes.

- Use 1½" screws to attach one-half of the mounting bracket (either half) to the back of the box; place it flush with the top of the back so its bevel is facing down *(inset)*. This creates a pocket for the other half attached to the windowsill.

- Attach the sides and bottom to the back, then to each other, with 2½" screws.

- Again using 2½" screws, attach the front to the sides and bottom.

- Drill three ½"-diameter drainage holes in the bottom.

4 LINE BOX

- To protect the wood from moist soil and prevent water stains on the outside of the box, line it with 4-mil plastic sheeting. Cut a piece to cover the bottom and go up the sides and ends.

- Poke a hole through the plastic over each drainage hole.

- To promote good drainage, spread a layer of gravel or clay pot shards over the plastic-lined bottom of the box.

5 INSTALL BOX

- Hold the box at the desired height, and mark where the other half of the mounting bracket will attach to the sill.

- With the bracket in place, drill pilot holes through it and into the sill; then secure it with five 2½" screws.

- Set the box on the bracket and add soil and plants. If you live in a climate where the box won't offer much of a display in the winter, use it as an off-season bird feeder, scattering birdseed over the soil surface.

Installing a Window Greenhouse

Enjoy flowers and fresh herbs at your kitchen window.

Few us have the budget, space, or time for a full-sized greenhouse. But envision a tiny greenhouse that hugs the house for warmth. That's a pretty good definition of what you see here. It's a glazed box that receives plenty of light, allowing you to grow sun-loving plants that would sulk on a windowsill. Another advantage is that spilled soil and water stay outside of the house, where they won't make a mess.

You can treat a window greenhouse as a beautiful display garden, with flowers year round. But I suggest that you try harnessing that sunlight to grow culinary herbs and even salad ingredients, just a few steps from the kitchen counter. Lettuce and Asian greens will take to the greenhouse's cooler temperatures in winter. In summer, switch to herbs and other plants that thrive on heat and can handle periods of low moisture.

You'll want to pick a window that gets sun at least part of the day. But note that this small box acts as a solar collector, sending temperatures above the safety limit for many plants. Regulate the heat by opening and closing the window to your house. Don't pick a window that is needed for cross-ventilation or as a fire exit. To allow full access to the greenhouse shelves, make sure both halves of a double-hung window are operable.

Tools

Tape measure
Carpenter's level
Electric drill and bits
Phillips-head and flat-head screwdrivers
Leather work gloves
Putty knife
Utility knife
Safety glasses
Caulking gun

Materials

Window greenhouse kit
Exterior silicone caulk
Foam caulk saver (optional)

Preparation

Measure the window opening, and contact a window greenhouse manufacturer *(see Sources on page 316)* to determine which window greenhouse will work best.

From the outside of your house, check whether the greenhouse would be subjected to falling snow from the roof above, or torrents of water from a pitch without a gutter.

LEVEL OF DIFFICULTY
Moderate

TIME REQUIREMENT
½ day, with occasional assistance from a helper

COST ESTIMATE
$500 to $1,000 and up, depending on the size of the window

1 REMOVE SCREENS AND STORMS

- You'll need to have access to the greenhouse from inside your home, so remove the screen and storm window.

- If an upper sash has been painted shut, use a putty knife to free it.

2 POSITION AND LEVEL THE FRAME

Have a helper hold the assembled greenhouse frame in place.

- Use a tape measure to center the frame over the window opening.

- Plumb the frame with a level.

- Mark the outline of the frame and the mounting holes used to anchor it.

3 ATTACH FRAME

- Remove the frame from the wall.

- Drill the anchor holes as marked. Use a masonry bit for brick, stucco, or stone; use a standard wood bit for wooden clapboard, or to go through siding into the sheathing or framing.

- With your helper positioning the frame along the outline marks, drive screws to attach it.

- If the kit comes with support brackets, attach them to the frame and wall.

4 CAULK AROUND FRAME

Before putting in the glass, seal around the frame where it meets the house.

- Run exterior silicone caulk around both the interior and exterior of the frame.
- To help seal the frame over wood, vinyl, or aluminum clapboard-type siding, insert strips of foam "caulk saver" or backer rod into the wedge-shaped opening before applying caulk.

5 ADD GLAZING TAPE

The greenhouse kit will most likely use glazing tape (coils of putty) to form a seal between the glass panes and the frame.

- Following the manufacturer's instructions, start applying the glazing tape in the groove in the frame near the top. Work your way down, pressing the glazing tape firmly into the groove.
- Cut off excess tape with a utility knife.
- Where it's necessary to use two strips of tape in a run, butt their edges together.

6 ADD GLASS

Again, follow the manufacturer's instructions for installing the glass. Wear gloves to protect yourself from sharp edges.

- Begin with smaller, rectangular panes rather than curved glass, in case you break a piece learning the installation process. If needed, a hardware store or home center can cut new standard panes.
- Most kits use compressible metal clips to press the panes into the glazing tape and create a watertight seal.
- Push the metal clips in place with a putty knife *(inset).*
- Install the shelves.

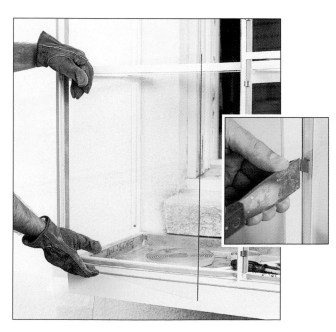

Painting Exterior Walls

Why would you want to paint your home? To save money, of course. And the professional house painters I've talked to mention other reasons. They like the peace and quiet, the breezes, the sunshine—qualities you don't find in every household task. So, consider taking on this job yourself. You'll make a dramatic statement by covering those wide-open surfaces with the hues of your choosing. And if you plan well, the work will go surprisingly quickly. Here's a tip if you aren't wild about heights: Some painting contractors will agree to do just the scary parts, leaving the lower story for you to handle. You still save some money, and you don't have to brave a wobbly extension ladder.

If your house is clad with aluminum siding, you may have found that the original paint is less than permanent, exposing the underlying metal. Fortunately, you can wash off the old powdering pigment, then use an additive to help the primer coat adhere to the metal. Your siding should look as good as new. The house shown on these pages is sided with aluminum.

Note: Pre-1978 houses may have been decorated with lead paint. See the Safety note on page 287 before beginning work.

Here's a big-scale project with big-scale do-it-yourself satisfaction.

Tools

Tarps
Ladders
Power washer (can be rented)
Paint scrapers
Paintbrushes
Airless sprayer (can be rented) and respirator
Caulking gun
Rubber and/or leather gloves
Protective eye goggles
Chisel and/or putty knife

Materials

150-grit sandpaper
Paintable caulk
Painter's tape or masking tape
Exterior primer and paint
Adhesion builder (for aluminum siding)

Preparation

Remove shutters, hardware, and vines from the walls.

Plan the job so that you won't be painting a wall under the midsummer sun; put off the job if rain is forecast.

Safety

When moving a metal ladder, make sure it does not come in contact with electrical wires.
If using an airless sprayer, make sure to wear a respirator.

LEVEL OF DIFFICULTY
One-story house: Easy to Moderate.
Multistory house: Moderate

TIME REQUIREMENT
2 weekends for a small house in good condition

COST ESTIMATE
$100 to $160 per 1,000 square feet of siding for 2 coats. A pressure washer rents for $55 a day, and an airless paint sprayer for $70.

EXTERIORS

1 COVER SHRUBS AND BEDS

The object of this project is to beautify the house, but not at the cost of giving a speckled finish to foundation plantings.

- Use tarps to cover plants, as well as walkways, the driveway, and any projecting roofs that will be visible from the ground or windows.

2 SET UP LADDER

- On uneven ground, take the time to dig out the high area beneath the rail of the ladder with a trowel or small shovel.
- The top rungs of a ladder are meant to serve as hand holds, not as steps. Switch to a longer ladder when necessary.

3 WASH SIDING

A rented pressure washer will speed up the job, but some professional painters use only a sponge and a bucket of plain water.

- Remove any mildew with a solution of 1 tablespoon non-ammoniated detergent and 1 quart household bleach to 3 quarts warm water; use waterproof gloves and protective goggles.
- Rinse well.

EXTERIORS

4 SAND/SCRAPE SURFACES

- Once aluminum siding has dried, remove any remaining powdery paint with 150-grit sandpaper. You can fill small dings with auto-body putty; allow the putty to dry, then sand smooth.

- For wood siding, use a scraper to remove old paint, then go over both rough spots and glossy, unweathered areas with 150-grit sandpaper.

TOOL
KNOW-HOW

Paint Scrapers

Removing flaking paint is nobody's favorite job, but a good scraper—one that's got a sharp blade and a handle that feels comfortable in the hand—can make the work go more easily. The standand scraper *(bottom)* has a steel blade that dulls quickly. I prefer a scraper with a replaceable carbide blade *(top);* they stay sharper longer, and replacing the blade is a snap. All scrapers require pressure to work. Try to use your body weight rather than relying on arm strength alone. This means being comfortably close to the area you're scraping. If you are on a ladder, move it as needed to avoid reaching out with the scraper—that long stretch not only is tiring but also risks upsetting your balance.

5 MASK TRIM AND HARDWARE

Apply masking tape to any areas that are painted a contrasting color or that should not be painted. (Paint stores stock a specialized masking tape that has just enough stickiness along one edge to keep it in place without lifting off paint that has been recently applied.)

- Mask contrasting trim if it has already been painted.

- Mask metal flashing and adjacent walls of brick or stone.

- Mask lighting fixtures and other wall-mounted items that won't be removed.

EXTERIORS

6 CAULK AS NEEDED

- Remove old, hardened caulk with an old chisel if it no longer makes a good seal.
- Use a putty knife to clean away any residue.
- Apply a new bead of a caulk that is specified as paintable and suited for exterior use.
- Allow the caulk to skin over before painting.

7 MIX ADDITIVES

Paint will stick better to the smooth surface of aluminum siding if you stir an "adhesion builder" into the primer coat. A good paint store will stock this product for both latex and oil-based paints.

- Pour off half a gallon of primer into a clean, empty can or bucket from which you will be painting.
- Following the directions on the can of adhesion builder, add the proper amount to the half gallon of primer you poured out.
- Stir to thoroughly mix the additive and primer.

8 APPLY PRIMER

Homeowners tend to dismiss primers as thinned-down versions of regular paint. In fact, a good-quality primer is formulated both to bond well with the surface and to offer a good grip for the topcoat.

- Brush on the primer, starting at the top of the house and working down.
- Apply paint along the bottom edge of each board or aluminum panel, then brush the face with horizontal strokes.
- Mix up more batches of primer and additive as you need them.

9 BRUSH ON FINISH COAT

- After the primer has dried, brush on a coat of exterior paint as a topcoat. Use the paint as it comes from the bucket; no additive is needed.
- If desired, mask siding when thoroughly dry and paint trim a second color.

10 OR SPRAY ON FINISH COAT

Although many pros continue to stick with brushes, some homeowners appreciate the speed with which they can apply paint with an airless sprayer from a tool-rental store. The model shown here draws its paint from a bucket.

- Before you spray, don gloves, safety goggles, and a respirator.
- Try to organize the job well beforehand so that you can rent the sprayer for as few days as possible; pick days when there's the least chance of wind.

Ron's
PRO TIPS

Spray Extender

Painting a house with a brush would go a lot quicker if the handle were a yard long. That would be unmanageable, of course, but an extender on a paint sprayer has the same benefit. It allows you to cover more area from wherever you're standing—reaching up from the ground, or to either side from a ladder. That flexibility means you get the job done even faster. Ask tool-rental stores whether they stock an extender before committing yourself to a sprayer.

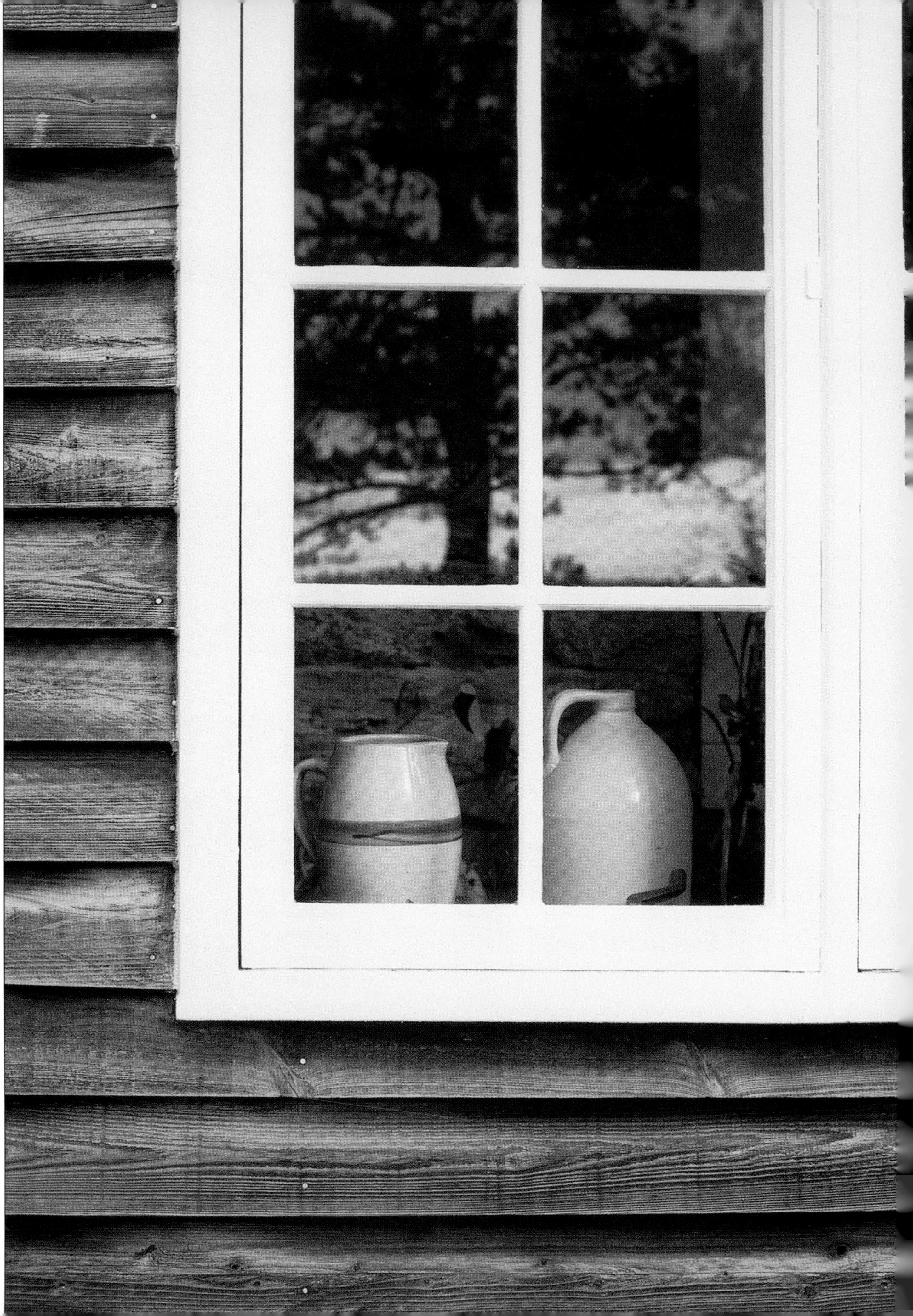

Painting Exterior Trim

It's the trim on a house that first catches the eye; so it make it worth looking at.

Have you ever noticed that the condition of the trim on a house can make or break the overall appearance? The walls can be in perfect shape, but if the windows and doors and their frames are neglected, the whole house can look tired and glum.

There are two main reasons that the paint on trim wears so quickly. First, trim gets a lot more wear and tear than the exterior walls: Doors and windows open and close, and little (and sometimes big) messy fingers tug at trim and molding. Second, trim has plenty of edges—and edges just don't hold paint very well.

I like to suggest to homeowners that they keep an extra gallon of trim paint on hand, waiting for a pleasant weekend when they'll have the time to sand a bit of trim and brush on a coat or two. Well-maintained trim will stand up better to the elements. And when freshly painted, these conspicuous details make the whole house look sharper.

Tools
Ladder
Drop cloth
Sanding block
Paint scraper
Putty knife
Nail set
3" sash brush
Caulking gun

Materials
80- and 120-grit sandpaper
Painter's caulk
Glazier points
Glazing compound
Wood putty
Masking tape
Exterior primer and paint

Preparation
You can scrape and sand trim in almost any weather, but plan the painting for a dry day with moderate temperatures, and out of the direct sun.

Safety
Up until the 1970s, household paints often contained lead, now known to be a neurotoxin. If you'll be removing paint that might contain lead, you can test for this element with an inexpensive color-test pen, sold at hardware stores. If the test is positive, spread a drop cloth below the work area so you can collect paint debris and dispose of it properly. Wear a dust mask, eye protection, and gloves when scraping and sanding paint.

LEVEL OF DIFFICULTY
Easy

TIME REQUIREMENT
½ day and up

COST ESTIMATE
$25 and up

EXTERIORS

1 PREPARE THE WOOD

- Lay a drop cloth below the work area to collect paint chips.
- Scrape away loose paint.
- Sand to smooth surfaces and remove wood fibers raised by scraping (*inset*).
- Remove dust and chips with a clean rag.

2 APPLY CAULK OR PUTTY

- Remove old, hardened caulk with a putty knife and check glazing compound.
- Apply paintable caulk rated for exterior durability according to the manufacturer's instructions.
- If any of the glazier points that hold the glass in place are missing, replace them and apply glazing compound.
- Set protruding nails with a nail set and fill recesses with wood putty or caulk.

Trim Painting Kit

Ron's
PRO TIPS

Painting trim is one of those jobs you can squeeze in whenever you find yourself with a few spare hours on a sunny weekend. But to take advantage of that opportunity, you've got to be stocked up with supplies such as masking tape, a caulking gun, a sash brush, sandpaper, a scraper, and razor blades. Otherwise you'll have to hunt around for the right paint and the right brush, then dash out to the store for sandpaper and masking tape—and before you know it, your spare time is up and nothing has been accomplished. Try keeping painting supplies handy in a separate toolbox or even in a plastic bucket.

3 MASK SELECTED AREAS

- With wide masking tape, cover adjacent areas that aren't to be painted. Paint stores sell a specialized tape with just enough adhesive along one edge to hold it in place.

TOOL KNOW-HOW

The Sash Brush

Painting trim requires you to be nimble. A sash brush (also known as a trim brush) can be a big help. Its bristles are trimmed at a diagonal so that you don't have to contort your wrist to make an even stroke of paint. And that pointed tip, with its acute angle, allows you to dab paint into crevices. Spend enough to get a high-quality sash brush. Then take the trouble to extend its life. Avoid dipping the bristles more deeply into the paint than necessary; this keeps paint from lodging near the metal ferrule, where it tends to harden and make the brush less flexible. Rinse the brush well immediately after use, using warm water. Finally, hang the brush to dry to avoid deforming the bristles.

4 APPLY PAINT

Allow caulk, glazing compound, and wood putty to dry before painting, as specified by the manufacturers.

- Again spread out a drop cloth, this time to protect shrubs, porches, and decks from paint splatters.
- For bare wood, first brush on a coat of primer and let it dry.
- Stir and brush on the paint—either one or two coats, as needed.
- To prevent the masking tape from leaving a residue of adhesive, remove it as soon as the final coat has dried.

Adding Shutters

Although shutters are no longer necessities, they are still pleasing to the eye.

Why do houses have shutters? Chances are you probably won't know the answer unless you're either an architectural historian or about two hundred years old. Shutters are a vestige of a time when both window glass and heat were very precious; by closing a pair of wood flaps over a window, homeowners of yesterday protected the panes and conserved the modest warmth their fires produced.

Today, most American houses continue to be built along traditional lines—siding, gable roofs—and we still tend to think that a window looks naked without shutters. To me, shutters don't seem quite right unless their dimensions are at least roughly in scale (that is, when closed would cover the entire window) and the hardware is somewhat realistic.

If you're planning on adding shutters to your home, I suggest you measure the opening to get the right size, then hang them with traditional hardware. You'll appreciate the difference—even if you aren't two hundred years old.

Tools

Tape measure
Electric drill
Twist bits
Phillips-head and flat-head
 screwdrivers
Claw hammer
Allen wrench

Materials

Shutters
Shutter hardware
Shutter dogs or holdbacks

Preparation

Choose between raised-panel shutters and those with slats; slats are available either fixed or movable. Although shutters can be found at many home centers, their selection is often limited. For a greater variety of styles and sizes, look in shelter magazines for companies that specialize in shutters.

Choose a paint color that either matches or complements the trim.

Plan on priming and painting the shutters before installing them.

LEVEL OF DIFFICULTY
Easy

TIME REQUIREMENT
½ to 1 day, depending on the number of windows

COST ESTIMATE
$50 to $100 per window

EXTERIORS

1 MEASURE WINDOW OPENING

Some shutters can be trimmed ½" from each side and 1" both top and bottom; check the manufacturer's specifications.

- Measure the height, from the top of the sill to the underside of the top of the frame.
- Measure the width, from the inside of one side of the frame to the other.
- Halve the overall width to get the width of each shutter.

2 ATTACH HARDWARE TO SHUTTERS

Shutter hinges are available for both frame and brick houses; those for brick houses allow for a window frame that is set in from the face of the wall.

- Have a helper hold the shutters in place as they would be when closed.
- Put each hinge in position, marking both the window frame and the shutter back for pilot holes.
- Drill pilot holes in the shutters, and attach the hardware.

CHOOSING
Materials

Shutter Hardware

Just as shutters accent a house, hardware accents the shutters. You can get chrome-plated items right off the shelf at most hardware stores, but you may prefer the more traditional look of hardware finished in flat black. Hand-wrought

reproductions are available through companies advertising in shelter magazines. And if you frequent flea markets and antique shops, you may find old hinges and shutter dogs that have been salvaged for reuse. The shutter dogs shown here were purchased from an antique dealer specializing in rescuing handmade hardware from houses slated for demolition.

3 ATTACH HARDWARE TO HOUSE

- Drill pilot holes in the window frame as marked. (If the hinges will be mounted on brick, use malleable iron shields in holes of suitable diameter.)
- Drive screws to attach the hardware. Or, if you are using a threaded pintle as shown here, turn it with the aid of pliers or an Allen wrench.

4 MOUNT THE SHUTTERS

- Hang the shutters.
- Position the holdbacks or shutter dogs and mark for pilot holes.
- Drill the pilot holes, attach the holdbacks or shutter dogs, and adjust their depth as necessary to prevent the shutters from rattling.

5 MOUNT DOGS OR HOLDBACKS

Traditionally hung shutters will flap in the wind unless anchored.

- Wall mounting is difficult on brick or stone houses, and they often employ "shutter dogs" that restrain shutters with arms anchored to the window sill.
- You can use holdbacks, often shaped like an S, complete with a hidden spring that prevents rattling; these mount directly to the siding.

Adding Low-Voltage Lighting

Highlight any part of your home, garden, or yard at night with low-voltage lighting.

There's something especially inviting about a house with carefully planned exterior lighting. The house says "come in, let me show you the way." Just a few years ago, lighting like this required an electrician and a serious investment. But with the advent of low-voltage lighting, installing exterior lights just got a lot simpler—and safer.

Adding low-voltage lighting to a home is a low-tech project anyone can tackle without fear. For power, all you need is access to an outdoor outlet. If you don't have an outlet in the area where you want to install lighting, consider hiring an electrician to install one. It should be a GFCI (ground fault circuit interrupting) outlet with a constant-use cover. If you have an older outlet, it's a small job to upgrade it to a GFCI.

You can find low-voltage lighting kits at most home centers, which contain the fixtures, a transformer, and a cable. Or you can buy the components individually to create a custom lighting system.

Tools

Electric drill
Twist bits (or a masonry bit if mounting transformer to brick or block wall)
Phillips-head and flat-head screwdrivers
Shovel or spade
Wire-stripping pliers

Materials

Low-voltage transformer
Cable
Light fixtures
GFCI outlet with a constant-use cover

Preparation

Install (or hire an electrician to install) a GFCI outlet with a constant-use cover on the house wall near the area to be lighted.

LEVEL OF DIFFICULTY
Easy

TIME REQUIREMENT
½ day

COST ESTIMATE
$30 to $50

EXTERIORS

1 LOCATE LIGHT FIXTURES

The first step is to define where the trench will fall and to make sure the cable that's provided is long enough for your plan.

- Place the fixtures where you want them and run the cable along the most direct route from the transformer to each of the fixtures.

- If one end of cable sheathing is already stripped (you'll see two strands of copper wire about ½" long), locate that end at the transformer.

2 DIG A TRENCH

How deep you dig the trench is up to you. I usually dig down about 6" to ensure that the wiring won't get damaged with future gardening or lawn care.

- Use a shovel or spade to dig a narrow (2"- to 3"-wide) trench along the path of the cable.

Ron's PRO TIPS

Cutting a Trench in Sod

If the trench for your outdoor lighting cable is located under part of your lawn, you don't have to end up with a gash of dirt across the lush sea of green. Instead, cut the sod out in a strip that can be laid right back in on top of the cable.

Use a hatchet or a small straight-edged shovel to make cuts that angle in slightly toward the bottom of the trench. Cut a wedge-shaped strip about 3" wide and remove the sod carefully. After the cable is laid, replace most of the soil so the sod will end up level with

the surrounding grass. Tamp the sod strip in place with your foot, and give the area a liberal watering to get the roots restarted.

3 ATTACH FIXTURES TO CABLE

Make sure the fixtures are close to the final location you want. Most low-voltage fixtures use a simple snap-on wire connector to connect the fixtures to the cable.

- Engage the two halves of the snap-on connector carefully. Once you start the assembly, the pieces can't be separated.
- Squeeze the two halves of the connector together as much as possible between your fingers and thumb.

4 SET FIXTURES AND BURY CABLE

- Push the spear base of each fixture into the ground. Step back and check that the fixtures are standing straight up.
- Gently fold the excess lead wire from the fixture down into the trench, but be careful not to crimp it.
- Replace the topsoil and/or sod into the trench.

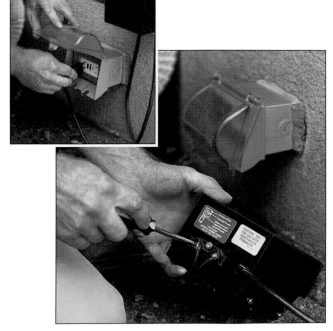

5 CONNECT TO POWER

Read the wiring instructions that are provided with your transformer kit.

- Loosen the terminal screws, slip the wire under the pressure plates, and tighten the screws securely.
- Position the transformer near the GFCI outlet, and mount it on the wall. Drill holes for the screws. On brick or block walls, you'll need to use a masonry bit.
- Plug in the transformer to the GFCI outlet (*inset*) and close the outlet cover. Adjust the timer that controls the on-off cycle to the desired setting.

Installing a Security Light

A brainy security light can make your home more hospitable after dark.

For many homeowners, a sensor-triggered security light is as indispensable as a doorbell, and not just for added security. Sure, the fixture will flood the area with light if an intruder (or the neighbor's dog) happens by, and that's a comforting thought. But these fixtures are also convenient. They turn on to welcome you when you walk out to the car, and then when you return home.

On top of that, most are programmed to turn themselves off after a certain period of time. They're usually photo-sensitive, too, so that they don't bother coming on in the daytime. For all this sophistication, they are amazingly inexpensive. And if you already have a standard no-brains floodlight on your house or garage, it's a quick job to replace it with a more intelligent sensor model.

Tools

Phillips-head and flat-head screwdrivers
Wire-stripping pliers
Ladder

Materials

Motion-activated security light
Silicone caulk
Caulking gun
Wire nuts

Preparation

If there isn't an existing light fixture on the outbuilding or side of your house, run the electrical cable yourself, or call in an electrician.

Safety

Make sure to turn off power at the main service panel before removing the old fixture and installing the new light.

LEVEL OF DIFFICULTY
Easy

TIME REQUIREMENT
½ day

COST ESTIMATE
$20 to $50

EXTERIORS

1 REMOVE OLD FIXTURE

- At the service panel, shut off power to the circuit serving the fixture. To ensure that no one turns the power back on while you are working outside of the house, place a note on the panel or a strip of tape over that breaker.
- Remove the old fixture, disconnecting its wires from those in the box.

2 ADD MOUNTING PLATE

As with most lighting fixtures, a security light attaches to a mounting plate instead of the box. The manufacturer will usually include a universal mounting plate with the light.

- Attach the mounting plate provided to the box, as described by the manufacturer's directions.

CHOOSING
Materials

Lighting Options

Security light fixtures tend to use incandescent floodlights (*center*); these bulbs don't take a long time to warm up—they come on instantly at full illumination. They aren't nearly as brilliant as mercury-vapor (*top*) or halogen fixtures (*bottom*), however. Both of these alternatives do need warm-up time, but they are considerably more efficient and have a longer life. That's why you'll often see them in industrial applications. For the majority of homeowners, standard floodlights will do the job if aimed carefully to make the best use of their modest power.

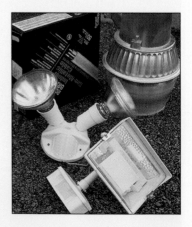

3 CONNECT WIRING

- Connect the new fixture's wires to those in the box, using either wire nuts or quick connectors: white wire to white, black to black, and green to ground.

4 MOUNT FIXTURE

- Mount the weatherproof gasket, if provided, between the fixture and the exterior wall.
- Screw the fixture to the mounting plate with the screws provided.

5 CAULK AROUND FIXTURE

- Apply silicone caulk around the base of the fixture to keep out water and insects.
- If the light is installed over siding (as shown here), take extra care to fill in any gaps under the fixture caused by the ridges of the siding.
- Turn on power and test the operation. Most security lights have a range of delays to choose from before the light turns off, as well as a sensitivity setting that determines when the light will be triggered. Select what works best for you.

626

WELCOME

Installing a Storm Door

Spruce up your entryway, and let the sun shine in, with an elegant new storm door.

Storm doors are more functional and attractive than ever. Both the frames and the glass panels are insulated, so they reduce heat loss in the winter and keep cool air in during the summer. Most doors have interchangeable screen panels if you prefer to let the breezes flow. On a "full-view" storm door, almost the entire door is screen or glass, so you can enjoy more sunlight year round, and it doesn't hide an attractive front door. (Note: Adding a full-view storm door may void the warranty on your front door; check the manufactrer's warranty before installing one.)

Storm doors come in a wide range of colors and styles to match any home. Most front door frames are made to standard dimensions, and storm doors are made to fit those standards. But there are built-in adjustment factors that make installing a storm door a lot easier than installing a new entry door in an existing frame. Most are reversible for left- or right-hand opening. The trickiest part of this job is cutting the aluminum frame pieces to length with a regular hacksaw—that and making sure you put the hinges on the right side of the frame.

Tools

Phillips-head and flat-head screwdrivers
Tape measure
Hacksaw
Elctric drill and twist bits
Sawhorses or other large, flat work surface

Materials

Wood shims
Storm door
Door handles and closer (if not provided with door)

Preparation

Most storm doors are made for one of several standard-sized openings. Check yours carefully before buying the door. Custom sizing is available from many manufacturers.

Also, as you begin the installation, remove the screen and glass panels from the door to reduce the weight and avoid damage.

LEVEL OF DIFFICULTY
Easy

TIME REQUIREMENT
½ to 1 day

COST ESTIMATE
$125 to $350, depending on the door you choose

EXTERIORS

1 SCREW HINGE-SIDE FRAME TO DOOR

A storm door should always be hinged on the same side of the frame as the main door is hinged.

• Hold the door upright in the position it will be installed, with the inside of the door facing the house. Then mark the side that will be hinged, as well as the top and bottom.

• Lay the door across a pair of sawhorses, and screw the jamb frame to the door.

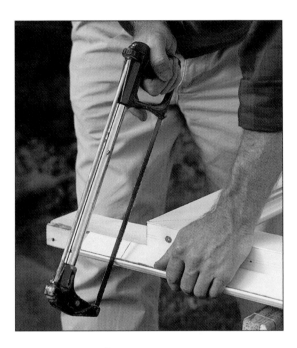

2 CUT OFF EXCESS HINGE JAMB

The two vertical jamb pieces are longer than necessary, to accommodate a variety of door openings and thresholds. The hinge-side jamb piece is to be cut at the bottom only.

• Measure the height of the hinge side of the door opening on the house.

• If the sill slopes away from the house, as is typical, transfer this angle to the measurement on the jamb.

• Cut the jamb piece as marked, using a hacksaw.

3 SCREW HINGE JAMB TO FRAME

If the door with the hinge jamb attached is too heavy or awkward, remove the door before mounting the hinge jamb, then remount the door after screwing the hinge jamb to the frame.

• Position the door in the opening so the hinge jamb wraps around the edge of the wood frame.

• If necessary, insert shims between the jamb and door frame until it's plumb.

• Secure the hinge jamb to the frame with the screws supplied.

4 SCREW HANDLE-SIDE JAMB TO FRAME

- Measure and cut the handle-side jamb to length, as you did the hinge-side jamb.
- With the door in its closed position, slip the handle-side jamb piece into position.
- Create a consistent gap between the door and the frame by inserting wood shims between the jamb and the frame; then screw the jamb to the wood frame.
- Screw the top jamb piece in place.

5 FIT BOTTOM SWEEP CAP

- Insert the rubber sweeps into the sweep cap if they are not pre-installed. I've found that lubricating the rubber sweeps with dish soap helps them slide easily into their grooves.
- Slide the sweep cap carefully onto the bottom of the door, high enough so the door can close.
- With the door in its closed position, snug the sweep cap down against the sill. Then screw through the slotted holes on the inside face of the sweep cap to secure the sweep cap to the door.

6 INSTALL HANDLE ASSEMBLY AND CLOSER

Follow the specific instructions that come with your door and hardware.

- Mount the handle assembly in the door.
- Screw the strike plate to the jamb.
- Check that the latch and lock operate properly before tightening all the screws on the handle, lock set, and strike plate.
- Install the closer (*inset*). You may need to drill holes both in the frame and in the door for the large screws that mount the closer.

Adding a Stone Path

A path of stone makes a handsome, long-lasting statement in your yard.

Stone is the original pavement, and it remains the most durable material. "Pavers" cut from stone in a geometric shape and fairly consistent thickness make laying out a walk a relatively straight-forward job.

The biggest challenge is moving the heavy pavers around the yard, and I think you'll find that even this is completely manageable if you follow a few easy tips. Best of all, once the pavers are in place, you don't have to worry about them. They are as close to maintenance-free as anything in a home landscape.

A stone walkway will be most useful in a high-traffic area, identifiable by the paths worn in your yard. The more traffic the path will carry, the wider you should make it. A width of 2' is adequate, but 3' will be more gracious.

The only challenge to using natural stone is locating it; ask at your local landscaping center. If it isn't readily available, consider using pavers made from concrete. They're available in various shapes, colors, and sizes and can be found at almost any home or building center. And just like stone, they're virtually maintenance-free and can be installed using the same techniques shown here.

Tools

Tape measure
Stakes
Twine
Claw hammer
Shovel or spade
Pry bar
Trowel
Garden rake
Gloves

Materials

Landscaping cloth
Sand
Stone or concrete pavers

Preparation

Buy bagged sand, roughly 50 pounds per 10 square feet of walk.

You'll be removing sod along the path's course, so look for bare places in the yard where you can use it.

LEVEL OF DIFFICULTY
Easy to Moderate

TIME REQUIREMENT
½ to 1 day

COST ESTIMATE
$150 to $500, depending on the length and width of the stone path

1 LAY OUT PATH

- Using stakes and twine, establish both sides of the path. If you place the twine a little to the outside of where the path is to go, you'll have more room to work with a shovel.

- Determine the pattern of the pavers. If you will be using pavers of various lengths, plan a mix of sizes; but remember that the longer the paver, the heavier it will be.

2 DIG THE TRENCH

- Using the twine as a guide, cut down through the sod to a depth that will allow the pavers to be flush with the ground when placed atop an inch or two of sand. A shovel with a pointed nose will penetrate the soil easily; you can switch to a square-bladed shovel to lift squares of sod and then make straight, crisp edges along the walk.

- Keep the squares of sod watered in a shady place if you're planning to reuse them.

- Smooth the bottom of the trench with a garden rake.

Ron's PRO TIPS

Laying Out a Curved Path

An easy way to guarantee a graceful arc is to "draw" it across the lawn with a garden hose. Once you arrive at a curve you like, preserve it by tapping small pegs along one side of the hose, or "draw" the line on the grass with spray paint.

There are two ways to make a curved path once you've laid it out. It's simplest to use rectangular stones and allow gaps at the ends. Or, you can cut the ends at an angle to permit butting the joints; either ask the stone supplier to make the cuts, or do it yourself with a circular saw and a masonry blade. If you do decide to cut the stone yourself, make sure to wear eye protection, gloves and a dust mask.

3 LINE WITH LANDSCAPING CLOTH

Landscaping cloth is a fabric that allows rainwater to penetrate but discourages weeds. It typically comes in 3'-wide rolls and can be purchased at most garden and home centers.

- Trim its width if necessary.
- Lay the cloth along the trench.

4 SPREAD SAND OVER CLOTH

Sand forms a bed to support the pavers and help keep them from rocking underfoot.

- Dump sand from the bags along the trench, reserving some to trowel under tippy pavers.
- Spread the sand with the back of a garden rake.

5 SET AND LEVEL PAVERS

- Lift the pavers with your legs, not with your back—a wheelbarrow or sturdy garden cart will be a big help in moving the pavers about.
- Once a paver is on the ground, "walk" it by holding it vertically and alternately moving one corner and then the other.
- Allow the pavers to settle for a week or two, walking on them often.
- If the paver rocks, have a helper lift a low corner with a pry bar while you trowel in a little sand. Lower the paver and test the result.

A Simple Brick-and-Sand Patio

You don't need to mess with cement to make a nice patio.

A brick patio establishes a civilized living area in the wilderness of the yard. It can be an inviting place to have meals, read the paper, play with the dog, or just soak up the sun. The easiest designs are rectangular; use a simple brick pattern, and stick to one level. If you're feeling more ambitious, you might have two or three levels or throw in a curved edge.

Patios typically abut a wall of the house, but I also suggest that homeowners consider freestanding designs. The freestanding patio shown here has no frills, and yet it provides a pleasant "no-mow" zone on which to place lawn furniture. The bricks are set in an uncomplicated running bond pattern, with an edging of vertical bricks to help anchor the patio, provide a clean look, and keep grass from infiltrating.

Tools

Shovel
Stakes and twine
4' level
Garden rake
Garden trowel
Brick set and claw hammer
Broom
Garden hose
Leather gloves
Safety goggles

Materials

Sand ("bar" or "washed concrete" sand)
Dry portland cement (optional)
Landscaping cloth
Bricks
2 by 4 screed board (as long as patio is wide)

Preparation

Pick the site with care. Level spots take less work, although a slight slope (1/4" per foot, away from an adjoining foundation) will improve drainage.

Order 20 pounds of sand per square foot of patio, for a 2" bed plus enough left over to fill between bricks.

For a more stable base, make a deeper excavation for a 4" layer of 3/4" crushed stone. Order 50 pounds per square foot.

Safety

Wear leather gloves and safety goggles when cutting brick.

LEVEL OF DIFFICULTY
  Moderate

TIME REQUIREMENT
  2 days, with a helper to work screed board

COST ESTIMATE
  $1.75 to $2.25 each for bricks and 20 cents for sand per square foot

1 LAY OUT PATIO

- Outline the site with stakes and twine, placing them 4" or so outside the excavation area to allow for digging.
- Check the squareness of the corners by measuring the diagonals, from one stake to its counterpart on the far corner. Both diagonals should be equal; if not, adjust the stakes until they are.

CHOOSING
Materials

Pattern Options

Running bond and offset bond *(below left and right)* are simple patterns suited to bricks that aren't half as wide as they are long.

Half-basket and double-basket weave *(below left and right)* save you the bother of cutting bricks.

Basket weave *(below left)* is another popular pattern that doesn't require cutting bricks. Herringbone *(below right)* is a challenging pattern to lay out, but it's one of the most visually interesting.

2 EXCAVATE AREA

- Begin digging around the perimeter of the patio; a square-bladed shovel makes a straight edge.
- Save the sod you remove; strips can be used to fill in around the edges of the patio. Keep sod watered and in a shaded spot until needed.
- Dig down to a depth equal to the depth of the sand bed (typically 2") plus the thickness of the brick. Check as you go by placing a 2 by 4 across the excavation and measuring from its lower edge.

3 DIG EDGING TRENCH

Edging bricks are placed vertically in a trench around the perimeter. Dig the trench deep enough to make their tops flush with the finished patio surface.

- Start by digging edge trenches on two adjacent sides to form a right angle.
- To accurately determine where the trenches opposite the first two should be, temporarily put in a few edging bricks and then lay out enough of the brick pattern (allowing ⅛" between bricks) to reach the far ends.
- Dig the remaining trenches and remove the bricks.

4 INSTALL EDGING BRICKS

- To help align the edging bricks, move the stakes closer to the patio edge and place the twine just above ground level.
- Lay the edging bricks upright so that their tops will be flush with the surface of the grass (or slightly above if you wish).
- Fill in around the bricks with enough soil to anchor them.

CHOOSING Materials

Bricks

You can use either of two kinds of brick. Pavers *(top left and lower two)* are made specifically for use on the ground; they measure exactly half as wide as long to allow for even spacing without cement; their edges may be chamfered to avoid toe-stubbing edges. Standard wall bricks *(top right)* are sized to accommodate cement, and because they are less than half as wide as they are long, it's best to lay them in a simple running bond *(see the opposite page)*. Wall bricks were chosen for the patio on these pages because of their warm, traditional look.

EXTERIORS

5 SPREAD SAND

- Before spreading sand over the trench, lay down a layer of landscaping cloth to prevent weeds from growing up between the bricks.
- Shovel sand into the excavation, and spread it with a garden rake.
- To level the sand, run a screed board *(see Ron's Pro Tips, below)* along the tops of the edging bricks.
- Add sand to any low spots and again use the screed board.
- Tamp the sand down to compact it.

6 LAY BRICKS

To avoid disturbing the sand bed, do your bricklaying from the lawn and then from the patio surface.

- Beginning at a corner by the house (or at any corner of a freestanding patio), place bricks in the sand according to your chosen pattern, leaving approximately ⅛" between bricks.
- Check often for alignment and level. Add sand with a trowel as necessary.

Ron's
PRO TIPS

Screed Board

A screed board is simply a 2 by 4 used to level the sand bed at the correct height. The board should be as long as the narrower side of the patio; cut notches in the ends, making them as deep as the brick is thick. With a helper at the far end, slide the board over the tops of the edging bricks, working it back and forth to distribute the sand evenly. If your patio is too wide for a single pass, you'll need to temporarily place a guide board down the middle of the sand bed at the same height as

the edging bricks; run the screed board along it and one edge, then along the other edge. Remove the guide board and fill in the space that it leaves.

7 CUT BRICKS AS NEEDED

Depending on the pattern you choose, you may or may not need to cut bricks. If you do, cutting them is easy.

- Rest the brick on firm ground or on sand.
- Place a brick set (a specialized broad-bladed chisel) across the middle of the brick, with the blade's bevel facing away from you.
- Strike the set with a hammer.
- Concrete bricks will need to be cut with a masonry saw (which you can rent).

8 ADD SAND

Filling in between the bricks with sand keeps out dirt that would support weeds and also anchors the bricks into a firm surface. (To add strength and longevity to the patio, consider using a mixture of 1 part dry portland cement to 3 parts sand.)

- Begin by scattering a few shovels of dry sand over the patio.
- Spread the sand diagonally across the patio with a broom to help it settle into the cracks *(inset)*.

9 HOSE DOWN SAND

- Wet down the patio with a hose to wash more sand between the bricks.
- Once the patio has dried, again add sand and sweep and hose it. Repeat until the cracks are filled with sand.
- Use strips of excavated sod to patch any gaps around the patio's edge.

Sources

Installing a Vented Range Hood (page 12)
Saber saw
Relaminating a Countertop (page 28)
Laminate trimmer and laminate roller
Sink Cabinet Storage Upgrades (page 50)
Cordless drill
Refinishing Trim (page 146)
Heat gun
Installing Ceramic Tile (page 202)
Tile cutter
Installing Wood Strip Flooring (page 208)
Flooring nailer
Installing Acoustical Ceiling Tile (page 244)
Staple gun

Tool Crib of the North

1550 South 48th Street, Suite 100
Grand Forks, ND 58201
(800) 358-3096
(web) www.toolcribofthenorth.com

House of Tools

#100 Mayfield Common N.W.
Edmonton, AB
Canada T5P 4B3
(780) 944-9600
(e-mail) mailorder@houseoftools.com

Home Hardware

34 Henry Street West
St. Jacobs, ON
Canada N0B 2N0
(519) 664-2252
(web) www.homehardwaredealers.com

Making a Built-In Window Seat (page 156)
Hardwood plywood—If you can't find a
local source of hardwood plywood contact:

Rockler Woodworking and Hardware

4365 Willow Drive
Medina, MN 53450
(800) 279-4441
(web) www.rockler.com

Sink Cabinet Storage Upgrades (page 50)
Sink tray and hinges

Woodworker's Supply, Inc.

1108 North Glenn Road
Casper, WY 82601-1698
(800) 645-9292

Installing Wood Strip Flooring (page 208)
Hardwood flooring—If you can't find a
local source of hardwood flooring, contact:

National Wood Flooring Association

16388 Westwoods Business Park
Ellisville, MO 63021
(800) 422-4556
(web) www.woodfloors.org

Installing a Window Greenhouse (page 276)
Window greenhouse

Texas Greenhouse Company, Inc.

2524 White Settlement Road
Fort Worth, TX 76107
(800) 227-5447
(web) www.texasgreenhouse.com

Hobby Greenhouse Association
For a directory of greenhouse
manufacturers, send $2.50 to:

HGA Publications Office

8 Glen Terrace
Bedford, MA 01730-2048
(web) www.orbitworld.net/hga

To find a contractor or a source of material for a
kitchen or bath remodeling project, contact:

National Kitchen and Bath Association

687 Willow Grove Street
Hackettstown, NJ 07840
(908) 852-0033
(web) www.nkba.org

Index

A

Access panels, in tiled tub wall, 89
Acoustical tile, ceiling, 245–249
Adhesives:
    Construction, 102, 131, 143
    Contact cement, 29, 30, 33
    Removing from floor tile, 197
    Sheet flooring, 184
Airless sprayers, 281, 285
Aluminum siding, repainting, 281–285
Anchors, hollow wall, 175
Appliance movers, 185
Applicator pads, restoring, 201

B

Backing blocks, 229
Backsplashes:
    Installing, 35
    Removing, 30
    Tiling, 55–59
Baseboard:
    Applying, 133, 145, 185, 191, 213
    Cabinet, 21, 65
    Removing, 130, 180, 200
    Wallpapering and, 122
Basements, finishing, 169–171
Basin wrenches, 39
Bathrooms:
    Exhaust fans, 91–93
    Flooring, 193–197
    Light fixtures, 75–77
    Medicine cabinets, 71–73
    Shower doors, 95–99
    Sinks, pedestal, 67–69
    Tileboard, 101–103
    Toilets, 79–83
    Towel racks, 95
    Vanities, 61–65
    Whirlpool tubs, 85–89
Bathtubs, whirlpool, 85–89
Bifold doors, 161–163
Blind-nailing, 137
Borders:
    Tile, 196
    Wallpaper, 125–127
Brick:
    Cutting, 311, 315
    Laying patterns, 312
    Patio, 311–315
    Types, 313
Building codes, 85, 151

C

Cabinets, kitchen:
    Islands, 19–21
    Painting, 47–49
    Refacing, 41–45
    Storage upgrades in, 51–53
Cap rail:
    Installing, 132–133
    Profiles, 133
Carpet, installing, 215–219
Caulk, applying:
    After tiling floor, 197
    To crown molding, 233
    Before exterior painting, 284, 288
    To greenhouse window, 279
    To outdoor lights, 301
    To shower doors, 99
    To thresholds, 269
    To tileboard walls, 103
    To toilet base, 83
Ceiling fans:
    Installing, 261–263
    Electrical boxes for, 262

Ceilings:
    Acoustical tile, 245–249
    Crown molding for, 227–233
    Painting, 113, 119, 125
    Skylights in, 255–259
    Soundproofing, 241–243
    Suspended
        hardware for, 239
        installing, 235–239
    Wallpaper borders and, 126
    Wallpapering, 223–225
Ceramic tile:
    Backsplash, 55–59
    Floor, 203–207
Chair rail:
    Installing, 135–137
    Profiles, 136
    Wallpaper border as, 125
Clamping techniques, for laminate flooring, 190
Closets, bifold doors for, 161–163
Contact cements, 29, 30, 33
Contour gauge, 197
Coped cuts:
    Filing, 232
    Making, 230–231
Coping saws, 231
Corner blocks, 152, 155
Countertops:
    Cutting for sinks, 23, 25, 30
    Kitchen island, 19, 21
    Relaminating, 29–33
    Scribing to wall, 33
Cove molding, 249
Crown molding:
    Fireplace surround, 152, 154
    Profiles, 228
    Wall/ceiling intersection, 227–233, 249

D

Doors:
  Bifold, 161–163
  Entry, 267–271
  Removing, 162
  Shower, 95–99
  Storm, 303–305
  Trimming
    exterior, 271
    interior, 191
  Wallpapering around, 123
Drawers:
  False, storage behind, 51–52
  Hardware, replacing, 45
  Refacing, 44
Drilling techniques, for pipe
  holes in vanities, 63
Drills, cordless, 53
Drywall:
  On basement walls, 169–171
  Cutouts in, 142
Ducting, for vented range hood,
  13–17

E

Electrical boxes:
  Ceiling fan, 262
  Extenders for, 131
  In new walls, 142–143
  Wallpapering around, 123
Electrical testers, 76
Electricity. *See* Wiring
Exhaust fans:
  Bathroom, 91–93
  Range hood, 13–17
Exteriors:
  Doors
    entry, 267–271
    storm, 303–305
  Lighting
    low-voltage, 295–297
    security, 299–301
  Painting, 281–289
  Shutters, 291–293
  Window boxes, 273–275
  Window greenhouse,
    277–279

F

Fans:
  Ceiling
    installing, 261–263
    electrical boxes for, 262
  Exhaust
    bathroom, 91–93
    range hood, 13–17
Faucets, kitchen:
  Replacing sink and, 26

Upgrading, 37–39
Faux wall finishes, 165–167
Fiberboard. *See* Particleboard
Filing, coped cuts, 232
Fireplace surround:
  Building, 151–155
  Materials for, 152
Flakeboard. *See* Particleboard
Flashing, around skylights, 258
Flooring:
  Carpet, 215–219
  "Floating" laminate, 187–191
  Resilient sheet, 179–185
  Tile
    ceramic, 203–207
    vinyl, 193–197
    wood, prefinished, 195
  Wood strip
    installing, 209–213
    refinishing, 199–201
Flooring nailers, 211
Foundation plantings, exterior
  painting and, 282
Framing:
  New interior walls, 140
  Around whirlpool tubs, 88
Furring strips, applying:
  On ceiling, 246
  On walls, 170

G

Garden path, stone, 307–309
GFCI (Ground Fault Circuit
  Interrupter), 85, 88, 295
Glazing tape, 279
Glue joints, for laminate
  flooring, 189
Greenhouse window, 277–279

H

Hacksaws, 97
Hardware:
  Hollow wall anchors, 175
  Kitchen cabinet, 45
  Shutter, 292
  Suspended ceiling, 239
Heat guns, 148
Hinge mortises, filling, 162

I

Inserts, hollow wall anchor, 175
Insulation:
  Basement wall, 170
  Interior wall, 140–141
  Safety with, 241
  Sound-control, 89, 241–242
Islands, kitchen, 19–21

J

Joints:
  Glue, 189
  Miter, 154, 271
  Scarf, 229
J-rollers, 31

K

Kitchens:
  Cabinets
    painting, 47–49
    refacing, 41–45
    storage upgrades in,
      51–53
  Countertops, 29–33
  Faucets, 37–39
  Flooring, 193–197
  Islands, 19–21
  Range hoods, 13–17
  Sinks, 19–21
Knee-kickers, 218

L

Ladders, safety with, 281
Laminate, plastic:
  Countertop, 29–33
  Flooring, 187–191
Laminate rollers:
  Described, 31
  For veneer, 43
  For vinyl floor tile, 196
Laminate trimmers, 32
Landscaping, exterior painting
  and, 282
Lawn:
  Cutting trench in, 296
  Scalping, for stone path, 307
Leveling compound, 180
Levels, laser, 236
Light fixtures:
  Indoor
    bathroom, 75–77
    on medicine cabinets, 71,
      72
    in new ceilings, 247
    track, 251–253
  Outdoor
    low-voltage, 295–297
    security, 299–301
Lock sets, 270
Lumber, for outdoor use, 274

M

Mantels, building, 151–155
Medicine cabinets:
  Adding wood sides to, 73
  Replacing, 71–73

Miter boxes, making, 212
Miter joints, 154, 271
Molding:
    Backing blocks for, 229
    Base
        applying, 133, 145, 185,
            191, 213
        on cabinets, 21, 65
        removing, 130, 180, 200
        wallpapering and, 122
    Cap rail, 132–133
    Chair rail, 135–137
    Corner, 145, 152, 155
    Cove, 249
    Crown, 152, 154, 227–233,
        249
    Door trim, 191, 268, 271
    Exterior, painting, 287–289
    Fireplace surround, 152
    Refinishing, 147–149
    For tileboard, 103
Molly bolts, 175

N

Nail guns, 211
Nail heads, hiding:
    In chair rail, 137
    In crown molding, 233

O

Outlet boxes. *See* Electrical
    boxes

P

Paint:
    Removing from trim, 148
    For stencils, 108
Paintbrushes:
    For exterior trim, 288, 289
    For stencils, 108, 109
Painter's tape, 99
Painting:
    Ceilings, 113, 119, 125
    Crown molding, 227
    Kitchen cabinets, 47–49
    Safety with, 281, 287
    Shutters, 291
    Sponge, 165–167
    Stencils, 107–109
    Trim
        exterior, 287–289
        interior, 227
    Wainscoting, 129
    Walls
        exterior, 281–285
        interior, 111–113, 165–167
Paint scrapers, 283
Paneling, installing, 139–145

Particleboard:
    Countertop, 30
    Vanity, 61
Path, stone, 307–309
Patio, brick-and-sand, 311–315
Pavers:
    Garden path, 307–309
    Patio, 313
Perforating tool for stripping
    wallpaper, 115, 116, 117
Pilasters, 152, 155
Plumbing:
    Bathroom sinks, 63, 69
    Flexible tubing for, 27
    Kitchen sinks, 27, 38–39
    Toilets, 83
    Whirlpool tubs, 87
Plywood:
    Hardwood, 158
    Underlayment, 194
Polyurethane, on applicator
    pads, 201
Power stretchers, 218
Pressure-washers, 282

R

Range hoods, vented, 13–17
Refacing techniques, kitchen
    cabinet, 41–45
Refinishing techniques:
    Trim, 147–149
    Wood floors, 199–201
Resilient channel, 241–243
Resilient flooring, 179–185
Roofs, safety on, 255
Routers, vs. laminate trimmers,
    32

S

Saber saws, 16
Safety:
    Ceiling fan, 261
    Cutting brick, 311
    Electrical work, 71–72, 75–76,
        91, 251, 299
    Insulation, 241
    Ladders, 281
    Painting, 281, 287
    On roof, 255
    Sanding, 199
    Wallpapering, 120
Sand:
    Patio, brick and, 311
    Stone path, 307
Sanders, oscillating, 199
Sanding techniques:
    Removing dust, 31
    Safety with, 199
    For wood floors, 199–201

Saws:
    Coping, 231
    Guides for, 141
    Hacksaws, 97
    Saber, 16
Scarf joints, 229
Screed boards, 214
Screwdrivers, power, 53
Scribing:
    Laminate to wall, 33
    Vinyl floor tiles to wall, 197
Seam rollers, for vinyl flooring,
    184
Security light fixtures, 299–301
Shelves, installing, 173–175
Showers, installing doors on,
    95–99
Shutoff valves:
    Bathroom sink, 67
    Kitchen sink, 38
    Toilet, 83
Shutters:
    Adding, 291–293
    Hardware, 292
Siding, aluminum, 281–285
Sinks:
    Bathroom
        pedestal, 67–69
        plumbing, 63, 69
        removing, 68
    Kitchen
        cutting countertop for,
            23, 25, 30
        faucets, 37–39
        plumbing, 27, 38–39
        removing, 30
        rimless vs. self-rimming,
            23
        upgrading, 23–27
Skylights, thin-line:
    Installing, 255–259
    Locating, 256
Sod:
    Cutting trench in, 296
    Scalping, for stone path, 307
Soundproofing:
    Ceilings, 241–243
    Whirlpool tubs, 86
Sponge painting, 165–167
Sprayers, airless, 281, 285
Stain, wood:
    Hiding gaps in paneling with,
        144
    On wainscoting, 129
Standards, installing, 173–175
Staple guns, 247
Stencils, for walls, 107–109
Storage, in sink cabinets, 51–53
Storm doors, 303–305
Stoves, vented hood for, 13–17
Studs, finding, 64, 229

T

Tack strips, 216
Tape, painter's, 99
Templates:
  Flooring, 181, 183
  Hardware-mounting, 44
  Sink cutout, 25
Thresholds, removing, 268
Tile. *See also* Tileboard
  Backsplash, 55–59
  Ceiling, acoustical, 245–249
  Floor
    ceramic, 203–207
    vinyl, 193–197
    wood, prefinished, 195
Tileboard:
  Installing, 101–103
  Types, 103
Tile cutters:
  Manual, 207
  Motorized, 57
Toggle bolts, 175
Toilets, upgrading, 79–83
Toilet seats, installing, 83
Tools. *See specific tools*
Towel racks, removing, 95
Track lighting, 251–253
Transition strips, 219
Trim. *See* Molding
Trisodium phosphate (TSP), 48,
  112
Tubing, flexible, 27

U

Underlayment:
  Carpet, 216–217
  Laminate flooring, 189
  Vinyl tile, 194
Utility knives, 122

V

Vanities, replacing, 61–65
Vapor barriers, 170
Varnish, on applicator pads,
  201
Veneer, 41–43
Vents, range hood, 13–17
Vinyl flooring:
  Sheet, 179–185
  Tile, 193–197

W

Wainscoting, installing,
  129–133
Walkway, stone, 307–309
Wall anchors, 175
Wallpaper:
  Booking, 224
  Borders, 125–127
  Hanging
    on ceilings, 223–225
    on walls, 119–123
  Safety with, 120
  Stripping, 115–117
  Types, 121
Wallpaper seam roller, 184
Walls:
  Basement, finishing,
    169–171
  Chair rail on, 135–137
  Framing new interior, 140
  Painting
    exterior, 281–285
    interior, 111–113,
      165–167
  Paneling, 139–145
  Stenciling, 107–109
  Tileboard on, 101–103
  Wainscoting on, 129–133

Wax rings, toilet:
  Replacing, 80–81
  Types, 81
Whirlpool tub, installing,
  85–89
Window boxes, making,
  273–275
Windows:
  Greenhouse, 277–279
  Wallpapering around, 123
Window seats, built-in, 157–159
Wire baskets, slide-out, 53
Wiring:
  Ceiling fans, 263
  Exhaust fans, 93
  Ground Fault Circuit Inter-
    rupter (GFCI), 85, 88, 295
  Lights
    bathroom, 77
    medicine cabinet, 73
    outdoor, 297
    track, 253
  Safety with, 71–72, 75–76,
    91, 251, 299
Wood floors:
  Refinishing, 199–201
  Strip, installing, 209–213
  Tiles, prefinished, 195